Lieutenant Commander James Newton has flown in the Royal Navy since 1991. Born in Sunderland in 1972, he completed his Basic Naval Training at the Britannia Royal Naval College. For most of his career he has flown armed helicopters with 847 NAS alongside the Royal Marines and he is no stranger to being shot at. He has flown prime ministers and all the current military commanders, and is still a serving Lieutenant Commander in the Royal Navy.

'In an unprecedented account, a serving Royal Navy pilot tells what it's really like to be at the controls of a £30m attack helicopter – and reveals the intense emotional aftermath of unleashing its fearsome weapons of war' *Mail on Sunday*

'Accounts of helicopter combat are few and far between. Lt Cdr Newton's story not merely plugs that gap, it's the best book on modern aerial warfare since Sea Harrier legend Sharkey Ward put pen to paper' *Navy News*

'Read *Armed Action* and get a taste of what battle's all about' *Daily Sport*

ARMED ACTION

James Newton

headline
review

First published in 2007 by HEADLINE REVIEW
An imprint of Headline Publishing Group

First published in paperback in 2007 by HEADLINE REVIEW

2

Cataloguing in Publication Data is available from the British Library

The views represented are those of the author and do not necessarily
represent the views of the Royal Navy or Her Majesty's Government.

Trade paperback 978 0 7553 1603 8

Typeset in Italian Garamond by Avon DataSet Ltd,
Bidford on Avon, Warwickshire

Printed and bound in Great Britain by Mackays of Chatham plc, Chatham, Kent

Headline's policy is to use papers that are natural, renewable and
recyclable products and made from wood grown in sustainable forests.
The logging and manufacturing processes are expected to conform
to the environmental regulations of the country of origin.

HEADLINE PUBLISHING GROUP
A division of Hachette Livre UK Ltd
338 Euston Road
London NW1 3BH

www.reviewbooks.co.uk
www.headline.co.uk

For Zulu 37

CONTENTS

Map of Al-Faw	viii
Prologue	1
Chapter One	19
Chapter Two	37
Chapter Three	71
Chapter Four	103
Chapter Five	141
Chapter Six	169
Chapter Seven	213
Chapter Eight	259
Chapter Nine	281
Chapter Ten	309
Where Are They Now?	329
Acknowledgements	333
Index	337

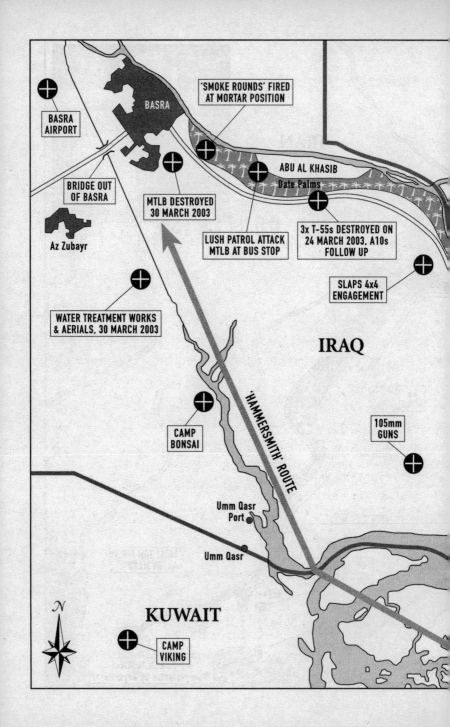

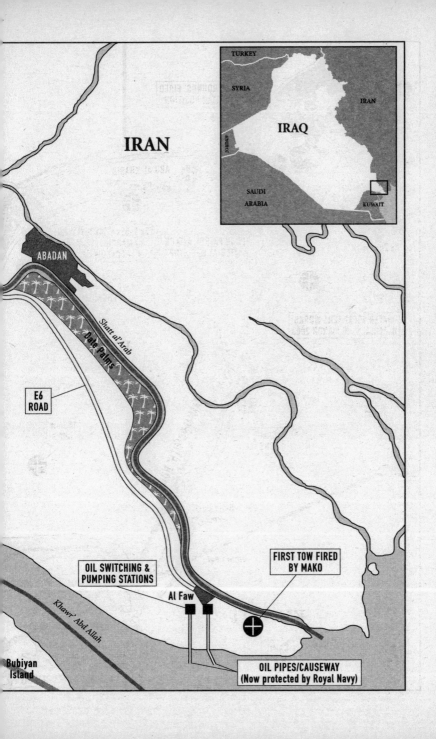

Prologue

The pristine sands of the Kuwaiti desert suddenly gave way to a vision of hell. Shell holes, the hulks of burnt-out tanks and troop carriers, and blotches of scorched, oily black sand – the detritus of the first Gulf War – littered the landscape as far as I could see. Up on the horizon, wobbling in the heat haze and looming ever larger, clouds of thick black smoke rose up towards the sky, punctuated every now and then by a huge fresh explosion on the ground. The shitty stench of rotting vegetation from the drained marshes blasted my nostrils, but as we neared the front line it was soon replaced by the unmistakable smell of cordite, mixed with burning oil. Just ahead of us I could see the little Scimitar light tanks of the Queen's Dragoon Guards, aka the Welsh Cavalry, fanned out in an arc across the heavily cratered desert, their muzzles flashing as they fired roughly one or two kilometres northwards towards the long string of date palms and low-rise buildings where the enemy were dug in, slightly to the east and south of Abu Al Khasib. Plumes of sand and smoke were bursting all around the QDG vehicles as I switched radio frequencies and heard the well-spoken tones of the officer commanding (OC): 'Hello, Cravat 33, this is Dobbin Zero Alpha. Over.'

I knew all about this OC even before we had gone out on a joint patrol with his troop the day before. He's one very cool cat, and even now, when he and his boys were right in the thick of a major engagement with the Iraqi T55s, he sounded totally unfazed. There was an almighty din in the background on his radio, and I could hear the *boom-boom* of the 30mm Rarden guns pounding away at the T55s and the rhythmical *rat-a-tat-tat*, *phut-phut-phut* of the mounted machine guns keeping up a steady stream of fire into the date palms. Engines were revving heavily, and I could make out strong Welsh and Scouse accents barking instructions at one another. And all the while, amid this orderly pandemonium, dozens of point detonation rounds were exploding around them.

'Any trade?' I asked the OC.

'Three-three, we have engaged one T55 with swing fire and destroyed it, but we've got more trade coming from grid 873684, if you're interested. It's a little sharp down here at the moment.'

If you're interested! *Does anything unnerve this guy?*

In 847 Naval Air Squadron we often like to think of

ourselves on the sharper end of operations, vulnerable not just to missiles, mortars and tank rounds but even small-arms fire (unlike the fast jets operating from 30,000 feet who, in Iraq at least, were as good as safe from attack once the missile defences had been destroyed before the war had even begun). But as we flew towards the QDG and I looked down at them in their little Scimitars taking a mauling from their heavier opponents, I felt a mild sense of relief, for once, that I was up in the air in my Lynx, and not down there on the ground getting pummelled. I thought we had it tough. I could feel myself tensing up and the blood starting to rise as we headed into the battle, but it steadied and steeled me to see this tiny, lightly armed troop of Welsh Cavalry, under a huge bombardment from a full tank division, steadfastly standing their ground and fighting like alley cats.

I quickly put my eyes to the roof sight and started scanning the date palms and buildings, trying to spot the enemy tanks. We were about four and a half kilometres away at this point and comfortably within the sixteen-kilometre range of the T55s' guns. I knew I had to find them fast because we were extremely exposed in this flat terrain with no hills or ravines to offer hiding places. To the Iraqi tank commanders we presented a lovely clear target set against a uniform blue backdrop, with only the heat haze to distort their judgement of our position.

There were battles raging along a thirty-kilometre stretch of land from the Al-Faw peninsula, next to Iran in the east, right across the outer suburbs of Basra where the scruffy little shanty towns border the desert and the drained marshland to the south. The risk of 'fires' from our own positions meant that, for the time being, we were confined to one of the pre-defined 4km square 'battle boxes' laid out on our maps.

Strictly, the role of 847 in Iraq was to act as a 'screen' in conjunction with the armoured reconnaissance vehicles below, observing enemy positions and then calling in fire from the Royal Marine artillery on the ground, or from the guns on the Royal Navy frigates and destroyers, or from the fast jet boys thousands of feet above our heads, returning from missions deep in Iraq. We were not meant to go into offensive mode unless there was no alternative or unless one of our TOW missiles was the most appropriate weapon for the task in hand. Held in our battle position (BP) as we were, there was, on this occasion, clearly no alternative if we were to come under fire. It was a battle.

I was talking to Geek in the Gazelle, the other helicopter in our 847 air patrol – who, like me, was scanning the date palms with his sight – when a shell exploded about 400 metres behind us. Four hundred metres may sound like a long way, but in a tank battle it is a bit too close for comfort. 'Aye, aye, this is getting pretty warm,' I said to Gizmo; he just nodded back at me, looking totally unbothered. He might as well have been deadheading his roses back in the West Country. Barely had the words left my mouth when there was a second, much louder explosion, this time

4

around 200 metres behind us, and a thirty-foot geyser of sand and smoke shot into the air. 'Fuck me!' The first, I suspected, had just been a random shot into the desert, but the second blast made me seize my controls, partly because of the shock of the explosion itself, but more because I understood instantly that a second shot along exactly the same angle, so quickly following the first, could mean only one thing: an Iraqi tank commander had us in his sights, and he was rapidly adjusting fire.

We didn't want to break away too hard because it was vital to get 'eyes on' the tank and then take it out, and in order to get eyes on we had to try and hold the hover position. So Gizmo, who on this occasion was actually flying the Lynx, took it drifting to the right as I carried on frantically looking up and down the date palms for the camouflaged tanks, which can be difficult to spot at the best of times, let alone when they are operating from under a uniform line of trees in a heat haze. 'It's like looking for a fucking needle in a haystack,' I muttered into my boom mike. We had moved a few hundred metres to the east and returned to the hover, still only about fifty feet above the ground, when a third round erupted right in front of us and the heady stench of explosive instantly filled the cockpit. Gizmo and I shot looks at each other, both knowing exactly what was going on: he was bracketing us. He'd put two rounds over the top and one in front, and now all he had to do was slightly adjust the elevation and lob one down the middle, and we were as good as fucked.

I had trained for this moment on countless occasions in recent years, but this guy was running rings around me. I hadn't got the faintest idea where he was firing from. He, meanwhile, was just a few yards, and a few seconds, from blowing us out of the sky. We might as well have been strapped to the end of his barrel. I could picture perfectly the scene going on in the T55. The tank commander would be barking orders and range adjustments at his gunner below, while sticking out of the turret and looking down his own sights, with us sitting slap bang in the crosshairs of his graticule. Like me, he had high-magnification sights, and I knew he would be looking right at my desperate face as I scrutinised the horizon to find him. This guy knew his stuff, and it was bloody obvious what was coming next – airburst. He was implementing basic anti-aircraft tactics: get your range with point detonation rounds and then switch to airburst, which is basically ack-ack, or flak: what armies have been using to bring down aircraft since the First World War.

It was so bloody hot in the midday sun that sweat was running down my face and into my eyes, and I was wiping it away with my sleeve so that I could see through the sights when there was an ear-splitting bang to the rear of the aircraft. Even Gizmo, a Royal Marine vet, raised an eyebrow at that one and we both instinctively knew that it was time to move – and fast. Gizmo broke hard to the right and we sped towards the back of our battle box as I tried to gather my thoughts and work out what the fuck to do. There was only one way of getting out of there intact and that was to find the tank – or tanks – firing at us and take them out with a TOW. I had never fired a TOW in anger, let alone killed anyone, and although I had scored two direct hits out of two during training in Oman on the way out to the Gulf, these missiles from the Vietnam era had an unpleasant but rare habit of 'roguing' on us.

Both helicopters made two laps around our battle box, each time searching for the tiny pinprick muzzle flashes amid the date palms as we sped towards the enemy. But to no avail; there was still no sign of him. We tried the 'split' manoeuvre next, whereby the two helicopters raced towards the treeline side by side and then split, one banking left and one banking right, so that, we hoped, the tank would be confused about which one of us to fire at, leaving one aircraft 'engaged' and the other free to help. The air was full of drifting smoke and puffs of airburst explosion as the Iraqis continued to fire at us for fun, pumping out shell after shell, one every five seconds. By the law of averages alone, this guy was due a hit sooner or later. He deserved one, too, because so far at least he was completely out-manoeuvring and outfoxing us.

'Geek, Scooby,' I said, calling up the Gazelle.

'Go,' replied Geek.

'Where *is* this guy?' I said as the airbursts rained down on us.

'Er . . . no tally,' came the reply, meaning he couldn't see him either. 'Do you want us to push forward and have a look for him, Scooby?'

To find this tank we would have to get up as close as possible to his rough location and stay in the hover. To be honest, when it comes to being shot out of the sky, there's not much difference between being one kilometre away or five kilometres. They're just numbers. If the tank commander has you in his sights, and you're within the range of his gun, then it makes little odds. My survival instinct was telling me to retreat the four kilometres to the back of our box, but the chances of spotting the tanks from so far back were much smaller. We had to get in there.

Gizmo pushed right up to within a few hundred metres of the front of the battle box, and we had only just gone into the hover when there was a loud crash a little to our right, followed immediately by what felt like a huge sack of gravel being thrown over the right-hand window . . . *One, two, three, four, five . . . BOOM!* Another blinding flash lit up the air in front of us, at our eleven o'clock: the explosion was so strong I could feel my armoured chest plate lift away from my body, and the Lynx bucked wildly as if a lorry had just rammed into us at speed. At the same time a deluge of what sounded like giant hailstones crashed against the windscreen and the helicopter quickly filled with the stench of cordite again.

'Scooby section, break right! Break right!' I yelled, ordering both aircraft to move. But I didn't need to tell Gizmo. He was already putting the Lynx into a hard manoeuvre, which was just as well, because a third airburst immediately erupted into the space we had just vacated, once again causing the helicopter to lurch and jolt as we veered away.

As we were speeding away from the immediate danger, a quiet voice appeared over my headset: 'Excuse me, boss.' It was Guns, the marine door-gunner in the back of the Lynx. I had almost forgotten about the young lad amid all the excitement of being blown to shit by an unsighted enemy.

'What's up, Guns?' I said, almost impatiently.

'Well, boss, I don't know whether you're interested, but I've just seen a muzzle flash.'

I swung round in my seat to see Guns down on one knee leaning on his mounted machine gun looking – well, looking quite bored really, like he was off in dreamland, making his holiday plans or thinking about his girlfriend.

'Interested!?! I'm fascinated! You may just have saved our lives. Where the hell is it? And try and look a little bit flustered or excited, will you, Guns? We're in a battle.'

'No bother, boss.'

Gizmo was moving the Lynx all around the box, desperately trying to disrupt the tank gunner's line and range, but now we swept back in towards the date palms as Guns started talking us on to the muzzle flash he had spotted: 'From the cream building come right two fingers [i.e. the width of two fingers held out in front of my face], low apex building with no front. Got it? Keep coming right, boss, keep coming right, that's it, just in there, boss, by the building?' He was virtually yawning.

My heart leapt with relief and excitement as I finally laid eyes on our tormentor. There he was, not right in front of us at all, but out on our nine o'clock over to the left. No wonder I couldn't find him. The bastard had outflanked us, which is exactly what you didn't want in a helicopter because you're generally moving forward and looking down the sight ahead of you. And, as he was firing at us from side-on, he had a much bigger target to hit. This guy was no rookie fresh out of tank college, that was for sure; he was a pro, probably a vet of the first Gulf War or the long conflict with Iran. He was brave, too, because he had obviously broken cover and come right out of the date palms to engage us. So far as I could tell, the rest of them had stayed put.

'I've got it! I've got it!' I blurted as I caught sight of a minuscule white flash. Almost immediately there followed a mother of an explosion right in front of us that made the Lynx jerk violently as Gizmo wrestled to regain control.

The bad news was that the tank was sitting inside the open end of what looked distinctly like some kind of school, because it had a kind of concourse playing area out the front. Crafty bastard, this one. Just as it wasn't great PR to shoot up an ambulance, neither would it look too great if I called in a J-Dam strike, or fired in a load of TOWs and wiped out a classroom for five-year-olds. I put the sight on visual and on to its highest magnification and then switched to thermal imaging just to make absolutely certain – and, thankfully, it was obvious there were no people inside the building that day. All the same, the Iraqi authorities could still use the images of shattered desks as a powerful piece of propaganda. They could be beaming them around the world by the time we landed back at base.

As we swung round and I fixed the building in my sights, it was clear that in order to fire at us the tank was having to drive out of the school and then quickly reverse back in before we could spot him. When he next sped out into the open to have a pop at us, that was going to be my window of opportunity. It was a small one, but it was at least a chance.

This was now a classic tank engagement: a straight gunfight. The best shot would win. The loser would die in flames. I wasn't thinking in human terms: it was helicopter versus tank. The training had kicked in and it was as if I had been pre-programmed to delete any thoughts about fellow souls. All I could see was 60 tons of Russian armour. The tank commander would have been in the same mindset: for him, it was just tank versus helicopter. Exhilaration had now replaced the fear and frustration that had gripped me for the past thirty minutes. The Gazelle moved to the relative safety of the back of the battle box to watch our six o'clock. I needed Geek to get word back to HQ that developments on the battlefield were moving fast. There was nothing that the unarmed 'whistling chicken leg', as we called the Gazelle, could bring to the battlefield now that we had our target. And it was perfectly clear that it was the bigger beast of the Lynx that this guy wanted as his trophy. With all our explosives on board, we'd make a far more satisfying bang than the little Gazelle.

There were two problems, however. First, the tank was partly obscured in its hiding place and difficult to identify positively. This meant that there was a chance, albeit a small one, that it might have been a friendly, perhaps one of the QDG Scimitars we were there to support. The last thing I needed was my first missile of my first war to take out some of our own boys. Second, it was sitting in an American-controlled zone and I would need to get the Yanks' permission to cross over to their patch and get a decent shot at it.

Perhaps sensing that we had finally spotted him, the tank commander opened up with a sustained volley of shells that erupted all around our airspace. How none of them had hit us yet was a miracle. I knew from our training over the years that, by rights, we should be lying in a mangled, charred heap in the sand by now. Certainly, if this had been the Norwegian lads whom we'd trained against, it would have been all over after a couple of minutes. But our good fortune couldn't last for ever. As Gizmo banked and dipped and lifted to try and avoid the endless barrage of incoming flak, I was desperately working the radios to raise the American controllers for clearance to cross boundaries into their area of operation and take a shot. 'Come on, come on, will you?' I muttered under my breath as I kept the sights glued to my face. Finally – probably after no more than thirty seconds in truth – the radio crackled into life and I heard that lazy Deep South drawl: 'Hello, Cravat 33, you're clear to proceed, but better get on with it. We have trade of our own.'

I immediately switched frequencies to talk to the QDG to make absolutely certain it was not one of them sitting in there. The doubt in my mind was minuscule, but I didn't want there to be any doubt at all. I don't think I could fly again after a blue-on-blue. I put out a request for them to confirm it wasn't one of their tanks and one by one, the Welsh boys came back over the airwaves: 'Zero One, negative . . . Zero Two, negative . . . Zero Three, negative . . . Zero Four, negative . . .' I was good to go.

I selected the first TOW missile as we retreated to the back of the battle position ready to turn and make a run for the tank. Taking a running shot at him was one option, but the chances of a direct hit were far greater if we closed in fast and then assumed the hover position, giving me a more solid platform to get the crosshairs on him before pulling the trigger. I would also have to hold the crosshairs on the target until the moment of impact, and that's easier if you're not hammering along at 100 knots and turning away at the same time.

The cat-and-mouse game of the last half an hour was now over. It was time for the Lynx to bare her claws. I felt a huge surge of adrenaline as Gizmo banked hard to the right, trimmed the cyclic forward and began to accelerate rapidly towards the tank, which was still pumping out round after round at us. I barely noticed the airbursts any longer as I focused all my concentration on putting the tank into the middle of the graticule and getting the missile away. When we were about 3,500 metres from our target, Gizmo brought the Lynx to the hover and put it into 'constraints', the pre-programmed flying parameters within which the computer allows the missile to launch. 'Roger that, firing,' I said into the radio, letting the QDG know that we were about to engage.

I saw the tank muzzle flash as I squeezed the trigger: we were both firing simultaneously. Our shots would be crossing in mid-air. The TOW flopped out of its tube about fifty metres to the right of the aircraft; I watched its motor furiously burning itself out and felt its heat on my cheeks. The tank commander, seeing the bright flash, would have known exactly what was heading his way. The motor burnt for about a second and a half before the missile raced away at about 700 mph into the distance, with its two copper guidance wires, attached to the Lynx, spooling out of its arse. Gripping the TOW controller in my right hand until my knuckles were white, I held the crosshairs on the tank, tracking it all the way, as Gizmo counted the seconds before impact: 'eight, nine, ten . . .' I held my breath as the sweat cascaded down my forehead. If we were buffeted by an explosion or a gust of wind, shunting the sight off the tank, the missile could also rogue and either flop into the sand or fuck off into the distance and cause horrible damage somewhere else, possibly to an innocent target.

It was just a matter of seconds, but the wait was interminable as the TOW rocketed at a slightly downward gradient towards the tank and Gizmo held the Lynx in post-launch 'constraints', which meant making sure not to turn the aircraft more than 110 degrees from the target. The tension was broken by a comic moment – almost surreal given the intensity of the situation – when one of the QDG tanks came over the radio. 'Hello, Cravat 33, this is Zero Five,' said the Welsh accent. 'Well, don't ask me if I'm in that building then, will you boss?' Bollocks! I thought there were just four Scimitars, but, having seen the T55 with my own eyes, I knew for certain it wasn't a friendly down there watching the TOW streak towards them.

I laughed nervously at the comment but the sound was barely out of my throat when a great flash filled the sight I was staring down.

'. . . Twenty, twenty-one, twenty-two . . .' continued Gizmo. Given the range, the fact he was still counting indicated that I had missed the target. I couldn't believe it. My heart sank heavily. Almost simultaneously another blast rocked the Lynx and another shower of gravel crackled against the windscreen. 'The next round's for us, Gizmo, let's fucking move!' I shouted: quickly we banked left – and the Lynx jolted as that next round exploded behind the tail rotor.

He didn't say anything, but I could feel Gizmo's disappointment as we retreated to the back of the box. 'Right, this time we're doing a running shot. Let's get close, Gizmo,' I said. The Lynx surged forward again, as Gizmo pushed it to about 100 knots, which was well short of the 250 mph the Lynx hit to set the world speed record for a helicopter, but about as fast as it would ever go in these conditions. I pressed the button to cut the wires from the first missile and quickly primed a second one. I could now see that the first shot had landed about fifty metres short: it wouldn't have even singed the commander's eyebrows. The explosion, however, had obviously put the shits up him because he had darted back into the building like a rat down a drain, and was now firing like a psycho from inside the concourse with everything he had left.

'You'd think this lad would be out of rounds by now,' said Gizmo as we sped back in, the blur of the desert rushing beneath us, like someone had pressed fast forward on the video recorder. I fixed the gap between the turret and the main body in the crosshairs and, when we were about three kilometres away, I squeezed the trigger and waited. Gizmo started counting again, 'One, two, three . . .'

It wasn't a big explosion like the first – just a small flare as the warhead penetrated the tank's armour. All the exploding was going on inside as the molten copper bolt bounced around the walls. After a few seconds there was a secondary explosion and smoke started pouring out of the turret as a figure jumped into the sand.

'Bullseye!' said Geek, who had been watching the engagement from the back of the battle position in the Gazelle. There was no joy, only relief, as I sank back into my seat – but then, just when Gizmo started manoeuvring to turn us around, we were both thrown forward as the tank's parting shot exploded metres in front of us. It was the closest one yet. The compression waves lifted my chest armour off, winding me for a second time that day as the nose of the Lynx reared up in the turbulence.

'Right, we're bingo [low on fuel]; let's get the hell out of here now, can we?' I said to Gizmo as he brought the aircraft back under control.

'That's not a bad idea that. Besides, I'm getting hungry.'

It took about fifteen minutes to get back to the camp from the front line, and we flew there in virtual silence. My hands were shaking so much I sat on them so that Gizmo wouldn't notice. We looked at each other and blew out our cheeks. Gizmo didn't say anything, but he gave me a look and a half-smile that spoke far more powerfully than any words. *Don't worry, Scooby, you're all right, you're not meant to feel relaxed.*

I was happy and relieved that my missile had eventually hit the target, but it was Guns who had saved our lives.

'Nice work, Guns,' I said over the comms.

'No bother, boss. I knew you'd get the bugger in the end.'

I craned my neck around to give the young lad a nod of thanks and congratulations and there he was, sitting at his door, one hand on the machine gun, legs dangling in the wind, like a bored kid killing time on the school wall . . . whistling.

CHAPTER ONE

'**C**an we have our pickled eggs as a starter, please?' asked Hovis politely.

'You what?' The elderly woman standing to the side of the counter had a fag hanging out of her mouth, and her bingo wings bounced up and down as she took it from her lips in amazement. 'Starter? You're in a bloody chippie, luv. It's not the effing Ritz, you know.'

We took our seats at the red plastic table and looked out of the window at the wet cobbled street outside. It was Wednesday night, 15 January 2003, and in less than twelve hours we would be standing on the deck of HMS *Ocean* as it pulled out of Plymouth's Devonport naval base and into the Channel. Officially we were sailing out to the eastern Mediterranean, but we all knew where we were really heading.

The woman returned and dropped two large plates on the

table, each with a single egg rolling around the edge. 'They'll be wanting meringues next, them two,' she muttered as she waddled back behind her fish bar.

Hovis is my oldest friend in the services and it wasn't necessary for us to talk in order to communicate as we picked up our plastic cutlery and tucked into our ridiculous starter. We each knew what the other was feeling. Part of it was the sadness of leaving behind family and friends for three months . . . or six months . . . or God only knew how long. At the back of my mind – at the back of all our minds, I presume – was the fear that it might only be our bodies that made it back, lying inside flag-draped coffins on a Hercules transport plane. I have pictures in my hallway at home in the West Country of my cadet classes at Dartmouth and flying training in the early 1990s. We are all smiling and waving at the camera; today, just over ten years later, four of them are dead. Some were killed in combat, some of them died in flying incidents. It's difficult to escape the feeling that as every year goes by, with every flight or mission that goes down in my log book, my chances of making it to middle age become just that little bit smaller. And that's before I even step into a combat zone. You never know when you're eating your last pickled egg.

'This is all right this, isn't it?' said Hovis, ending the silence as we munched through our cod and chips. He wasn't talking about eating a pickled egg in a crap chippie on a cold January evening. What he meant was, 'This is better than being shot at, isn't it?'

We had been so busy preparing for war over the previous two months that there had barely been any time to sit back and consider what lay in store for us out in the Gulf, which was probably just as well. It's not good for the soul to dwell on the uglier eventualities of war. In the build-up to our departure a non-specific uneasiness underscored all our preparations, but at the same time, pulling in the opposite emotional direction, was a sense of boyish excitement about the prospect of heading into a proper battle for the first time. Northern Ireland, the Balkans and Central America had all had their moments for me, and most of us had at least half a dozen near-death experiences to recall with a shudder. Several among us were veterans of the Falklands and the first Gulf War, but for all the younger officers on 847, including Hovis and me, this was possibly going to be our first experience of a full-on war. Try as I did, there was no escaping the excitement of it. After all, we hadn't joined up to spend a few decades flying around Salisbury Plain, with the odd week spent lying in frozen ditches on Dartmoor eating squirrels, before ending our careers filing papers in a net-curtained office in High Holborn. That would be fine in years to come, but first I wanted a slice of the real action, to put myself on the line. Imagine training every day for ten years as a Premiership footballer but never getting to play in a competitive match. That's how it comes to you after a while. Why am I *doing* this?

I'm sure Hovis was feeling the same thrill of anticipation, mixed in with the dread, the self-doubt and the inevitable gloom that follows all the farewells. This, for heaven's sake, is a man who still points at sports cars and shouts: 'Wow! Look at that! Hoofing!' Hovis gets excited about everything, even wars. He gets especially excited if you feed him processed cheese, to which he is highly and hilariously allergic. He goes nuts. The additives in blue Smarties and Sunny Delight have the same effect on him, and he has provided the squadron with much amusement over the years whenever we have gone ashore for a night out and one of us has spiked his food with crushed-up Smarties or a few slices of Kraft.

One of the best examples happened on Bonfire Night one year, when Hovis was dancing around the huge fire, happily labouring under the illusion that he was, in his own words, 'a cat monkey boy'. When his embarrassed and long-suffering wife Kate tried to usher him into the car to take him home, he rugby-tackled her and pretended to maul her. On another occasion, she woke up in the middle of the night to hear strange noises emanating from the wardrobe; when she opened it she discovered her husband, back from the pub, crouched in a ball with his arms above his head pretending to be in a space rocket. When he had stopped making his rocket engine revving noises, he said: 'I'm going to the moon. Do you want to come?' His wife just shut the door, went back to bed and left him to his cheese-induced fantasies.

We all loved Hovis even before he had joined the squadron after word reached us of an incident on a skiing holiday in the French Alps. A combination of processed cheese and large quantities of lager had combined to push our new colleague over the edge of reason. Kitted out immaculately in full dress uniform, Hovis was seen bombing down the slopes of Courchevel at twilight, stopping every now and then to let off fireworks in all directions. Unfortunately, when he arrived at the foot of the slope he skied straight into an admiral. The slurring explanation he gave for his behaviour impressed the admiral still less than the collision. The good news for his new colleagues was that when he flew out to the Far East to join us on *Fort Austin*, a Royal Fleet Auxiliary supply ship, he was put on 'extra duties' for the full two weeks of our tour as part of his punishment, meaning that the rest of us could put our feet up when it came to what would have been our turns on the duty roster.

If you met Hovis in the middle of one of his 'cheese trips', you might be surprised and alarmed to learn that he was 847 Squadron's electronic warfare instructor or EWI (pronounced Ee-Why) – and a very fine one to boot – responsible for anything inside the aircraft that flashed or beeped, including radar warning systems, radios, computer systems and all the secret 'crypto'. He had been given the call sign 'Hovis' by the senior officers of the squadron, aka the Secret Six, on the grounds that he was 'a loafing bastard'. In truth, he quickly proved to be one of the most hard-working and dedicated officers among us, in spite of his weird food allergies and love of practical jokes. My call sign is 'Scooby' as in Scooby Doo, Cockney rhyming slang for 'he hasn't got a clue': a name I earned while on exercise in the jungle shortly after getting my wings, when I somehow managed to get detached from the rest of the formation on the way back to the ship.

Hovis and I walked around the corner to join the other officers of 847 Squadron, who had congregated in one of the many pubs that line the cobbled streets of Plymouth's Barbican district. Like thousands of British sailors, marines and aviators over the years before us, we had headed to this historic area down by the docks to enjoy a final drink on terra firma before taking to the high seas, bound for distant lands and waters for a good dust-up with Johnny Foreigner. 'Enjoy' is perhaps the wrong word, though, because there wasn't exactly a party atmosphere in the pub that night. Most of the squadron were family men who at some point in the previous few hours had said farewell to their wives and children without any idea when, or if, they might see them again.

There was a lot of suppressed emotion in that room. Marines, with whom we other navy pilots live and work and go to war, aren't in the business of sharing their more tender emotions, at least not in company, but we all understood the anguish of saying goodbye. Outwardly, everyone put on a brave face; psychiatrists would say we were in denial. It's worse for some than others, particularly bad for the ones with children, and I tend to look away or go somewhere else when the mums, wives, girlfriends and families come down to the airbase or the docks to see off their loved ones on the eve of a departure. It's always the same awkward scene of tear-stained faces, bear-hugs, quiet moments with the kids on the knee, and lots of forced humour, plastic smiles and crap wisecracks. As soon as the farewells are over and the families have been squared away we all try to put them from our minds and get busy. Most take refuge in humour, and the banter begins almost instantly we're on our own. It's the same when you hear about the death of a colleague – you mourn his loss properly at the appropriate moment, but at work you try and crack on and keep busy. It's too painful to think about, let alone discuss.

That night, as always on these occasions, there was a posse of lads propping up the bar, roaring with laughter and getting the beers in. This small group tends to be a mixture of the young single lads, the one or two who love killing people and the ones who are just delighted to be sailing the next day because they can't get away from their girlfriends fast enough.

They warn you in the navy that the most difficult time for relationships is the two weeks before you go away and the two weeks after you get back. When you took into account the fact that in 847 Squadron we were away for roughly three-quarters of the year in total – in recent years – to an unlucky few, this did not leave enough days out of three hundred and sixty-five to enjoy a 'normal' relationship.

'So how did your missus take it?' Slaps was saying to one

of the other boys as I squeezed in with a pint of Speckled Hen at one of the tables in the corner.

'Oh fine, she was great actually,' came the stock reply, accompanied by a nervous laugh. 'I think she's getting the hang of it after all these years. Kids were a bit teary, but they'll be fine once they're back home . . .' But I knew he was talking utter bollocks, because just a few hours earlier I had seen the guy's wife weeping her eyes out in the car back at the airbase. I also knew full well, from the experience of previous tours, that his kids were going to be worried sick until their dad was safely home again.

'And how did yours take it, Scoobs?'

My stomach tightened. 'Who? Suzi? Oh, she was absolutely fine. She took it pretty well, I think, considering . . .' I replied unconvincingly. Hovis, aware that not everything was great in my home, quickly cracked a joke and changed the subject.

There was probably a time, not that long ago even, when on similar evenings in Plymouth the rum and the ale would have been flowing and the whores would have been working the tables while salty, leather-faced seadogs hammered out a medley of classic songs of the sea. But on that cold, damp January evening in 2003 there was just a hum of subdued chat around the tables while the jukebox played quietly in the background, interrupted from time to time by the noise of a win on the fruit machine in the corner, or a burst of laughter from the few lads putting them away at the bar.

We're all good, clean-living family men these days, of course, but we also had a daunting schedule of work to complete on the voyage out to the Gulf in order to get ourselves ready for the possibility of war. Sailing away with a monstrous hangover, followed a few weeks down the line by a dose of the clap, wasn't even on our radar screens. The technical side of Royal Marine warfare had moved on a little since the days when our ships would pull alongside the enemy and the boys in red, fuelled by a few bottles of rum, would jump aboard and run through as many Frenchmen and Spaniards as possible.

The marines on the ground still fight at pretty close quarters but our roles, as combat helicopter pilots, were technologically complex and challenging, and it was as much our brains as our brawn that would see us through the coming months. The better we could operate our helicopters, weapons and general equipment on the battlefield, the greater our chances of surviving would be. For us it was more about computers than cutlasses. Having a few beers and going out on the razzle would have to wait until we were allowed ashore on the way home.

In late November 2002 Clubs, the squadron's Commanding Officer (CO), had called the senior officers into his office and sat us down on his big leather sofas and told us that we should be 'combat ready' for desert conditions by mid-January. That announcement marked the beginning of a period of feverish preparation. 'This time we'll be turning left,' he said, and we all knew what that meant. Normally when we headed out on exercise on HMS *Ocean* we would push south into the Atlantic and then turn right towards America. 'Turning left' meant we would be passing through the Strait of Gibraltar and steaming towards the Middle East.

In truth, the whole atmosphere at our Yeovilton base had changed significantly fifteen months earlier, within hours, minutes even, of those two American airliners smashing into the World Trade Center. Our aircraft were quickly assigned to aid the civil authorities, who feared a similar major terrorist attack against Britain. As we were scrambled to protect power stations, cities and various other institutions and facilities, speculation flew around the base that we were all about to be put on Home Guard duties. Contingency plans had been drawn up for our role in the event of chaos occasioned by a massive terrorist strike. Once a few weeks had passed and those fears had died down, our attention quickly turned to the Gulf, and there was a sense in the camp of heightened activity and purpose, almost of urgency. It seemed inevitable that British troops would be involved in the American-led invasion, which in turn meant that the 'theatre entry troops' or 'shock troops' of the Royal Marines would almost certainly take part in any airborne or amphibious assault; and that, in turn, meant that the Commando Helicopter Force (CHF) would have to be there to support them from the air, including 847 Naval Air Squadron as well as the Sea King transport and medium-lift squadrons.

It is true that, as advertised, the marines can drop whatever they are doing and be ready to deploy anywhere in the planet within twenty-four hours, but ideally the more time you have to prepare the better. We had about six weeks on this occasion, and we had barely caught our breath by the time we walked into the dockside pub that evening. We put ourselves, and our equipment, through an endless series of tests. There were weapon-handling drills, NBCD (nuclear, biological and chemical defence) drills and gas-mask drills (sitting in a small room while someone lobs in a CS canister); wet and dry dinghy drills and abandon aircraft drills; escape and evasion exercises. We collected our desert camo gear and picked up our personal weapons, which we had to keep clean and zeroed; we had dozens of jabs and medicals; we prepared our ops boxes, containing maps, technical manuals and some supplies; and we collected and studied piles of maps and other miscellaneous publications, manuals and documents necessary for fighting wars in the twenty-first century. And the aircrew of 847 Squadron flew the helicopters as much as we could, practising various techniques and disciplines.

Meanwhile, the engineers stripped down six Lynx AH7 and six Gazelles AH1 into a thousand pieces before painstakingly rebuilding them so that they were in pristine operational condition. They also began fitting what new kit had arrived before we set sail – all the while doing their day jobs of servicing the aircraft before and after all the dozens of extra sorties the aircrew were now flying.

Like the other officers with specific training responsibilities, I had been putting in days of twelve, fifteen, sometimes eighteen hours at the base to try and get every one of our forty-four pilots up to speed. By the time I had arrived in Plymouth and walked up the gangplank of HMS *Ocean* with my Bergen on my back earlier that day, I was already feeling pretty shattered, physically (from work) and emotionally (from home). Throughout our preparations I had felt two powerful tugs of responsibility on my conscience, pulling in opposite directions. At one end there was my wife; at the other there was a squadron of pilots who had to be trained and primed to the highest standards so that they could execute their tasks in the battlefield as safely and successfully as possible. I don't think it's an exaggeration to say that if we went into battle undercooked and ill-prepared, then casualties were inevitable.

Were we ready – *combat* ready? That was the big question nagging away at me in the pub that evening. The enormity and gravity of the task ahead hit home now that we were just a few hours from setting sail, and it was ultimately my responsibility to ensure that everyone in that room was all set to go into battle. When I looked around at 847 Squadron I saw the most experienced helicopter unit ever sent to war by the British armed forces. They were mostly marines, but there were quite a few navy pilots too, plus the American exchange Cobra pilot and a couple from the Army Air Corps. Going through them, man by man, reminded me that it was certainly an impressive outfit.

There were a handful of young guns among us, but most were old sweats who had seen plenty of action in one arena or another over the better part of two decades or so. Every single man in that room would have put his life on the line to save another, but that wasn't the same thing as putting your life in someone else's hands. Pilots who hadn't flown and practised enough, who weren't up to scratch, were as great a liability to their comrades as a T55 or a Roland missile. One stupid mistake, one moment's inattention, could bring down disaster. Any highly aggressive behaviour or anyone losing their cool in the heat of battle could compromise the lives of others.

My training team, all experts in their specialised fields, was as good as you could hope for. I was TO1 (Training Officer One), in overall charge of all our training programmes, including the warfare training. Lush, my right-hand man, was TO2, an identikit Royal Marine with big tash, big muscles and big attitude. He was one of our best pilots – not that I would ever tell him that – and he didn't take shit from anyone, least of all me, his cabin mate on *Ocean* and a mere sliver of a navy pilot next to his bulkier frame. We had bonded quickly since he transferred to 847 after an exchange, instructing with the Army Air Corps, and had only one run-in – there's a limit to how long you can fall out with Lush for. He doesn't bear grudges, and he can't resist a joke. If anyone personified the famous marines' sense of humour, it was Lush. A former member of the Royal Marines parachute display team, he had once taken to the air for a public display with Sonic, another top 847 pilot (and one of our Flight Commanders). The aircraft was at about 15,000 feet, the door was open and the green light had come on, indicating it was time to jump, when Lush tapped Sonic on the shoulder and said: 'Just the one jump today then, Sonic?'

'No, I'm doing the full dozen!' he replied, a little bemused, heading towards the door.

'Not without a parachute on you won't be.'

Having already loaded his battery pack for filming on his back, Sonic had then forgotten to put his parachute pack on . . . it was typical of Lush to wait until the last second before telling him.

Then there was Slaps, the TO3. More Devonian than a cream tea, he was a former sergeant-major who had risen up through the ranks and was a good link between the officers and the NCOs, who had full respect for him. He was one of the most experienced men on the squadron, a Royal Marine down to the soles of his regulation size ten boots, and had flown every kind of helicopter in the British services. In normal company he would not be difficult to spot, with his big moustache, bald head and big frame, but he had about two dozen doppelgängers in the room that night: big men with no hair on their heads, but lots under their noses. (I learned fairly quickly that Royal Marines came in two sizes: big and built like a house, or small and built like a house.) At first I had found the task of motivating a man of such experience and strong character a bit daunting – I didn't imagine that a man of forty-five was going to be too keen on being told what to do by an officer fifteen years his junior – but we quickly developed a good working relationship. He never let you down.

Then there was Cindy, our helicopter warfare training officer, responsible for training us in how to fire the aircrafts' weapons and coordinate fires by the artillery and jets. On the face of it, Cindy looked like an archetypal marine, which is to say he was built like a house. In many ways, though, this eighteen-stone monster was a highly unlikely character to be teaching us how to bring violence to the battlefield . . . for Cindy, weirdly enough, is a sort of hippy. When he's not firing missiles and blowing up tanks, he spends his time communing with nature, collecting crystals, reading poetry, celebrating the summer solstice at Glastonbury or Stonehenge, and studying the legend of King Arthur. Cindy got married dressed as a clown, which tells you just about everything you need to know about the man. Always calm and mellow, fazed by nothing, going about his work slowly and methodically, Cindy's a great person to have around camp to bring some tranquillity to an often frenzied and intense atmosphere. You will meet some marines who are never happier than when they're leopard-crawling through a swamp or bayoneting a division of infantry to death, but Cindy is a man with genuine, unembarrassed respect for the value of human life. For him, violence is always the very last resort, not a reflex reaction. In short, he is one of the most genial and gentle characters you'll meet; but, weirdly, very good at blowing things up too.

Hovis, the EWI, was our in-house electronics geek, a man who can erect an IKEA wardrobe before you have even had time to groan at the thought of it. With all the new kit arriving, Hovis had his work cut out over the coming weeks.

Another highly important member of the squadron was Sweetcorn, the operations officer for the upcoming conflict, responsible for the daily hands-on supervision of our missions. He was going to be the single most important man on the squadron after Clubs and Spidey (the senior pilot) once we arrived in the Gulf and went to war. Sweetcorn and I hadn't been getting on of late. In fact, a row had been brewing over the previous few weeks; and Sweetcorn is not a man you want to have any kind of conflict with, for the simple reason that he usually wins and he's very, very scary. He is – surprise, surprise – an extremely large man with a large shaven head and huge tash under a huge nose. Frankly, Sweetcorn terrifies the wits out of people, friend or foe. To paraphrase the Duke of Wellington talking about his own troops: I don't know what Sweetcorn'll do to the enemy but, by God, he frightens me. He is the alpha male silverback gorilla of the troop, and if he wants to eat all your bamboo and shag your wife, then fine, you just let him go ahead and do it.

Sweetcorn doesn't talk, he shouts: generally about six inches from your face, while standing on your toes. He doesn't negotiate, he commands. He never backs down. If

I saw him on Yeovil High Street, I'd cross the road – but if I found myself down a dark alley with a dozen Fedayeen or IRA charging at me, there's no one I'd rather have for company. This is a man born to bayonet. He loves his Marlboro Reds, which he smokes by the carton-load, but he can still bench-press his own weight all day long. Everything he does, he does aggressively. He even shits aggressively, as I discovered when I sat in the adjacent cubicle to him at Yeovilton one morning. If I saw him striding into work one morning with raw meat hanging out of his teeth I wouldn't bat an eyelid. Away from work he's a pussycat, a really decent man with good values; but once he puts on his uniform in the morning, people throw themselves against walls when he passes by.

My biggest anxiety that evening sitting in the pub was not biochemical warfare, or getting shot out of the sky, or being captured and tortured; it was Sweetcorn. If the squadron was to operate smoothly, he and I would have to resolve our differences about the best way to go about training in the final, crucial weeks before the conflict began. I had strong views on the subject; but so did he, and unfortunately, 'compromise' was one word he was not in the habit of using.

CHAPTER TWO

The winter sun was low on the horizon but there wasn't a cloud in the sky when we started to emerge in long disciplined files, like ants out of an anthill, from the depths of HMS *Ocean* and out on to the giant expanse of the flight deck. Roughly a thousand men, most of them the Royal Marines of 40 Commando, dressed in camo gear and green berets, marched to their pre-arranged standing positions for what is known as 'Procedure Alpha'. Thousands of well-wishers, mainly family, friends and locals, had thronged the quayside to wave us off and there were hundreds of others, including television crews and journalists, packing all the vantage points around Plymouth Sound. I was one of the lucky ones with a view of the scenes below, but others had to spend the two hours that were to follow standing stock-still in the January cold, staring at the back of someone's head.

I spotted a small handful of protestors holding up Stop The War! banners, which isn't really what you want to see when you're about to leave home for half a year and set sail for a potential war zone. They were waving their placards at the wrong people, though, because it wasn't exactly within our power to decide whether we wanted to go and fight this war or not, or to question its legitimacy – in just the same way that it wasn't within the gift of the men who once left England's ports for the Crimea, or the Transvaal, or Flanders, to question why they had been asked to fight. The politicians have always made the decisions, and we – soldiers, airmen and sailors – fulfil our contract to the state. We are paid to fight, with taxpayers' money; we are not paid to have a crisis of conscience. Those protestors might as well have locked themselves in their bathrooms at home and waved their banners behind the shower curtain for all the difference it was going to make. Did they really think all the lads on deck would see all the slogans ashore and say: 'Hey, those guys are right! Sod the war, let's all go back home'?

All the same, it was mildly amusing, and no surprise, to see that the brave dissenters had positioned themselves at a spot some way from the families and other well-wishers, who were unlikely to have looked upon their cause with a great deal of sympathy, to say the least. In fact, they would have been about as welcome as a fart in a biochemical suit. There was a lot of raw emotion in that crowd, and many proud, apprehensive fathers, brothers, sons and ex-servicemen who would have happily torn them limb from limb and thrown them into the Sound. And that's after the mothers, wives and children had had their go.

On deck, the presence of the protestors prompted a few sarcastic mutterings and giggles from the lads: 'Oops, don't fall off that ledge now . . . I hope those courageous young men and women are going to be all right while we're away . . . Come on, you've got to admire their bravery coming out like that on a cold January morning to do their bit for Queen and country . . . They must be in the RAF . . .' Beneath the banter, it was a little galling to be reminded, at that difficult moment of setting sail, that not everyone back home was rooting for us as we headed off.

I knew my mother and father were in there somewhere, but the crowd was so great and the flight deck was so high above the waterline that it was impossible to pick out individual faces. Mum, who is – how shall I put this? – a touch eccentric these days, said she would be carrying a ten-foot plastic poppy so that I might be able to pick her out, but try as I did, I couldn't spot it anywhere.

The week before, I'd been down to Dartmoor to say goodbye to them in the house where I'd spent so many happy years as a child, from which I had run wild on the moors with my best mate Bruce – camping, fishing and, when I was a little older, shooting our lunch and tea. For the first time in my twelve years in the navy, I saw a fear and a tenderness in Dad's look and manner. Unlike Mum, my father, who was a master mariner in the merchant navy for forty years, knew exactly what I did for a living, and he understood as well as I did that this deployment carried far greater risks than any other I had undertaken. He's a hard man, my Dad – South Shields born and bred – and it was strange to see him welling up as he gave me a big hug and told me to look after myself.

It was the same when I had said goodbye to my sisters Laura Jo and Victoria, my brother Ben, and my best friends Stuart and Bruce. Everyone hugged that little bit tighter and longer. Mum, bless her batty socks, probably thought I was heading out to EuroDisney, or going on a Club Med cruise with a few of my mates. She knew I flew helicopters but I don't think she understood – or perhaps she didn't want to understand – that I also fired missiles and machine guns, and that people fired them back at me.

I've never liked Plymouth that much. It's an alien world to me because I'm used to air stations, not naval bases. My Dad, who spent much of his career on the other side of the world, sometimes for a whole year at a time, always takes the mickey because, in his eyes, I've never really been to sea. Over the years I have come to associate Plymouth with the pain of departure, the start of a very long haul, months on end living in a coffin-sized cabin with a twenty-stone marine two feet above my head. The best thing about Plymouth was seeing it heave into view again from the cockpit window and knowing you were almost back home.

The Royal Marine band struck up on the quayside, and the crowd began cheering and singing and frantically waving their Union Jacks and St George crosses as *Ocean* prepared to pull out of the Sound and slip over the horizon. There were people wiping tears from their faces, but there was lots of good humour too. One girl was holding a banner that read: 'Hurry Home Tookie, I want some Nookie!' I couldn't wait to go, to be honest, because the emotion of it was starting to get to me. At the best of times, there is a limit to how much fun there is to be had standing for two hours in the cold winter air, legs astride and arms behind your back, but it's that much worse when you're heading off into an unknown world, where death, danger and destruction await, and all you can hear and see is a crowd of family and friends, almost hysterical with emotion.

As *Ocean* started to slide slowly out of the Sound, we broke from Procedure Alpha and began to file back below deck. I turned my head for a final look at the slowly receding crowds – and there on one of the promontories I saw a bloody great big plastic poppy, bobbing ridiculously in the wind above a sea of heads. The sight of it gave me a start as I imagined Mum standing in the throng, with the tears sure to be rolling down her cheeks; quickly I looked away and headed down through the hatch.

'Mum' is also the affectionate nickname given to HMS *Ocean*. 'We're running a little low on fuel, let's head back to Mum' . . . 'Mum's rolling tonight,' we say. Mum was thoughtful and subdued at that particular moment – she always was in the few hours after departing on a deployment – and there wasn't much banter as, two abreast, we

41

headed down through the hatches and along the 'assault lanes' back to our cabins.

In a few weeks *Ocean* would join a flotilla of over forty ships carrying 31,000 troops – Britain's largest maritime task force since the Falklands War – but for the time being we had only the Type 23 frigate HMS *Northumberland* for company as we powered out into the Channel at full speed of eighteen knots. There are no portholes or windows, except up on the bridge, but I didn't need my eyes to know that very soon the craggy cliffs and bays of Cornwall would be no more than a faint pencil line on the horizon.

At 204 metres long and with a beam of 35 metres and a displacement of 22,500 tonnes, *Ocean* is the biggest ship in the navy, a tad heavier than the aircraft carrier *Ark Royal*, but there certainly wasn't a great feeling of space on board her during the voyage out. She was packed to the gunwales with men and equipment. In addition to the 450 men of 40 Commando, there were 300 aircrew and engineers from 847 and 845 Squadrons, living cheek by jowl with the 250 men and women of the ship's company. The ship is effectively a floating town, with its own bakery, its own shop, its own bank, a cafeteria (nicknamed Starbucks), a gym, a chapel, several canteens and enough provisions on board to serve 4,000 meals a day, or feed a family of four for half a century.

Strictly speaking, *Ocean* is not an aircraft carrier but a helicopter amphibious assault ship that has been fitted and equipped specifically for the type of operations undertaken by Royal Marines. There are only six landing spots up on the flight deck, but in addition to the twelve Sea Kings from the CHF that made up 845 Naval Air Squadron, there were the six Lynx and six Gazelles of 847 Squadron. There were also half a dozen landing craft to ferry ashore troops for the amphibious element of the assault, plus the big 105mm guns, the mortars, the ammunition, the medical back-up teams and the 'Wimics': converted Land Rovers with mounted heavy machine guns, used by special forces and the brigade recce force (BRF). In short, we were carrying a serious amount of equipment. It was absolutely stacked down in the hangar below the flight deck where the engineers had their work cut out to find room for all the aircraft, even after folding in the blades.

The hydraulic platform which lifts the aircraft to and from the deck was closed when I went to seek out 'Engines', the air engineering officer, and his right-hand man 'Deps', to find out when the aircraft might be ready so that we could get cracking on our training as soon as possible. I opened the tiny hatch leading from the corridor and suddenly found myself standing in a space the size of a full football pitch. Walking through *Ocean*'s maze of corridors, with no natural light, you feel like a mole in a network of underground tunnels, and it's a pleasant surprise when you emerge into the enormous open space of the hangar.

'The lads', as the aircrew called the engineers and mechanics, were already busy at work in there, manoeuvring the aircraft in and out of holdings bays with the mini-tractors as they set about opening crates and fitting the new equipment. This cavernous hall was going to remain a hive of activity until the day *Ocean* returned to port, even when the squadron went ashore and set up camp, first in Kuwait and then, not long afterwards, we hoped, in Iraq itself.

All the work would happen down in the hangar, not on the flight deck, where the salty spray of the sea and the often powerful winds of the Arabian Gulf were no help to man or machine. The engineers also needed a safe environment in which to work, free from the risk of both accident and attack.

Engines and Deps, together with their thirty-strong team of engineers and mechanics, were going to be vital over the coming months, as important in their own way as the men who would be doing the flying and the firing. The aircraft were going to be under enormous stress in the desert, flying pretty much around the clock in extreme heat and harsh conditions, and they would have to be fixed, serviced and refuelled at breakneck speed in order to keep two air patrols (each comprising one Gazelle and one Lynx) up in the air from dawn to dusk, and often at night as well. Every time one of us landed back on *Ocean* or in camp, Engines and his boys would have to be waiting to swarm all over the machine, like a Formula One pit-stop team, to get the aircraft back out again as quickly as possible.

The squadron had learnt from past experience that the biggest problem where we were headed was going to be the powdery sand of the desert, which soon finds its way into

every part of the machines, with potentially fatal consequences. Within hours of sailing, the lads had already come
up with a laughably simple ploy to prevent the inevitable
damage caused by millions of glassy shards of sand wearing
down the tail rotor blades: they were going to stick Fablon
tape along the blades of the rotors and then replace it after
each flight! Every time you have to replace the main or tail
rotor blades of a helicopter it effectively costs the taxpayer
hundreds of thousands of pounds; Engines and his team
had just solved the problem at a total cost of about twenty
quid. The pilots may take the piss out of the ground crews
for their evening entertainment, but beneath the banter we
all had massive respect for their resourcefulness, ingenuity
and hard work.

One of the major worries for the ship was storing the
many high-explosive missiles 847 were taking with them. If
just one of them went off by accident, there would be an
almighty firework display that would dwarf any damage and
loss of life caused by an Iraqi Seersucker cruise missile.
There was a small risk of salt corrosion or the heavy
vibrations of the ship triggering an accidental explosion, but
the biggest threat came from the massive amount of energy
emanating from the ship's powerful radar system.

There are thirteen decks on *Ocean*, each of them resembling a racetrack running around the perimeter, and each
containing scores of twin cabins for the men. The decks are
numbered in descending order from thirteen down to one,
and the various sections, running lengthways, were assigned

the standard NATO alphabet letters: Alpha, Bravo, Charlie, Delta and so on. Six Juliet, just below the dreaded water-line, was to be the postcode of my cramped, windowless home over the coming months, in a cabin the size of a railway sleeper berth that I would share with a marine the size of a train.

Unlike those on *Ark Royal*, *Ocean*'s passageways have been designed with width as a priority, so that two fully laden marines can come up the assault routes side by side through the maze of passages, ladders, hatches and stairwells, out on to the flight deck and into the helicopters waiting to fly them into action. The thinking behind the design is that the troops waiting down on the mess decks with their Bergens and guns should be able to get into the helicopters as quickly as possible, without running, so that the craft already up in the air do not have to wait too long in the holding position, circling round and round the ship.

Ocean is a superb ship, what the enemy would call a high-value asset, with a highly efficient company, but it has one drawback: although the hull design is based on the *Invincible* carrier class, it is built using commercial methods. However, it is defended by accompanying frigates and destroyers, and it also has an excellent defence system known as Phalanx designed to stop incoming missiles by firing a circular pattern of bullets, not unlike an old Gatling gun, creating a wall of lead that aims to explode the incoming strike before it hits the ship. There would still be plenty of damage caused by the shrapnel, but the Phalanx, if fired at the right moment, would probably save the ship from a fatal blow. There were also a number of bog-standard general purpose machine guns (GPMGs) mounted around the deck to see off possible suicide attacks by enemy crashing into the ship on jet skis.

As the engineers began the task of fitting the new items of equipment to our helicopters, including a new radio system and state-of-the-art laser system known as LTDRF (laser target designator and range finder), we pilots set about starting to learn how to operate the kit as quickly as we could. Lush had also managed to get hold of a crate of hand-held GPS devices at a good price from one of his contacts in London. We were cleared to use them, but unfortunately we were going to have to operate them by hand.

It was frustrating, as Britain's foremost attack helicopter unit, that we didn't have GPS fitted into our control panels, even though half the population back home were driving around in their family saloons with the instruments sitting on their dashboards. You won't often find me having a pop at the MoD, but this was one piece of kit that we really needed, and preferably not the fiddly hand-held type. Our hands had quite enough to be getting along with in the cab of the aircraft as it was, what with map reading, using the TOW roof sight, firing missiles, and working half a dozen radios and frequencies to talk to the other helicopters, the tanks on the ground, the jets, the artillery, the ships and the AWACS controllers, as well as the team back in the operations room. It did seem incredible to us that while the Americans were climbing into their titanium-protected aircraft fitted out with every imaginable cutting-edge mod con, because we couldn't get an internal GPS fitted in time, we were going to war with a hand-held GPS and a bundle of maps on our knees.

Whenever we apply for new kit to be installed or for any major modifications to the aircraft to be made, there is (a) no guarantee that our request will be approved by the brass in charge of the money and (b) even if it is approved it can take time to reach the Squadron that needs it. The system is tangled in red tape, budgetary constraints and testing procedures at Boscombe Down. The guys who work there do a great job in difficult circumstances, but the inevitable delays from above are a source of constant frustration for us. For instance, for several years the 847 pilots have been pushing to have a PTT (press to transmit) installed on the floor of the Lynx, as on the Sea King, by which we can transmit on the radios using our feet, thus freeing up our hands to look at maps, or work the GPS, sights and missiles; but it has just never happened. There is no end to a pilot's wish list for his aircraft, but there was no doubt that we could carry out our jobs more efficiently if we had an internal GPS and a PTT for operating the radios. A titanium shell to protect us from small-arms fire would have been nice too, but that, for the foreseeable future, is just the stuff of wild dreams.

So, in a typically British military fashion, we just cracked on, making the best of what equipment we had and adapting our flying techniques accordingly, while relying on the imagination, hard work and DIY skills of our ground crew. Those engineers and mechanics, so often the unsung heroes of a deployment, did an incredible job on the way out, getting the aircraft in tip-top condition. We did get a PTT fitted to the TOW left hand grip – it was a great help and arrived just in time, and the engineers fitted it really quickly.

Over the coming weeks, in addition to trying out all this new equipment, there was a multitude of other daily tasks and challenges to address, both in airborne training and back on the ship. The sheer scale of what we had to achieve was overwhelming. For a start, we had to begin to practise flying in our chemical suits and gas masks, which we all hated wearing because they were so heavy, clumsy and hot. Flying the aircraft, and fighting from them, in the extreme conditions of the desert, often in appallingly high winds and in the heat of battle, was going to be difficult enough as it was, but doing so dressed up like Mr Chuckletrousers or Sir Ranulph Fiennes in the Arctic would be almost impossible.

Furthermore, all of us had to improve our night-flying skills as well as our methods for taking off from the ship and 'landing on' – even Spidey, the senior pilot and a man to whom the helicopter is just an extension of his body. This is a far greater challenge than you might imagine, especially in the dark when you have no idea how close to the water you are, you're dizzy with fatigue after two or three days with little sleep and you've just spent the previous ninety minutes dodging rounds of ack-ack, mortars and machine-gun fire. We also needed at least two or three days of live-firing practice in the desert and an assault rehearsal – probably in Cyprus – as well as regular personal weapon training off the back of the ship. Squeezed in among the flying and firing, there was a packed schedule of daily lessons and talks covering a wide range of subjects.

Maps of Iraq with probable enemy defensive positions needed studying; Iraqi fighting tactics, weapons, strengths and weaknesses demanded detailed scrutiny and analysis; and fresh intelligence was coming in all the time. There were escape and evasion guidelines and procedures to run through, as well as advice about biochemical warfare and endless injections to guard against such an attack. There were fitness programmes to complete, personal weapons to clean and prime, specialist flying techniques to perfect, radio frequencies and call signs to learn; lessons on Islamic culture, Iraqi history and basic Arabic language classes; reports to write up, assessments to make, briefings to attend . . . the list was endless.

It was deeply annoying, then, that as *Ocean* headed out of the Channel and into the Atlantic towards the Bay of Biscay the blue skies gave way to heavy cloud and strong winds. With a 300–foot cloud base sitting on top of us, and *Ocean* lurching from side to side like a sailor on shore leave, flying was out of the question for the first three days. Instead, we attended endless planning meetings and ground training lessons. It was Groundhog Day every day as we settled into a monotonous routine, waiting for the weather to clear. We rose between six and seven, shaved in our little basins in the cabins and then queued for the showers (each section of the living quarters had four showers for roughly four dozen men) before joining another queue for breakfast in the officers' dining area. Here you could help yourself to sausages, bacon, baked beans, eggs and tomatoes, or you could go the less popular, healthier route of cereals and fruit. (I was loading up on the fresh fruit, partly because I needed to get into shape, but also because there are only a few days of it at sea before the canned versions start appearing!)

After breakfast all the pilots filed into the briefing room, where we were given an update on the weather and forecasts for the days ahead, the serviceability of the aircraft and the overall training programme for the day. (This daily meeting has been known as 'shareholders', 'shares' for short, since the Korean War, when the Fleet Air Arm lost so many pilots that those who survived took out 'shares' in their squadrons.) The rest of the morning was spent in refresher lessons, most of them given by me and the other training officers . . . and it was remarkable how everyone was now paying full attention. It's not quite the case that back in Yeovilton people were in the habit of throwing paper aeroplanes around or staring out of the window during ground training, but as we headed towards a potential war zone all the pilots were particularly eager to learn and log every last detail we put to them. For us, these small details, and the split seconds saved by having the knowledge to react quickly, meant the difference between life and death.

After a short break for lunch, if we still couldn't fly it was back to ground training and further rounds of briefings. There was no set beginning or end to the working day on the way out, but during those early days of the journey we would start to head back to our cabins between six and seven. There isn't much to do on the ship apart from work, eat and sleep; what 'leisure' time we had was spent in the gym, watching DVDs in our cabins or having a couple of beers in the officers' wardroom, down on two deck.

Security restrictions meant that mobile phones were banned, and calls home on the ship's phones were confined to certain assigned days and times. On the way out to the Gulf, each of us was allowed one free twenty-minute call per week when the security window was opened – and there was of course, no guarantee that any one would be at home when you called. There was also a television in the wardroom, and at the outset we used to tune into the news every evening to find out how the negotiations with Iraq were progressing, hoping a political deal might be reached. There were a small handful who were straining at the leash for some action, but most of us still held out hope, up until the very last minute, that some kind of peaceful resolution to the stand-off might be found.

As for the newspapers, they were next to useless, because

they tended to be a fortnight old by the time they were delivered. When the first set of papers did arrive, there was one article in the tabloids which caused widespread amusement throughout the ship – except, that is, for the boyfriend of the girl who had taken the Murdoch shilling in return for getting her bangers out on page three, wrapped in a Union Jack. It was the same girl who'd been holding the banner in Plymouth that read 'Hurry Home Tookie, I want some Nookie', and the paper had promised the couple a weekend in a luxury hotel to fulfil her desires when he got home. Tookie apparently failed to see the humour or generosity in the offer.

The wardroom was probably the most popular room on the ship, partly because you could find beer and good company in there, but also because it was located at the stern of the ship, by the quarterdeck, where you could stand outside and either enjoy a smoke or get a lungful of fresh sea air while taking in the view as the foamy wake of the ship rushed into the distance just a few feet beneath you. The rest of the marines and matelots relaxed on their mess decks, listening to music, watching films and going to the gym. They're allowed a couple of cans of beer to help unwind but, in contrast to the days of old, mess decks today are largely alcohol-free, mainly due to operations.

If an officer wanted a proper dinner aboard *Ocean*, there was one sitting a day when the stewards served a three-course meal in the dining area, but as the days became ever busier we normally made do with a quick plate of food from the wardroom canteen. The stewards and chefs of the ship's company, whom we've got to know well over the years, look after us superbly and generally do a good job with the provisions available to them, but there comes a point at sea, after a week or so, when you start finding unexpected vegetables and curious combinations on your plate, like lasagne and swede, or spaghetti Bolognese with a side dish of sweetcorn or carrots.

After dinner most of us headed next door – or rather, through the dividing curtain into the wardroom – for a couple of beers and a chat. The wardroom isn't exactly the last word in luxury, but it develops a certain homeliness after a few days at sea. It's about fifty feet square and looks a little like the lounge bar of a 1970s pub on a council estate, without the jukebox or swirly carpet. There are a couple of built-in sofas up against the wall and a scattering of tables and padded chairs around a half-moon bar but, of course, no windows. A flickering television monitor mounted on the wall provides the only view of the outside world. There is one small fridge for 'goffers' (fizzy drinks), one beer pump (70p a pint), a choice of red and white wine, and a few bottles of spirits and mixers. It was a lively place for the first week or two, as we made our way down the Atlantic and across the Mediterranean, but as our working days got longer and our nights got shorter, many of us were too tired, or not in the mood, for beer and banter and headed straight to our cabins after dinner to get as much sleep as possible.

For those who wanted it, however, the wardroom provided the only opportunity for the officers to get together as a group in an informal setting, both to unwind and to discuss the challenges facing us over the weeks ahead. Generally, the talk on these evenings was constructive; but, as we sailed ever closer to the Suez Canal and the tensions and strains started to mount, heated discussions and even the odd argument erupted.

Most of us rarely drank more than two or three cans of beer, or a couple of pints or glasses of wine, because we were generally flying the following day, but there were one or two bigger drinkers in our midst. By and large the wardroom was a very happy place where we sought refuge in company, and found comfort in a drink or two, after a long day. I tended not to go there every night, however, knowing from previous long deployments that much as you may like and respect your colleagues, you inevitably begin to tire of talking to the same people in the same place at the same time day after day. Our working hours were long, and became longer by the day, but that was far preferable to sitting around inspecting our navels, because the boredom of the evening routine and the lack of distractions started to eat away at us fairly quickly. There is a limit to how many times you can watch a DVD of *The Office* or *Phoenix Nights* on a small laptop computer.

Most evenings we retired to our cabins at about midnight. On some older ships to which we are deployed six of us may be allocated a single room to share, but on *Ocean* the officers' cabins are designed for two people, which for me, at least, is the ideal arrangement. Strangely, much as I craved my personal space at times, I didn't want my own cabin because I enjoyed the chat and the company. Still, it can be a terrible experience, particularly on long deployments, if you are assigned to share a cabin with (a) someone you dislike or (b) someone with personal hygiene issues or (c) someone who can't go to sleep until he has pleasured himself and then hands you down a sock from the bunk above, saying, 'Get rid of that willya, sonny, there's a good lad?' I was lucky because my old friend Lush, who showers at least once a day, failed on only one of those counts.

The cabins on *Ocean* are reasonably comfortable, if a little claustrophobic, especially when you are on one of the decks below the waterline and there is a risk of mines and missiles. They are so small that even a couple of dwarves would feel cramped, let alone a pair of outsize marines. When I lay down for the night in my pit in Six Juliet I was able to reach into the sink from my bottom bunk, and sitting upright was completely out of the question, even though I am one of the smaller members of the squadron at five feet eleven. Lush never forgave me for grabbing the bottom bunk, complaining that a man of his age (forty-two) and build (stocky brick shithouse), should not have to climb a ladder in order to go to bed at night. He also had to sleep on his back or front, because if he lay on his side his shoulder got wedged on the deck head.

Other than the beds and the sink, the cabin contained a small wardrobe, two drawers under the bottom bunk and an air vent in the middle of the room; and if I folded my bed up against the wall, I could then pull down a small table the size of a laptop to use as a desk. The cabins, in short, were for sleeping and for storing personal belongings and little else. If you wanted to swing a cat, you had to head up to the flight deck.

With so many of us squashed into such close quarters, within a few days of sailing *Ocean*'s airtight decks and corridors inevitably started to honk, but the ship's company kept her spick and span. However, the smell was especially bad in the hot, fetid atmosphere of the tiny gym down on deck two, where dozens of marines hammered the weights and bench presses until their veins and eyes started popping. It smelt like a dairy at milking time – this was the worst of it though!

For the first few weeks of the voyage, the further we sailed away from home the more I wanted to return. Or perhaps it was more the case that *the closer I got to war*, the more I wanted to return. It's difficult to put a finger precisely on what I was feeling at any one time because there seemed to be so many powerful emotions, pulling me in so many different directions: missing my family and friends, boredom, fear of death, fear of professional failure or letting down my colleagues, determination to acquit myself well, anxiety about my wife coping by herself, worrying about Mum and Dad worrying about me, uncertainty about how long I would remain in the services and what I would do if I did not extend my commission, frustration with stubborn or difficult colleagues, elation after a successful sortie or a breakthrough in the training programme, relief that pilots were making progress in their weaker areas, relief too that, unlike most men on the squadron, I didn't have any young children to miss, mild apprehesion when I went to collect my personal weapons and stored them in my locker, admiration for the uncomplaining professionalism of the guys just getting on with business . . . A ship packed to the gunwales with a thousand men and women is a cauldron of emotions in any circumstances, but heading into a potential war zone every feeling is heightened, every tension soon ratcheted to the maximum.

On the fourth day we 'turned left' as Clubs had promised and passed through the Strait of Gibraltar, and the atmosphere on board reached a new level of intensity. It was then that I started having the odd cigarette out on the quarterdeck in the evenings. Others started writing their wills and 'last letters', handing them to friends to give to their loved ones in the event of their deaths. Conversations started to take a more solemn turn every so often; I remember one strange exchange with another pilot, who said to me over a beer, 'Jim, if I never make it back home, will you tell my wife she was right about the conservatory. Tell her that we should have got one after all, and I was just being tight.' What he was trying to say was, 'Will you tell her how much I loved her?' but, being a big, hairy-arsed killing machine of a marine, he felt he could only express his more tender feelings through the medium of an unbought conservatory extension.

On a separate occasion, another pilot, one of the juniors, sought me out to ask if he thought we'd be back in England in time for the annual air show at RAF Fairford in Gloucestershire. It was a peculiar question, coming as it did apropos of nothing whatsoever, but I could see how his anxious mind was working. He wanted an event in the future on which to fix his mind and his hopes, as if he were throwing a rope ashore to tie him to the life he had left behind and to which he wanted to get back as soon as possible. It was about this time, too, that the onboard chaplain, the Reverend Peter Scott, or 'Bish' as we affect-ionately called him, started to hand out dozens, then hundreds, of crosses and camouflaged bibles. He even blessed our aircraft. (He's not so busy in peacetime!)

A couple of weeks later the 'Dear John' letters started to appear on the notice boards. There is a weird, seldom-used tradition in the navy that when sailors receive letters from girlfriends breaking off relationships, they post them on the wall for everyone to read. Not everyone goes public with their break-ups, but for some this old custom helps them to deal with the sadness. Curiously, these letters tended to have quite a positive effect on morale, because they under-lined that we were all in the same boat, literally and figuratively. They brought us closer together.

Any excuse to bond is welcomed, because the tighter and

the stronger we became as a group of pilots – or soldiers, or just plain fellow passengers – the easier it would be to get through the weeks and months to come, and the better we would execute our jobs. By the same token, what you don't want is discord or division and, worryingly, we had one or two strong personalities sailing on that ship with the capacity to cause a rumpus and upset morale on the squadron. One was Bozo, a fiery old sweat with his fair share of personal problems back home, who had started to seek solace in the tankard in recent months, and we worried he would continue to do so on board *Ocean* – something not tolerated – raising a real danger that he was going to be a liability once we started flying missions over Iraq. You don't want a troubled, angry, sleep-deprived, depressed marine for a co-pilot at the best of times, but least of all when you are flying into a wall of bullets and flak.

It says something for the quiet, mature way that 847 goes about its business and looks after its own that none of us rushed to criticise or berate Bozo, or even to discuss his problems behind his back. Instead, we all just kept a very close watch, raising the odd eyebrow if he started getting grumpy, while trying to lift his spirits and steer him on to a better course. He was, after all, a brave, experienced pilot who had seen plenty of action in his career; he was a good man and a good airman who happened to be having a hard time in his life. However, you couldn't help feel sorry for the man sharing a cabin with him, and we tended to swerve him in the evening if he looked like he planned on a few too many. There was no reason to hasten to judgement on him, because we all knew that if it became obvious that Bozo was going to be a serious liability in the air the CO would have no hesitation in grounding him. Until we arrived in the Gulf, it was best to humour, tolerate and help him through a tough period. Which the ship's company did – brilliantly.

Ginger was another potential source of unrest among us, and it was no surprise that he and Bozo loathed each other with a passion. This character was a young officer on exchange, who, it is fair to say, had done little to endear himself to Bozo since his arrival on the squadron. There has always been a healthy rivalry between the Fleet Air Arm and the Army Air Corps – not to mention the RAF – but the unpopularity of this particular officer had nothing to do with inter-service tensions. It was a question of personality, and Ginger had already had a number of clashes with other pilots before we'd even set sail.

You'd have thought that a man on an exchange in a squadron of pilots who had grown into a tightly knit group of friends over the years would tread carefully and go to some lengths to accommodate himself with his new colleagues. But Ginger proved to be confrontational with some pilots from the moment he arrived. He never drank while we were at sea but once, on exercise in Norway, he'd flown into a rage after a couple of drinks and attacked another pilot. Picking up a ski, Ginger hurled himself at the pilot and almost cut him in half as he swung it into his midriff. He ended up needing stitches to sew up his wound, even though he had been wearing several thick layers of clothing to keep out the cold. Needless to say, from then on Ginger faced an uphill struggle to win the respect and affection of his new colleagues. He was another character we'd be keeping a close eye on once we had reached the Gulf, because there was the feeling he could be a serious liability if he lost his cool in the air.

I had only had one 'fight' in the military. During my first tour with 847 in the late 1990s I ended up having a brawl right in the middle of my own leaving do. This character, the son of a high-profile public figure, was a first-rate pilot, and we had become very good friends by the time my first tour with 847 was over. DJ loved a good night out on the booze and he certainly hadn't kept away from the bottle on the evening we came to blows. We were in a smart hotel some-where in Dorset and everyone had been drinking fairly heavily, enjoying the opportunity to let off some steam after a hard few weeks. Suzi and I had been going out with each other for about two years by then and I knew he had developed something of a soft spot for her. He had spent a lot of the evening chatting her up and finally, in front of everyone in the room, he went down on one knee and 'proposed' to her. I was on the business end of a few pints myself and had been growing increasingly irritated by the flirting, so at this point I saw red and waded in. There followed lots of schoolboy pushing and shoving and swearing – to the great delight, needless to say, of all our colleagues.

DJ and I decided to settle our differences in time-honoured fashion with a good bare-knuckle scrap outside. Everyone else filed out to watch as we took off our black tie jackets and rolled up our sleeves. They were loving it. It was like being back in the playground. I've never been a brawler and most of the marines would have me for breakfast if I were ever daft enough to come to blows with any of them. But that night DJ, though fairly tidy with his fists, and quite large with it, was drunker than me and I fancied my chances. With everyone laughing a little nervously and egging us on, I let fly with the first punch – and completely missed him. My momentum swung me around in a circle and I fell to the ground like a screen drunk, but at the same time he leant back to avoid the blow and also fell over, leaving us both groping at the air as we tried to get back up. It was a scene straight out of Laurel and Hardy.

At this point, the adjutant arrived on the scene. You don't mess with adjutants: they perform a similar role to sergeant majors, only they're officers and have the responsibility and the right to enforce discipline on everyone in the squadron, including the other officers. This particular adjutant, the CO's right-hand man, was a very large, battle-hardened marine, only a little smaller than the hotel itself. He picked the pair of us up by our scruffs, like we were newborn kittens, and then turned a deep blue colour as he screamed a tirade of abuse in our faces, along the lines of 'You two are a bloody disgrace . . .' He then proceeded to punch us both in the stomach as hard as he could before marching back inside, leaving us writhing on the floor desperately trying to catch our breath. I was so badly winded I couldn't get up for about ten minutes. Finally we staggered to our feet, shook hands, slapped each other on the back, went back inside and carried on as if nothing had happened. (We are still great friends today.)

That's the way it tends to be in 847 Squadron. It doesn't normally come to blows, but whatever the nature or intensity of the row, you settle your differences quickly, shake hands and then move on.

As *Ocean* powered towards Cyprus my simmering row with the operations officer, Sweetcorn, potentially far more serious than that childish fracas in the Dorset hotel, was threatening to boil over. The tension between us was getting worse by the day, because at the heart of it was a very significant issue: namely, how we were going to make best use of the crucial upcoming weeks in training. It wasn't so much a personality clash – although it can be difficult to pass the salt and pepper to Sweetcorn sometimes without having a personality clash; it was a question of correct procedure, with lives on the line. In crude terms, Sweetcorn wanted to go straight into operational war training, and I wanted to concentrate on making sure all our flying skills were completely up to speed before we started firing the missiles and working on battle procedures and so on.

It may sound daft, but I believed our main priority as a squadron was to ensure that landing on and taking off from the ship, in any weather, became second nature for our pilots. You'd think that getting airborne and landing again would be pretty straightforward, even elementary, for experienced, elite helicopter crews. But it's not. It's not like driving a car, where you just get in, fire the ignition and away you go – or if it is, it's like driving a car in pitch black at 130 miles an hour with no headlights through an assault course of hazards. You can't see the water below, and you're trying to find a ship which has always turned off all its lights and is constantly on the move to guard against attack. Sometimes the ship might have to manoeuvre sharply as you're closing in to land, and all too often there will be powerful winds buffeting the aircraft as the ship pitches and rolls in the darkness. It was likely, too, that we would all be fairly exhausted even before the conflict began, and fatigue can be a killer for helicopter pilots. Most deaths in the Gulf were likely to be caused by crashes, collisions and people ditching on take-off or missing the ship in the dark following a malfunction. So getting to and from ship safely was one of our biggest challenges. Furthermore, most of us had never flown in the desert, and most of those who had hadn't had more than a few hours of training experience in those conditions. Flying in temperatures up to 50 degrees inside the helicopter was going to be a shock, especially wearing night vision goggles (NVGs): another new skill to learn.

Back in Yeovilton, over the couple of months before we sailed, I'd been inundated with requests for extra training from pilots who had been perfectly happy with their flying skills up until then. These requests continued to flood in after we had set sail, and there was one evening in the wardroom when a handful of the boys turned on me, angry that they weren't getting enough practice. (There is nothing like the prospect of a war to concentrate the mind so keenly!) Also, we had five pilots on the squadron who had not passed all the relevant tests to render themselves combat ready (CR). To gain CR status pilots have to prove their competence in a wide range of tasks and skills, including an amphibious assault exercise, Arctic training, firing live missiles, calling in artillery and jets, operating as an air observation platform, moving troops and equipment, flying at night and flying in tactical formation, as well as 'nap of the earth' flying, whereby pilots fly as close to the ground as possible, under radar, to avoid detection. If, as had happened a year earlier, our annual trip to the Arctic in Norway was cancelled through a lack of money and some units were deployed elsewhere, the pilots who had been scheduled for assessment lost the chance to become CR that year. These men were not meant to fly combat missions in the Gulf, but there were others who could make the CR grade if they came through various exercises during training on the way out to Iraq. We needed these boys.

At the time we set sail, night flying was still the biggest cause of anxiety, because it is by far the most difficult and stressful form of flying that we do. At night, you rely for your survival not on your own senses but on a heavy pair of

NVGs sitting on the outside of your helmet through which the world appears as a light green image with little depth perception and with a few blotches of haloed light. It is virtual reality for real, and it can be discomfiting and disorientating to be manoeuvring through the darkness in a sky thick with air traffic, surrounded by radars and missile systems that are poised to blow you out of the sky at the first hint of an air controller's suspicion.

Flying a combat helicopter is not just something you learn once and then forget about. It involves constant practice, hours of it. In 847, the standards are as high as any in the British services because the roles of the squadron are so many and so varied. Most helicopter squadrons exist for a single purpose such as transportation, airborne early warning operations, search and rescue, anti-submarine warfare and so on, but at 847 we are trained for a broad range of different tasks we might be asked to carry out by the commandos we support: armed action, reconnaissance and observation, the direction of fire on to enemy targets, night flying, casevac and medevac (the evacuation of casualties or patients) and, to a limited degree, the movement of men and equipment, all performed flying at under fifty feet. Our primary role, however, is 'to deliver violence to the battlefield'.

Originally known as 3 BAS (3 Commando Brigade Air Squadron), 847 and the rest of the CHF earned the nickname 'Junglies' for their early operations in the tropical conditions of the Far East. Today, though, we are trained to fly in any conditions, wherever our skills and firepower may be needed to assist the Royal Marines: in the Arctic, in the desert, in the mountains . . . The whole point of 847 is to be as flexible as possible, prepared for any eventuality and, like the marines, ready to deploy anywhere in the world at seventy-two hours' notice. As we prepared for the Gulf, no one needed to tell us that our role would be to provide armed support for an amphibious or air assault by 40 and 42 Commando. That was going to mean a great deal of flying between *Ocean* and our forward operating bosses in the desert, often at night, and often at short notice.

My view was that before we moved on to any other form of training, flying the helicopters had to be something we could do while barely thinking about it, as if we were operating on automatic pilot. People refer to this instinctive ease of flying as 'strapping the aircraft to the back', as though we just threw a Bergen on and got going. The pilot, not the helicopter, must be in control. We didn't want to be struggling with the flying because there was going to be so much else on which we'd need to be concentrating. In order to get everyone up to these very high standards, we would have to use up many man-hours of flying – and this was what infuriated Sweetcorn. I understood that, as operations officer, he felt a different responsibility, an urgency to start prosecuting what he felt was a more important aspect of our preparations. He had a good point, too, because most of us had never fought in a war; but in my judgement, my priority shaded his. I also felt that Cindy was already doing a superb job in preparing us for warfare. And so Sweetcorn and I clashed, again and again: we clashed after the morning 'shareholders' meeting, we clashed in ground training and briefings, and we clashed over drinks in the wardroom in the evening – and in between there was just an awkward silence. Unfortunately, Sweetcorn doesn't do backing down or compromise, and on this issue, nor did I. But the dispute had to be resolved as quickly as possible, partly because time was running out, and also because it was threatening to cause a split in the squadron.

CHAPTER THREE

When we sat around over a few beers in the wardroom in the evenings, with war looking increasingly likely by the day, the reality of all the risks facing us in the Gulf began to rise to the surface of our conversation like the bubbles in our warm lagers. The Al-Faw was not Plymouth Sound, Basra was not Yeovil, the desert was not Salisbury Plain – and the figures jumping out of a building to take a shot at us were not going to be pop-up cardboard figures; they were going to be real soldiers with real weapons who would be defending their land, their home towns, their families and their brothers-in-arms every bit as furiously as we would defend ours.

In terms of flying the helicopters, our greatest concern was operating over the sea at night as pairs of aircraft, but there were plenty of other grave dangers too, apart from the obvious one of being shot or blown out of the sky. Friendly-fire incidents, whether we were on the receiving or the delivering end, ranked highly in our list of anxieties. In other conflicts the fear of the helicopter being hit by an air defence missile would be a major issue too, but we hoped that the special forces and the fast jet boys would have taken out most of the Iraqi air defences by the time we went in.

Mines in the Gulf would always be a threat, but the British and the Americans both had minesweeper ships and teams of men operating to prevent such an attack. With tens of billions of dollars' and pounds' worth of coalition hardware floating around in the Gulf, not to mention tens of thousands of men and women, it was highly unlikely that the war planners would let an old-fashioned mine slip through the net and cause serious damage to any of our assets. An attack by a Scud or Seersucker (aka Silkworm) missile on *Ocean* or on our camp in the desert, however, was a real danger. Even though these weapons have to be fired from giant transporters, which are visible by satellite and easy prey for special forces if they could get there in time, they pose a particular threat because they can be fired from a long way off, even several hundred miles behind the front line of the battle. These Scuds and Seersuckers are capable of causing immense damage but their accuracy is not always guaranteed and it is often good luck if one manages to make a direct hit.

Then there was the threat of a biochemical attack, which

was almost too hideous to think about, but at the time loomed large in our conversations. We were, after all, going to war on the grounds that Saddam Hussein was in possession of such apocalyptic instruments of mass destruction, so we had to assume that they were at his forces' disposal. Furthermore, we figured that if he had been prepared to use them against his own people, as he had done in the Kurdish village of Halabja, then surely he would be even happier to deploy them against an invading force attempting to unseat him from power. For over twenty-five years Saddam's political *raison d'être* had been simply to hold on to power at all costs, and he had shown he was prepared to go to any lengths to achieve that. We had been receiving our Naps and Bats injections and boosters for weeks on end to guard against some forms of biochemical attack, but they offered only limited protection against certain types of agent. We had all seen the images of blistered, choking victims of biochemical strikes and needed no reminding of the potentially appalling scenarios that might unfold. Our bar-room reasoning, however, was that because biochemical weapons come under the highest category in military planning, if Saddam so much as lobbed in our direction a single rocket containing biological or chemical agents, then our brass might have no option but to retaliate, immediately, with the most powerful weapons we have to bring the conflict to an abrupt, albeit awful, conclusion.

All these scenarios were regarded as real threats, but if

you had carried out a poll among the forty-four pilots of 847 Squadron heading towards the Gulf, you would have found that the greatest fear among us was the fear of being shot down and captured. Endlessly, we discussed what we would do in such an event. There were, broadly, three options open to us: (1) try to escape, then stand and fight to the last bullet, then surrender; (2) try to escape, stand and fight, then keep the last bullet for yourself; (3) surrender immediately, in the hope that you would be treated more leniently.

Needless to say, many of the marines signed up to the options involving leopard-crawling their way through the burning desert and fetid swamps to the Kuwaiti border and, if caught, then fighting to the death while bayoneting as many as possible of the enemy along the way. Most of the others chose the fight-to-the-last-bullet-then-top-yourself option. I was one of the few who thought the best altern-ative was to fight to the last bullet and then surrender, my thinking being that there was always a chance that you might be able to cut a deal with a senior officer who was keen to cross over to the coalition side to secure his family's survival and safety. Getting captured by regular forces would certainly be an unwelcome development, but the worst-case scenario was falling into the hands of lawless insurgents.

You certainly couldn't accuse the Fleet Air Arm of failing to prepare their pilots for the worst. Like all cadets, I had to pass courses in both escape and evasion (E&E, as it is more commonly called), and resistance to interrogation, or R2I, before I was awarded my wings. The two weeks we spent living rough, trying to evade capture before being 'interrogated' by our gaolers, were by a very considerable distance the most difficult challenge of my life up to that point. Nothing in my previous experiences in any way prepared me for the stress and pain this exercise entailed. By the time it came to an end, I was an emaciated, hollow-eyed, shivering wreck . . .

Different parts of the services go about E&E training in different ways, but the Fleet Air Arm (FAA) takes a greater interest in the process than most owing to the distinctive nature of our work. The likelihood of an RAF jet, flying at 40,000 feet, being shot down and the pilots having to eject is minimal compared to the risks facing helicopters flying a few dozen feet above the ground and often landing in hostile terrain, including jungles and deserts, on reconnaissance or troop transport missions. We could be shot down by a 9mm pistol. (The RAF exercises, they like to remind you at Dartmouth, are a far cushier affair: they take place over two or three days, and at the end of each day the cadets head back to a hotel for a hot dinner and a good soak in the tub.)

It is with good reason that the courses we have to pass in the FAA are very similar to those undertaken by special forces. Like the SAS and SBS, we often operate right up to and beyond the front of the battle, or FLOT (forward line own troops), deep inside hostile territory, or past the FLET (forward line enemy troops). These acronyms are the clearly demarcated battlefield zones they teach you on a blackboard at Dartmouth, Sandhurst and Cranwell, but in truth most battles do not fall neatly into those categories any longer, and in the Gulf it was very unlikely to be the case that our troops were going to line up, Waterloo-style, on one side of no-man's-land, with the Iraqis taking up their neat formations a few kilometres away on the other. For the first few days there was likely to be a semblance of coherence to the positions, but thereafter there would be no clear lines showing us where the friendlies ended and the enemy began. The battlefield was going to be fluid and ever-changing. 'No plan survives the first contact with the enemy,' we say.

A further reason why our superiors want to ensure that we are never captured is that all pilots, as officers or non-commissioned officers (NCOs), are privy to highly valuable information. The general infantryman on the ground doesn't need to have specialist knowledge, he only needs to know about the job in hand. Aviators, though, are regarded as high-value assets (HVAs), because we have to be given a great deal of information in order to be able to execute our jobs. I need to know, among other facts, where all the other friendlies are positioned on the battle front, as well as the exact location of our engineering and operations base, how many and what jets and helicopters are out there that day and what weapons systems are on board. I also know all the tactical call signs and radio frequencies of the other pilots and units on the ground, which is knowledge the enemy would be very keen to get hold of for 'spoofing' purposes. (Spoofing is a ploy whereby communications experts tap into a radio channel, record the voices, and then edit and doctor them to send false information back out to the enemy over the airwaves, perhaps to lure an aircraft squadron or a tank troop into an ambush, for example.)

Most important of all, though, is the fact that aviators are also apprised of our CO's mission plans, which are known as 'one-up' and 'two-up'. 'One-up' is information relating to a short-term or daily objective of my CO, such as a mission to seek out and destroy the enemy's communications network. If they can find out that that was our aim for the day, then they can take steps to prevent it from happening. 'Two-up' refers to the wider, longer-term intentions of the land component commander – such as, for example, a plan not to take the battle into Basra itself but to secure the area around the city instead and hope for an uprising. All this type of information is gold dust to the enemy, but they need to get it out of us quickly because they know that after twenty-four hours the current missions end and fresh ones are launched. They also know that hasty modifications to the battle plan might be made as a result of our capture, in the fear that we might give away the plans under interrogation.

My E&E training began very soon after I had arrived at Dartmouth as a nineteen-year-old cadet in 1991. There is sound logic behind the decision to throw cadets into the course so early in their training. E&E is one of the hardest aspects of all FAA training, and the navy doesn't want to spend the better part of three years and several million pounds training you, only for you to collapse in a forest at the end of it and decide that, in fact, perhaps you did want to be a landscape gardener after all.

The course starts with two weeks of lectures and demonstrations teaching you the basics of fieldcraft, the knowledge that will enable you to survive in the wild. You learn how to make a silk map to sew into your flying jacket, how to snare animals, how to fish, how to collect condensation for drinking by tying bags around plants, how to bury yourself quickly in a shallow grave (and even make a straw to breathe through if you need to), how to make a compass with a needle and thread. (I don't think I'd be giving away too many state secrets if I reveal to those who didn't already know that to make a compass you simply magnetise the needle by rubbing it, and then lay it into a puddle of water. It should spin to align north/south.) They also told us how to kill an attacking dog (either stab it in the throat, or put a fist in its mouth and then down its throat) and how to kill a person with a blade (stick it up through the ribcage from behind or in through the back of the neck and into the brain). They even teach you how to take a crap and leave behind no evidence of it for your pursuers.

The instructors who supervised our fortnight-long practical exercise, which started in the wilderness and ended back at the interrogation centre, were a highly experienced team of Royal Marine and special forces officers. I had total respect for them from the moment the exercise started to the day I was finally released, even when they were pushing us to the outer limits of our endurance. The only equipment they allowed us to take was a small tobacco tin, in which we could store whatever we liked (it's the same amount we'd be able to fit into the foot pocket of our flying overalls). Most of us took a few boiled sweets for energy, a fishing line and hook, a tampon (which is just very compressed cotton wool and ideal for fire-starting), a small piece of flint for a spark and some condoms for storing water. The smokers tended to find room for a small amount of baccy and rolling papers. One colleague on the previous course was caught digging up some food he had buried in a field before the exercise began and was instantly failed. When he was put through the course again, they made his life hell.

In an attempt to simulate a real scenario, they break you down into units of two, three or four men, which are the sizes of most aircrews in the FAA. There were three in our group, and the first thing the instructors did was strip us naked and look under our foreskins and up our arses to make sure we hadn't hidden anything useful there.

We were then blindfolded, put into the back of a truck and driven around for two hours in the middle of the night. Any dim hopes I might have been harbouring that our instructors would treat us with even a modicum of leniency or sympathy were painfully dashed in the back of the truck.

After roughly an hour, I lifted my blindfold to sneak a look to find out where we were (answer: on the M27) and promptly received a punch in the guts from one of the marines that left me lying on the floor, coughing and wheezing.

We were dropped off in what appeared to be the New Forest, judging by the trees, flat terrain and general feel of the place. (OK, OK, I already knew that from looking out of my blindfold.) 'Right, you've been shot in the leg,' said the instructor, pointing to one of my fellow cadets, the biggest of the three of us. 'And you two are going to carry him to this grid reference where you will be met by a friendly contact. You can either make a stretcher or take it turns to carry him over your shoulder. Be there in four hours, or you've failed the course. And don't forget that we have men out there watching you, so don't think you can get way with not carrying him!' With that, they jumped into the truck and drove away. The aim was to exhaust us and put us under as much stress as possible at the outset, because that would be the likely scenario in a real incident, when we'd be running like the wind to get as far away from the enemy as we could.

The run that followed nearly killed us, and when we arrived at our pre-arranged grid to meet our contact, we collapsed on the ground, soaked to the bone with sweat, gasping and dizzy with exhaustion. There was, however, no contact waiting for us there: just a note under a brick by a post, telling us we'd been compromised and to hurry to another grid by sunrise. And so it continued for the first few days. There never was a contact waiting for us: just another note with further instructions. So we just ran, and ran, and ran. At each grid reference we had been instructed to leave a sign, like a stone pointing in a particular direction, indicating that we were safe and also that none of us was in need of medical treatment. As the exercise wore on, our contacts at last started to appear; we'd see our man 100 yards or so away and lie up on the treeline or in a ditch to await his signal, praying that he would give the message to stop running. If he lit up a cigarette and immediately stubbed it out it meant that we were safe to emerge; if he took three quick drags he was telling us that there were enemy around and we'd have to find further instructions at the location. Every time our increasingly desperate hopes were dashed, and on we would run. One night, a week or so into the exercise, I was lying in a stinking drain under a road, surrounded by turds and piles of pink toilet paper, when the contact emerged right in front of me, and my heart jumped: he was so close, surely he was just going to turn around and say 'OK, sonny, it's all over, you're safe now, out you come!' But then he took three quick drags and disappeared back into the woods. I wanted to weep.

Each day we had short intervals in which to rest and, if it was still daylight, we quickly dug shallow graves and gratefully lay down in them, breathing through the leaf litter as we tried to get some sleep. We had to sleep in the graves because normal life was still going on in the forest during the day: people were out there walking their dogs, taking picnics, foraging for wild food or just going for a stroll to enjoy the beauty of the natural surroundings. We knew that if any of them spotted us and reported it to the police, then we would fail the course and have to start it all over again. On several occasions we were almost compromised by civilians coming within just a few feet of us. It's amazing how close people get without seeing you. (Remember that the next time you go blackberry picking or dog walking . . . You never know who's lying in the bushes a few yards away!) One day I was lying in a trench, my face blackened with mud, my hair wild and my clothes filthy from days and nights sleeping rough, when an elderly man stood within a few inches of me as he bent down to pick up a stick for his dog. I could see his blue eyes and hear his breath as he leant towards me, and I lay stock still until he had gone – partly because I didn't want to fail the course, but also because if he had seen me the poor chap would probably have had a heart attack.

A few days in we lost track of time, aware only that several nights had passed, so it was difficult to say what day it was when our instructors left notes for all the units on the run to meet at a particular grid in the morning. We had completed the first phase of the escape exercise, which was based on the principle of trying to get as far away from the 'aircraft crash site' as possible. We were still technically behind enemy lines, and over the following days we convened at various locations to be shown how to put the theory of fieldcraft, or bushcraft, into practice. We had not been given any food up to that point but they had provided us with plenty of fresh water with which to fill up our water bottles at the different locations to which we had been sent. They allowed us this small luxury because they didn't want us going down with dehydration, or illness from drinking infected water, in the first few days of the exercise. This wasn't kindness on the instructors' part, however; it was all part of the realism because, in a genuine crash and escape scenario, we'd all be carrying fresh water with us. (We also used condoms to carry water. One of the guys in my unit, when filling his up, turned to the instructor and said: 'It's amazing, isn't it? You put three fluid ounces into one of these little rubbers and they burst, but pour in a gallon and they're absolutely fine.' He received a size twelve boot up the arse for his bit of banter.)

There are four main priorities out in the field in a temperate climate: protection, location, water and, lastly, food. In theory, you can go up to a month without food, but you're as good as dead without water after four or five days in a normal environment. In the desert or the extreme cold (where you dehydrate even faster than in the heat), you can survive for only about twenty-four hours without water, and you are encouraged to drink about ten litres a day in those conditions if you can. We were constantly thirsty during the exercise, and you have to resist the temptation to drink too much at one go, as I found to my cost when I downed my water bottle, promptly vomited it all back up and had to go several more hours on the run before I could stomach my next drink.

Shelter was crucial, too, because if you are exposed to the elements, and you are exhausted and weak, illness will soon set in and render you incapable of escaping, compromising not just yourself but your comrades. Keeping dry and warm is of paramount importance when you are on the run, and that was one thing that wasn't too challenging there in the New Forest, because there were plenty of branches and ferns with which to make a basha and a comfortable bed to lie on. It is imperative, though, to build your shelter in an appropriate location where there is access to water, and food to hand as well, if at all possible. Ideally, too, you want to be in a position from where your rescuers can pick you up, preferably near an open space where you can lay out an SOS signal with stones or other materials and which is big enough for a helicopter to land.

Even though I was shattered, weak, starving, dizzy and disorientated by this stage, I actually enjoyed the fieldcraft element of the course because it wasn't that different from all the times I'd spent living and sleeping wild on Dartmoor throughout my childhood. I already knew how to fish with a basic line, how to snare and how to collect water, and I had a reasonably good idea what flora and fauna were safe for us to eat. Boiled nettles I knew made a nutritious and weirdly delicious soup. I knew the poisonous berries to avoid and the edible mushrooms to collect, and I knew that sorrel, pig's nut, dandelions, hawthorn and young beech leaves, and many other plants, were not just OK to get by on, but positively good to eat.

Food is the least important of the four main priorities of survival because it's generally the easiest to get hold of and you can survive long periods without any. That said, it is more difficult to forage for food in some environments than in others. In the desert, for instance, food is hard to come by, but in the jungle, it's like living in a supermarket – as I discovered on an E&E exercise in Belize one year, when I actually managed to put on weight.

On this exercise in the New Forest, in spite of the abundance of plants to eat, I was amazed by how quickly and how far our energy levels dropped. Within a few days we were all working in slow motion, taking an eternity to carry out relatively simple tasks like chopping logs or collecting firewood. We quickly began to crave carbohydrates and high-protein foods like red meat. When I managed to catch a squirrel, the other two were so excited I thought they were going to try and make love to me when I brought it back to camp. I had identified a squirrel run across a stretch of forest floor and up a tree, and so laid a snare overnight at the foot of the trunk. When I returned the following morning, grinning from ear to ear, holding Squirrel Nutkin by his bushy tail, my colleagues stared at me in awe, their mouths wide open, before jumping to their feet to hug me. (For those who might be concerned for the squirrel, it died a painless death as the loop through which it put its head tightened hard and throttled it instantly as it tried to run away.)

For some reason, my abiding memory of this episode was my amazement at the size of the squirrel's testicles, which looked far too big for an animal of its size. After skinning and roasting it over the fire, using sticks to hold it in place, we ate every last part of it with a Stone Age relish (well, almost!), sucking its bones until our mouths hurt. I didn't think much of it at the time, but it's interesting now to recall how quickly we descended from civilised human beings into near-savages, savouring every tiny morsel of a meal we would never have dreamt of touching back at home.

As soon as we had finished our feast our energy levels went through the roof, as if we were high on drugs, and we immediately started running around chopping logs and gathering wood in a frenzy of activity. Later we boiled up the tiny bones for a stock and used it to make a perfectly reasonable soup with mild mushrooms and nettles. I then tied the tail into my hat, Davy Crockett-style, but regretted that a few days later when one of the instructors ripped it from my head, with lip-curling contempt.

Officially, we were not allowed to rummage through bins outside houses and pubs, and you would fail the course if you were caught. We tried that only once and found it counterproductive because we expended more energy getting there and back than we gained from eating the scraps, delicious as they were.

After about ten days, on one of the mornings when we

were instructed to meet the course leaders they gave us a demonstration on killing and skinning chickens and rabbits. We had all lost over a stone by this stage and we must have cut very sorry, dirty, skinny figures when we staggered to the meeting point that morning because, at the end of the session, they let each unit keep one of the animals to eat. Only a bucket of Kentucky Fried Chicken could have made us happier. It was the sole act of kindness we were shown over the entire four weeks. Our chicken tasted truly, mouth-wateringly incredible, probably the most enjoyable meal I've ever eaten, but it came at a very high price.

There was a guy in our unit called Bruce who had never killed a chicken, and so the instructors showed him how to pick it up by the legs and hang it upside down before killing it. In this position, the chicken tries to turn its head upwards, presenting the holder with a lovely clear stretch of neck to whack with a stick. But Bruce, like all of us, was so exhausted and uncoordinated, virtually hallucinating, that when he came to hit the chicken, he completely missed and shattered his knee as he followed through. The impact made a noise like gunshot and one of the other cadets threw up almost instantly at the sound of it, while Bruce himself collapsed on the ground in agony and went white as he writhed from one side to the other. 'Great,' I thought, assuming the instructors would take Bruce straight to hospital. 'More chicken for the other two of us.'

Not a bit of it.

'Right,' said the instructor. 'Get on with it. You're in the field. This could happen for real. See you in two days' time.'

Although I didn't know it at the time, the last task they set us during the escape element of the course was a night navigation examination, 'Night Navex' for short. I'd been looking forward to this part because I'd always fancied myself as a pretty impressive navigator, both on the ground and in the air. The trick, I like to tell my less talented colleagues, is to keep it all very simple. Don't necessarily go the most direct way, but take the route with the least risk of getting lost . . . *Just follow the telegraph poles, turn left at the river, turn right at the farm, stick to the road heading south and bingo, you'll come to the target* . . . I've often found, tempting though it may be, that if you simply follow the crow's flight, the shortest and most obvious-looking route to your target or destination, you are more likely to go wrong because you do not have the clear landmarks to guide you there.

I was so confident in my outstanding navigation skills that I immediately volunteered to lead our unit on the Night Navex . . . and promptly managed to get us all completely, utterly, hopelessly lost, having taken a wrong turn at the outset. After a couple of hours of fruitless wandering, the three of us decided to split up and go our own ways, with the other two muttering something under their breath about 'a useless, cocky wanker' as they staggered off into the undergrowth. Being the genius navigator that I am, a Lewis and Clark character for the modern era perhaps, I then proceeded to get even more lost. I couldn't even find one of the checkpoints where you report in, admit you've screwed up, take an ear-bashing and then get dropped off somewhere else to try again. I knew now that the instructors would be out looking for me, in case I was injured or had fallen ill, and I knew, too, that when they found me they'd be sure to give me a proper fucking hiding in the back of the truck for the inconvenience I had caused them.

There is a safety routine we were told to follow when you are as utterly off course as I was: head south until you hit the main road and walk east along it until you come across one of the instructors in his Land Rover. I finally found the road, and as I was stumbling through the bushes to the side of it I saw a car parked up: the interior light was on, and inside was a young girl, looking deeply distressed. The situation presented me with a massive dilemma. For two weeks I had managed to avoid being compromised by a member of the public, but did I now risk failing the course by helping her? God only knew what had happened to her – or what might happen to her – but she looked almost hysterical.

I lay up in the bushes and considered what to do. After a few moments I found my moral bearings: it was obvious that I couldn't leave her there, sitting on a dark, empty road in the middle of the New Forest at three o'clock in the morning. If it were my wife, sister or mother in distress, I'd hope that someone would do the decent thing and go to her aid, so I stumbled out of the bushes and crossed the road towards her car. For the rest of my days, I will never forget the look of absolute terror on her face when I walked up to the car and knocked on the window. I had not seen a mirror for two weeks, but I knew that I looked like a caveman. My hair and beard were matted with dirt, my drawn face and ripped clothes were caked in filth and my eyes had sunk into bony hollows. The poor girl screamed and screamed and screamed for so long I almost gave up and left her. 'LEAVE ME ALONE!!!' she yelled over and over again as she cowered over to the side of the vehicle.

After about ten minutes I managed to calm her down enough for her to open the window an inch or so and I was able to explain to her that I was in the military and I took out my ID card to prove it. I wasn't convinced that she believed me when I told her that I was going to go to one of the instructors who would call the police out on his radio. I imagined she thought I was just a weirdo in the woods and was keen to be shot of me, but as I began to walk away she called me back and asked if she could return the favour in any way.

I joked that I could murder a Big Mac meal and then jogged off down the road to find help. (When I recounted this story a few days later, one of my fellow cadets, with a dark, ribald sense of humour, said: 'You should have replied: "Sure, do you mind if I play with your breasts for a bit?"' Somehow I don't think she would have seen the comedy in the comment.)

I found the instructor asleep at the wheel in his Land Rover. After bollocking me for my awful Navex skills, he contacted the police, and then dispatched me back to the woods for the rest of the night. The following morning I turned up at the pre-arranged meeting point with the other cadets, and we were sitting and lying around on the grass when the instructor arrived and got out of his Land Rover holding a large McDonald's bag. Words cannot describe the truly incredible smell of that bag, and I sat there salivating as the instructor gave a little talk to all of us, praising me for TCUP (thinking clearly under pressure) in helping the girl. When he had finished he walked over to me and opened the bag, and I almost passed out with hunger and excitement as he approached. The big matelot bastard then proceeded to eat the entire contents of the bag while standing about one foot from my face. He chewed every mouthful of his Big Mac, large fries, and apple pie as slowly as he could, and pulled theatrical faces to show how much he was enjoying his meal. After swallowing the last mouthful he wiped his chin, and then with a big smile handed me another McDonald's bag from his jacket pocket. I tore it open, delighted, but inside there was just a single large stone. His face was still only a foot or two from mine, and for a split second I felt a powerful impulse to lean forward and introduce my forehead to the bridge of his nose – but a little voice in my head told me that my doctor, plastic surgeon, careers officer and lawyer would all have strongly counselled against such a move.

On empty stomachs and no sleep, then, we were sent out to complete the final phase of the exercise: testing our evasion skills. The object was to reach the grid reference they gave us without being caught by a twenty-strong hunter force of Royal Marines and special forces, backed up by MoD police with killer Alsatians. We'd heard that these police handlers didn't mess about, to say the least, and needed no second thoughts before giving aspiring officers of the Royal Navy a good shoeing when they finally caught up with them.

The exercise was weirdly exhilarating. Even though we were exhausted and weak with hunger, the fight–flight adrenaline surged into our bodies and carried us far greater distances at far greater speeds than we could possibly have imagined ourselves capable of when lying around on the ground, half-dead, a few minutes earlier. We set off in a group and headed straight to the nearest river and began wading through it. I was aware that it's something of a rural myth, or Hollywood myth, that dogs can't smell you when you're in the water because you also give off a scent in the air that they can pick up. Wading through moving water on a stony uneven river bed is also slow going and exhausting, so I and two others (Nick and Colin) decided to peel off and go our own way.

We were moving fairly fast, or at least it felt as if we were, as we pounded through the trees, criss-crossing the river from time to time, and stopping only occasionally for a breather. When night began to fall there was still no sight or sound of our pursuers, and so we decided to dig our shallow graves and rest up for an hour or two. I fell into a deep sleep almost instantly, but it was still pitch dark and I had no idea how much time had passed when we all sat bolt upright in the earth at the sound of dogs barking in the distance. Under different circumstances, it would have been a mildly comic scene – three men emerging from the ground like the living dead – but this was not a moment for laughs, and we stared at each other for no more than a second before jumping to our feet and hurling ourselves headlong into the undergrowth. As we ran and stumbled and fought through the branches in the dark, the sound of the dogs started to get louder and we could see long beams of torchlight flashing through the tree trunks and branches.

The sound of the barking dogs seemed to trigger some deeply buried primeval fear in me because my heart, already pounding from the effort, suddenly began to race so fast I thought it was going to explode. We knew that as soon as we were caught the dreaded resistance to interrogation exercise would begin, so we had the extra incentive that the longer we could evade our hunters, the less time they had to interrogate us.

These policemen have to be very fit and very fast to keep up with the pace set by their slavering dogs, and it was also to their advantage that they hadn't spent the previous two weeks living off nothing but a few berries and nettles. We were shattered while they were well rested and well fed, and it was inevitable that they would close in on us eventually.

I was splashing across a river when I turned around and saw the dark figures of the policemen for the first time, roughly 500 yards away, with their yelping Alsatians dragging them through the trees like huskies with a sledge. We must have been going for another fifteen minutes or so when Colin, who was the furthest behind, fell to the ground and let out a scream. I think he had injured his leg in the fall, but he got up and managed to hobble for a short while longer before the dogs got him. There was a commotion of growling, snapping and barking when I turned around, and I could just make out a dim image of three dogs pulling Colin down and pinning him to the ground before the policemen arrived, a minute later, to pull them off. (The handlers aren't allowed to let the dogs off their leashes until they're confident that they can get to them before they start tearing you to pieces. That was what they told us before the course began, and for some reason I found it only mildly reassuring.)

I felt a perverse sense of delight that Colin had been caught because I knew that this bought Nick and me some more time, as the police would have to bind and blindfold him before one of them escorted him back to the truck to be taken away for interrogation. Nick and I put our hands on our knees, gasping and heaving to get some oxygen into our lungs, before setting off again as fast as our jellied legs and hammering hearts could carry us.

We survived the rest of that night and then a second day on the run, until at nightfall we stumbled across the beautiful sight of a hay barn in the middle of an open field. To us, it might just as well have been the penthouse suite in the Hong Kong Mandarin and, without a second thought or a moment's consultation, we dashed inside, collapsed in a heap and plunged into sleep bordering on coma. It was raining quite hard outside and the temptation of warmth and proper shelter was too much for us to resist. The mind starts playing tricks when you are that tired, and it wasn't difficult to convince ourselves that the barn was a safer option than the bushes.

It was, in fact, a basic mistake on an evasion exercise because it was the first place our hunters came to search in the morning. The barn was out in the open, giving us no cover and nowhere to run, so when we heard the rumble of an approaching Land Rover, just after daybreak, we knew our number was up. We made a pathetic attempt to get away, lolloping across the empty field like rag dolls, but the marines just drove alongside us, laughing and scoffing at our stupidity. We had done well to evade them for that long, and we scored good points as a result, but they were in no mood to congratulate us when we gave up the chase. I was expecting them to blindfold us and sit us in the back of the truck, but no such luck: in fact I was amazed by how roughly they treated us. As soon as they got out of the Land Rover they started manhandling us, throwing us to the ground before they ripped our boots off, Plasti-tied our hands behind our backs, put bags over our heads and literally hurled us into the back of the truck. Nick was still lying on top of me in the cramped space as we drove off in total silence.

After two weeks on the run, we were physically and men-

tally on our knees. We had become completely disorientated and had lost our sense of reality to the extent that we
forgot that what was happening to us was just a military
exercise, from which we could have pulled out at any time
to go off and become farmers or accountants. This new
'reality' hit me hard in the back of the truck when I tried to
ask for some water and one of the marines put his mouth to
my ear and started screaming in a heavily foreign accent.

We reached some kind of detention centre, where they
stripped us naked, blindfolded us and tied our hands
together at the front. I was shivering with cold when one of
our 'captors' started pulling me by the thumbs, like they
were a joystick, and pushed me into a room where a
woman's voice barked questions at me. In those days we
were taught to reveal only five pieces of information –
name, rank, serial number, date of birth and nationality –
and to reply to any other question, 'Sir (or Madam), I
cannot answer that question.' If you said anything else, then
you had failed the whole E&E course and would have to
start it all over again in a few months' time. Since then, the
procedure has changed.

The course instructors tried every trick to get us to yield
even apparently harmless information. They asked me
questions like, 'So, is your squadron still based at
Yeovilton? . . . It's a shame about your brother Ben, isn't
it? . . . And what about your poor Mum down in Devon, I
hear she's fallen quite ill since you've been gone . . . Please
sign here because we need the Red Cross's permission

before we can treat your wounds . . .' The aim is to get you to say as much as possible so that they can record your words and then mix them up and edit them into an alleged statement, or confession.

When they had finished asking questions, one of the guards grabbed my thumbs again and ran me down a corridor, still with the blindfold on, and pushed me into a room where they put me in the Lotus position with my hands on my head and left me. In the room there were speakers blasting out white noise at 150 decibels, the equivalent of standing next to a jet taking off. After several hours – it was impossible to assess the length of time exactly because I was delirious – I felt someone grab my thumbs again, lift me off the ground and put me into a new position, leaning with my hands against the wall at a steep angle. I learned very quickly that it was not a good idea to move from the stress position when one of the guards slapped me over the legs with a truncheon as I tried to wriggle into a more comfortable posture. The aim of the interrogation is to dislocate your expectations and fracture your grasp of reality so that you become so confused and you're in such pain that you eventually start gabbling. We had been told back at Dartmouth that anyone who genuinely couldn't take any more was to raise his left hand. The interrogator would then push it down, and if you put it up again straight away then you were taken out, failed and made to do the whole fortnight again later.

I was seriously wobbling at one point in the white noise

room when I looked down underneath my blindfold and saw that someone had collapsed next to me. Up until then I had had no idea that there was anyone else in the same room, let alone standing right next to me. I assumed he was unconscious because his hand was lying at my feet, and I instantly recognised it by the wedding band as that of my best friend at the time. The knowledge that there were others in the room and that they were struggling at least as much as I was gave me a big boost of energy and confidence that I could get through it.

Over the hours that followed – or was it days? – I was pulled out of the white noise cell and put into rooms with three different types of interrogator, who could be summed up as Mr Nasty, Miss Flirty and Mr Indifferent. It was the same procedure each time: someone grabbed me by the thumbs (which is very painful, by the way) and ran me down endless corridors and through dozens of doors before they sat me down in a room and pulled off my blindfold.

'Hello, I'm from the Red Cross. I'd like to do a medical examination on you,' said one man, all friendly and sympathetic. 'You are not well. How are you feeling?'

'Sorry, sir, I can't answer that question,' I replied after a short pause in which I almost let slip an answer.

After twenty minutes of different questions and the same answers, it was back to the stress position, and so it continued for hour after hour: stress position, white noise, thumbs pulled, down corridors, in and out of rooms, back and forth, the odd truncheon across the legs . . . Much of it is just a nightmarish blur today, just as it was then. But I distinctly remember one room in which a very pretty woman, revealing a truly magnificent pair of breasts in a low-cut blouse, leant right up to me so I could see down her cleavage, with her hot breath all over my face, asking me all sorts of friendly questions in a sexy whisper. I was stripped stark bollock naked again and just sat there, almost weeping, as I replied over and over again, 'I cannot answer that question.' After about ten minutes she exploded in fury: 'Call that a fucking penis!?! You're a fucking eunuch! Fuck off, you pathetic little man! Get out of my sight!' And then the blindfold was back on, someone grabbed my thumbs and off we went again, running crazily down corridors, bouncing off walls.

On another occasion two of them grabbed me from the stress position, ran me down a corridor, pulled off my blindfold, threw open a door and held me out over a 100 foot drop to the ground below. They then hauled me back in, ran me around for another five minutes, opened the door again, this time leaving the blindfold on, and then pushed me out. I screamed – by now I was so screwed up I was convinced everything was for real – and then hit the ground about three feet below. It was a different door. They pulled me back in, shouting, 'You fucking poof! You fucking big poof! Call yourself a pilot!'

A few hours later they ran me down a corridor and sat me down in a room where a man with a nice face and a big tash – he looked a little like Professor Robert Winston – smiled at me from behind his desk on which there was sitting a plate of steaming hot curry. It was my favourite, too: chicken korma. We had been told beforehand that if there was ever any food or water within reach, we were to grab it and wolf it, but if it was out of reach we had to leave it. The curry was out of reach. For five minutes Mr Indifferent asked me a series of bland questions and then – and it truly shocked me – he went absolutely psycho and started smashing up the room with astonishing violence. He took a baseball bat and set about destroying everything in the room, bashing walls and screaming at the top of his voice that he was going to kill me. He shattered the curry bowl into a thousand different pieces and I honestly thought I was next and he was getting ready to let me have it as he ran towards me holding the baseball bat behind his back as if about to take a mighty swing at me. But then I was grabbed by the thumbs and off we went again . . .

I came very close to failing the course right at the death, when I was taken into a room where one of the course instructors was standing there smiling with a red band on his right arm (we'd been told it would be on the left, but I was deranged now and couldn't think straight.) 'It's all over, Jim,' he said. 'Well done. Have a drink, let me shake your hand and let's discuss how you got on. Why didn't you tell us about the squadron?' I leant back with relief and was just about to start my explanation when I noticed their expressions had changed and I twigged that this was just another ploy in the interrogation, so I shut up, utterly deflated, before I was returned to the stress position and the exercise continued.

Finally, thank God, the next time I was run into a room, it was genuinely all over and I was congratulated by an instructor with a red band on his left arm. There was also a doctor in the room who gave me a full going-over before the instructor asked me how long I thought I had been at the interrogation centre. 'Ten or twelve hours,' I replied. In fact, I had been in there for thirty-six hours.

For the following forty-eight hours we were left in a house to wash, eat and recuperate. We were each given two cans of beer, which I relished, but strangely I didn't feel that hungry, I suspect because my stomach had shrunk to the size of a tennis ball and even a modest amount of food made me feel sick and bloated. As I shaved off my beard and enjoyed my first shower for two and a half weeks, I felt as proud as I ever have done: as a nineteen-year-old, fresh out of school, I had survived the same course to which the SAS candidates are subjected, and passed with a good point score in spite of my disastrous Night Navex. From the moment I finished that E&E course my confidence grew enormously, because I had been pushed well beyond what I thought was my capacity for endurance, and come through it. Just! And if I learnt one thing and nothing else from that experience, it was this: don't get shot down, and just never, ever, get caught.

CHAPTER FOUR

It took *Ocean* just ten days to reach the waters off southern Cyprus in the eastern Mediterranean, and there was a dramatic shift in atmosphere on board from the moment she dropped anchor there. The dull, overcast mood that had sat over the ship after setting sail was blown away in a cloudburst of action. The Groundhog Day feel, the sadness of leaving home, the classroom frustrations of ground training and the petty rows and squabbles were all swept overboard in a torrent of frenetic preparation as we primed ourselves for a simulated assault on the island's coastline. We all knew that the next time we did this it would be a real operation, and this was our only chance to try and get it right. Screw it up, and morale would sink; but perform it well and our confidence was sure to soar.

There was simply no time to be bored, frustrated or rueful

any longer as we focused all our energy on a packed schedule of specific tasks and challenges, culminating in the simulated assault. The sense of purpose was palpable throughout the ship. People walked more briskly along the corridors and talked in clipped, professional tones to one another; there was less banter, there were fewer people in the wardroom supping on beers after dinner, there was no daytime dawdling over coffees from 'Starbucks', no sitting around in cabins idly passing the evenings in front of DVD sitcoms – and no more taking the piss out of the ground crews, that time-honoured diversion from the monotony of our routine. It was time for action.

Choreographing a rapid, night-time assault involving so many men and machines represents a logistical challenge of the highest order for the men tasked with its coordination, and its success or failure can turn on one small detail or event. If, for example, 'H' hour, when the helicopters go in, is set at 3 a.m., and all the marines are down below on the mess decks, fully armed, camoed and psyched up, ready to be led up through the assault routes on to the flight deck, while the aircrew are ready to roll out the aircraft, one by one . . . and then one of the first troop helicopters goes U/S (unserviceable) and has to be removed and replaced with another from the hangar, a delay of thirty minutes or so is caused and, at a stroke, the whole operation is thrown into disarray, because the helicopters already up in the air, circling the ship in a racetrack pattern while waiting for the others to get airborne, only have enough fuel for about ninety minutes. Plan 'A' is then ripped up and the men running the show, down in the amphibious operations room in the centre of the ship, quickly have to put Plan 'B' into action to keep the operation going. Apart from anything else, such a scenario plays havoc with the nerves of the troops, who are completely pumped up to go, and then utterly deflated if the operation goes wibble and has to be cancelled or delayed. If you can imagine a team of footballers or rugby players at a World Cup final, in the tunnel under the stadium, being told just before they take to the pitch that the match is off or has been postponed, then you will have just a small insight into what it is like for marines about to go into battle.

A Raidex (raid exercise), particularly at night, is daunting for a number of reasons. First, it pulls together all the many different strands of our training, all the various skills we work on, into one single, concerted challenge. In regular training, we tend to concentrate on one area at a time, but in a Raidex we are doing everything at once, under pressure, to a minutely devised timetable, in coordination with a score of other aircraft and troop units (albeit imaginary ones in this instance). It's all systems go, and there is no room for error.

On Sunday 26 January the ship went into action stations and all of us were assigned additional roles on top of our 'day jobs' – tasks such as firefighting, or casevac or working as medical orderlies, assisting the doctors and surgeons who suddenly became a far more visible presence around the ship. I had barely taken any notice of the dozens of medics aboard up to that point, but when we reached Cyprus they all seemed to appear from nowhere, like ghouls from the shadows, forcing our unwilling imaginations to remind us exactly why they were there each time we passed them in the corridor. Try as I did, I couldn't help but think, 'That man could be amputating my leg, wrapping my burnt body in gauze or pumping my heart in a month's time.' There was always a good deal of gallows humour in evidence when we fell into conversation with the surgeons, and the lads never missed an opportunity to put in a string of surgical requests – most of them on the same lines: 'Hey doc, after you've sawn my leg off in a few weeks' time, while you're about it can I have a penis transplant, a new set of pecs and some liposuction on my beer gut . . .?'

It was at this time that we were ordered to pack our Bergens with everything we were to take into the field in Iraq. We also went to the armoury to collect our personal weapons – the SA80 assault rifle and Browning pistol – together with several bandoliers of rounds, magazines and grenades, and stowed them in our lockers up on the flight deck, ready to pull them out at a moment's notice before getting airborne. Everything we did from this time onwards represented one step closer to war, ratcheting up the tension notch by notch.

In the middle of this intense and focused activity came an episode so absurd it might have been considered even too ridiculous for a scene in a *Carry On* film. Clubs had assigned me the task of sorting out all the practical arrangements for our four days in Cyprus, including living quarters and flying programmes. I planned to fly ashore to RAF Akrotiri the day before our training began in earnest. However, a message came through from an official at the base that it was not within his gift to provide us with either accommodation or any airspace over the following days, because the Red Arrows were in town for training.

The reaction on board *Ocean* was one of dumbfounded astonishment. Well, fuck us then, we're only going to war! So long as the Red Arrows are nice and comfortable and have got their airspace, everything's going to be just fine with the world. Don't worry, we'll just stay on board and watch telly, and then go and topple Saddam Hussein when we can be bothered, hoping, of course, that the Red Arrows won't be needing the airspace in Basra that day! It was unbelievable – we were about to conduct our only joint exercise before going to war, but our demands were considered to be inferior to those of the air display lads on winter training. I needn't bother painting the picture when news of this rebuff was relayed to the commanders back in the operations room on *Ocean*; suffice it to say that there was much steam emerging from ears, expletives from mouths and eyeballs from sockets. You could have the heard the verbal explosions back in Whitehall. One phone call later, clearance was granted.

Starting at dawn on the Monday, 847 Squadron began two days of intensive flying practice, first rehearsing what is known as relief in place, or RIP to give it its grim acronym. In short, this is the handover between two air patrols, where the one returning from the front to refuel meets the one up coming in to replace it, quickly passing on information from the battle and talking the new team on to targets it had discovered. We flew all day and all night, packing in as many hours in the air as we could, and trying to make our imaginary scenarios as realistic as possible.

It was there in Cyprus that we had to make quick and wholesale changes to our normal flying practices. In temperate or tropical conditions, i.e. the flying environments in which the vast majority of us had spent most of our careers, the standard procedure during observation of targets was to fly low to the ground and come into the hover where it's difficult for the enemy to get sight of us. Ideally, you want a hill or another large feature behind which you can hover, popping up every minute or so to observe the enemy or get a missile away before disappearing from sight again. We call this 'dead ground', where the enemy can't see you. In the flat, featureless landscape of the desert there is no dead ground.

Furthermore, in the desert sands of Iraq, as in the snow-clad mountains of the Arctic, hovering low to the ground was not an option, for two reasons. First, the clouds of sand or snow kicked up by the rotor blades make us more easily visible and therefore more vulnerable to attack. If it was very early in the morning and the dew was still flattening the powdery sand, then you might be able to hover about forty or fifty feet off the ground, but the sun quickly burns off the overnight moisture. Second, the intense heat of the desert meant that the engines would run too hot if we tried to maintain long periods at high power and maximum weight.

Going high up was not a sensible option either. If I'm flying a helicopter in a combat zone, the last place I want to be is high in the sky – or 'skylined' as we call it – for the simple reason, again, that I present far too easy a target for the enemy, who have clear visuals on me at all times and can pick me off with their guns far more easily than if I'm low down. If I'm flying at 100 knots at one or two thousand feet, gunners have all the time in the world to take aim and fire as I move across the backdrop of the sky; but if I can get up close, low and fast they have only a second to fix and strike as I speed through the narrower window of their vision, even though at that height I'm still in range of the enemy's CIWS (close-in weapons systems).

Hovering somewhere in the middle, neither too high nor too low, was not a possibility either, owing to the power problems caused by the heat, and we were right in the middle of the threat band – in danger from all weapons. So we were faced with a conundrum; and Cindy, our warfare instructor, empowered by his crystals and forever thinking laterally, came up with a typically imaginative answer to it – not that it went down very well, at first, with the rest of the boys, who groaned at the thought of having to learn yet another technique on top of fine-tuning their other skills and procedures in the short time available.

At the heart of Cindy's thinking was what is known as 'dislocation of expectation': that is, doing something that the enemy is not expecting you to do. This is a concept that had been hammered into our heads from the first day we signed up for the navy and the marines, along with the principle of maintaining 'eyes on' the enemy at all times. It is one of the great features of the Fleet Air Arm that, within broad guidelines and established practices, we are given freedom to create our own techniques and flying practices, working out those that we feel are suitable for the job in hand. Our superiors trust our skills and intelligence.

The enemy, dug into their camouflaged bunkers and revetments, will know that before we can strike, we have to fix them in our sights; and to fix them we have to spot them, which can take time as you scan the landscape and the horizon for the smallest clue of their presence. They might, for instance, be the crew of a tank dug into the sand amid some date palms, or a communications post inside an abandoned building or partially destroyed watchtower, or a mobile mortar unit hiding in a hole in the ground. The enemy would be expecting our air observation platform (AOP) to take up the hover position. This was the expectation that Cindy planned to 'dislocate' with his new system, which went by the highly technical term . . . 'Hamster–Rat'.

In the Hamster–Rat technique, a single air patrol (one Lynx and one Gazelle) establishes an aerial racetrack pattern with the two aircraft at diametrically opposite positions to each other at all times. The location and observation of enemy targets is 847's core business and the beauty of this system, if we could make it work, was that between the two helicopters we would have 'eyes on' the target, or suspect position, at all times. It works like this. The first aircraft, say the Lynx, speeds towards the enemy, with the commander in the left-hand seat looking through his sight to identify potential targets and his co-pilot at the flying controls. As the helicopter calls 'off right' at the front of the battle position and heads back to the rear of the racetrack, the commander has a minute or so to talk the incoming Gazelle on to the target. The Gazelle will do exactly the same in return, and this continues until the target has been positively identified and a grid reference established; then a decision is taken as to what type of 'fire', if any, should be brought to bear. It sounds simple, but the timing of the two aircraft, as well as the 'talk-on', has to be spot-on in order for it to work effectively and prevents the helicopters coming into a power-sapping hover.

After weeks of discussion on the subject, Cindy's brain-wave was a real breakthrough, and despite the odd groan from some of the pilots the plan was widely considered to be a safe and sensible way to tackle the first priority of our missions, namely, to find targets threatening the advance of coalition troops.

The brief stopover in Cyprus turned out to be crucial to subsequent events in Iraq. It's no exaggeration to say that what we learned from our intensive training there, and the brainstorming sessions that took place among all the pilots between sorties, almost certainly saved some of our lives a few weeks later. It was there, too, that we made the huge call to take our S10 respirators in the aircraft instead of wearing our AR5 biochemical flying suits – the 'whistling handbags' as they were known, owing to the funny noise made by the motor attached to the oxygen filter packs. None of the pilots needed to express their frustrations with these cumbersome outfits in words; I had only to see the look on their faces when they returned from a sortie, stepped out of the cab of the aircraft and ripped off their rubber helmets to work out their feelings on the subject. Their eyes were imploring me to go in to bat for them with Clubs. In the event, it was not a difficult argument to win because, in addition to the flying dangers the face masks presented, they seriously diminished our fighting capability. As pilots operating complex machines in difficult conditions, we were going to have precious little spare capacity as it was; dressed as Jacques Cousteau except for the flippers, literally with no room to manoeuvre, we would have none whatsoever. The general consensus was that, on balance, there was a greater chance of dying from making a flying error as a result of the cumbersome charcoal-lined rubber suits and helmets, especially if we were flying at night and looking down the two toilet-roll tubes of our NVGs, than there was of dying from a chemical attack.

The Raidex itself ran continuously for the final thirty-six hours of our time in Cyprus. 'H' hour began at 3 a.m., the time when the enemy are at their groggiest and least vigilant, with wave after wave of Chinooks and Sea Kings forming racetrack patterns around the ships before sweeping into land in long columns. This was a 'dry run', with none of the 1,500 marine ground troops taking part, but it was still a highly impressive sight and sound as dozens of helicopters took to the night skies, the steady boom of the rotors growing louder each time another one lifted from the flight deck.

Once the imaginary troops had been dropped at the mock-up oil installations, the helicopters returned one by one in rapid succession to transport the casualty evacuation and medical teams, together with all the heavy equipment, including artillery, mortars, ammunition, general supplies and Land Rovers. The amphibious operations room in the heart of *Ocean* was a tense place that first night as the commanders of the various troops and squadrons, in tandem with the operations and warfare training officers, busily worked the walls of screens and radios to choreograph what turned out, in the end, to be a well-rehearsed show.

An exercise on this scale, just like a real operation, is controlled via a giant matrix known as HEALT (helicopter employment and assault landing table), and the challenge for those in charge is to get the right balance of men, weapons and support systems ashore in the right order at the right time. It is a highly complicated undertaking which can go wrong at any time. For instance, if one of the first helicopters to land is shot up, then it is vital to get the casualty evacuation and medical teams on the ground as soon as possible, but that can be difficult if there are not enough troops already in there to beat back the enemy. These rehearsals often go wrong, which I suppose is why we do them, but the Cyprus Raidex went beautifully. However, it ran for only thirty-six hours: in Iraq, the operation would continue until such time as the oil installations and the wider area of the Al-Faw peninsula were secure and the UK Armoured Division had driven up from its base in Kuwait and joined the battle. That could take several days, maybe even a week or longer.

At this stage of the assault, the role of 847 Squadron, with its 'find, fix and strike' capability, is to provide an armed escort for the transport helicopters and the amphibious landing craft that go in simultaneously or follow in behind a few minutes or hours later, depending on the plan. If the Raidex concentrated the mind in a professional, practical sense, it also had a telling impact on the emotions. The realism and intensity of the exercise served as a dramatic wake-up call, a powerful reminder that in just a few weeks we would be flying into a proper battle zone. It was a difficult enough challenge in mere simulation, flying into an empty beachhead with mock targets, so what would it be like with real bullets, rounds and missiles flying about our ears in the inevitable chaos caused by a sudden eruption in fighting?

The enormity of what we were being asked to do hit home

hard when we all gathered in the wardroom for a beer once the exercise was over. Since the Normandy beach landings of 1944 it has become an unwritten rule in British military planning that we don't do opposed landings any longer for the simple reason that they are a recipe for carnage. It takes only a handful of machine gunners, even a single nest, to wreak havoc on the invaders, and our brass have long been reluctant to put men through the shredder as their predecessors had to do in France sixty years ago.

In the Al-Faw, however, there was simply no alternative to an opposed landing. Ideally, you'd want the enemy defences to be pummelled from the air before the troops are sent in, but the very purpose of our assault was to *preserve* the oil installations from destruction, so bombing them was out of the question. The only way to pull it off was to break the unwritten rule and use 'theatre entry troops', as they are known in technical military parlance: in this case, the Royal Marines, who were chosen to land in the middle of the Iraqi defences and secure a foothold, under heavy fire, until the infantry and cavalry boys poured in behind, however many days later. Or, as one of our team put it so eloquently, 'We kick down the door, then fuck off when the grunts arrive.'

From Cyprus we headed due south towards the Suez Canal to take us into the Red Sea; from there we would eventually emerge into the Indian Ocean and turn the corner into the Arabian Gulf to join the dozens of other British and US seaborne aircraft starting to congregate in those troubled waters. Once we had gone through Suez, we knew that there was to be no turning back. The coalition governments weren't now going to suffer the humiliation of standing down their troops and sailing all their hardware back home. That, in a way, would have been a victory for the Iraqi regime and made monkeys out of Bush and Blair. Saddam's brinkmanship had gone too far; he was going to get a bloody nose now, come what might.

When we passed through Suez on 1 February the gunners took up their positions on deck and the rest of us were ordered below to stay out of sight, just in case anyone decided to take a pot shot at us. There were, of course, a great many people throughout the Arab world who did not appreciate our presence in their waters, and it wouldn't have been very difficult for them to fire a few shots across our bow to let us know their feelings. I had been through Suez a few times before, but had seen nothing on the last transit as I was holed up in my windowless cabin; this time I was one of the few fortunate enough to catch a view of the world's most famous canal after making up a feeble excuse to join the men and women up on the bridge. Emerging from the giant lock at the Port Said end into the man-made gateway between East and West was an incredible experience I'll never forget. After two weeks sailing through the Atlantic and the Mediterranean, largely oblivious to our location, it gave me something of a start when I looked out of the bridge windows and saw the continent of Africa a dozen or so metres to one side, and the Sinai desert and the Middle East a few dozen metres to the other.

Aboard a ship the size of *Ocean* this part of the journey was almost surreal, because we were so high above the waterline and the canal was so narrow at some points that it looked and felt as if we were sailing across desert. Except when I looked forwards or backwards, there were long stretches where I couldn't see the water below, just dozens of sprawling, dusty villages and towns, scattered along the flat, arid Egyptian landscape, some reaching right up to the water's edge. It gave me something of a weird thrill to see hundreds of Egyptians going about their daily lives, literally just a stone's throw from where I was standing. I can't quite explain it, but it felt like I had woken up on another planet, in a world very far removed from my own.

At several points men and boys pedalled frantically along the canal banks to try and keep pace with the ship, some of them waving frantically to get our attention. Others, mainly young, dusty children, just stood there, looking up at *Ocean*'s towering bulk. They seemed so close I felt I could reach out and shake their hands. The children had probably seen a thousand giant ships in their lifetimes already, but I imagine the sense of awe at the size of these vessels diminishes only a little. I still get that feeling of wonder whenever we come alongside one of the American aircraft carriers, which are so huge they make our largest ships look like remote-control toy boats on a park pond. The sheer scale of these maritime skyscrapers is something to behold.

Everywhere, however, there were grim reminders of war. Littered throughout the baked terrain were dozens of burnt-out hulks of tanks and other military vehicles, which had not moved an inch since the moment they burst into flames and were destroyed in the intense fighting between Egyptian and Israeli forces during the Six Day War of 1967.

Before the Suez Canal was constructed in the mid-nineteenth century, ships had to sail an additional 6,000 miles around the Cape of Good Hope to reach the Arabian peninsula; it took us roughly twelve hours to cover the 100 miles between our entry point and the gigantic lock at the southern end of the canal, from which we emerged into the Red Sea. Soon we laid eyes on the Kingdom of Saudi Arabia a few kilometres away on our port side. Egypt was still to our starboard, but within two days it gave way to the parched coastline of Sudan and then Eritrea, both shimmering in a heat haze on the horizon, before we squeezed through the Bab El Mandeb ('Gate of Tears' in Arabic), the narrow waterway separating Yemen from the tiny outcrop of Djibouti on the Horn of Africa, and out into the Gulf of Aden and the Indian Ocean. From there it was just four or five days' sailing to our next ports of call, Oman and the United Arab Emirates at the southern end of the Arabian Gulf, where we were to complete the final phases of our training with live-firing practice in the desert.

By the time we entered the Red Sea, some of us had been laid low by the cocktail of bugs and colds that inevitably break out when there are so many people living together at such close quarters. Unless you were incredibly lucky, there was no avoiding the sneezes and coughs. It didn't help that it was becoming increasingly difficult to get a decent night's rest as the ship's crew went about their various tasks at all times of the day or night, while we in 847 began to start work earlier and finish later, in an effort to cram as much practice time as possible into our programmes. There was all manner of noise twenty-four hours a day, as people got up and went to bed at different times and the crew carried out various maintenance tasks.

One night, for instance, I had just descended into a deep sleep when I sat bolt upright in bed and smashed my head on Lush's bunk, woken by the sound of a team of grunting matelots heaving an enormous chain along our corridor. The following night the maintenance men set about repairing the faulty lighting on our deck. The night after that there was fire practice and all the alarms went off at once. Another night I was late to bed after working on 'Tabletop', my computerised flying programme for ground training, but a few hours later Lush had to get up just before dawn for the first flight of the day. Rarely did any of us go to bed and sleep uninterrupted until six in the morning. Such is life aboard a ship of war. And yet it was very important for us to get as much sleep as possible if we were to be at our sharpest for flying, and so we soon fell into the habit of snatching an hour's kip during the day whenever our schedules allowed. Nobody frowned upon this practice – it was even encouraged – because everyone understood the dangers of fatigue.

As we sailed down the Red Sea, I entered into an

intensive diet and daily fitness programme down in the smelly gym. Over the next month I cycled and rowed for about sixty to ninety minutes a day, but I didn't dare touch the weights for fear of embarrassing myself. Most of the marines in that claustrophobic hellhole barely broke into a sweat or a grimace as they happily bench-pressed their own weight for hours on end, but I can barely bench-press a bench without the veins on my neck bursting. I was burning off so much energy that my appetite began to increase considerably, and I was able, every now and then, to succumb to the greasy charms of a full English breakfast and the odd burger, knowing I could work it off in the gym later.

We started to feel the heat now as well. Up in the Mediterranean, it had been no more than mild, cold even at times, but from the Red Sea, as we began to steam south towards the equator, the temperature rose steadily. We began to sweat – heavily – and we knew that we wouldn't stop sweating until *Ocean* sailed back through the Strait of Gibraltar and out into the squalls of the Atlantic, in however many months' time. It was only just February, but the thermometer was already climbing into the upper twenties Celsius. God only knew what it would be like in two months' time out in the desert, but at least the journey out gave us the chance to acclimatise slowly from the freezing cold back home to the scorching heat of the Middle East. (One afternoon I even managed to slip past the CO in my flip-flops and shades and steal a couple of hours of sunbathing in a quiet corner of the flight deck.)

With the weather perfect for flying, all the pilots managed to get in the many hours of training that we so desperately needed, and we were able to fine-tune the various techniques and flying formations we planned to employ in Iraq, as well as work on the essentials like deck training (taking off and landing) and night flying. There is no better feeling in the world than a good flight in clear weather in a beautiful setting, but since becoming chief training officer at 847 I rarely had the chance to relax and enjoy the ride, because when I was in the air I was generally concentrating on teaching or assessing the other pilot. But on the morning of 4 February I was reminded of why, twelve years earlier, after leaving school in Devon, I decided not to join the Royal Navy as a seaman officer after all but apply to the Fleet Air Arm instead.

A family friend was a keen glider pilot and he offered to take me out flying one weekend. I can't say I was overly excited by the prospect, and it was more out of politeness than anything else, not wanting to rebuff his generosity, that I had agreed to go along. But that first flight blew me away. I was a little nervous at first, as the wheels bumped along the runway, but when we lifted from the ground and the little engine was cut, high up above the sweeping expanse of Dartmoor and the patchwork fields of north Devon, I was mesmerised by the experience. I went back the following week, and the week after, and soon I was hooked. It then began to dawn on me, as the pressure mounted at home to make some sort of a career decision, that people actually get paid to fly! Within a few months I was leaning out of the carriage window, waving goodbye to my tearful mum on the platform as the train pulled out of Newton Abbot station taking me on my way to Dartmouth . . .

I relived something of that first joyful flying experience when I went up with Spidey, the senior pilot, for a ninety-minute sortie out over the Red Sea in one of the Gazelles. With Spidey in the cockpit I could just sit back and relax, because there's nothing much I could teach him about flying that he didn't already know, or that he couldn't perform much better than me. It's difficult to evaluate aviation skills to an exact degree, but I think it's fair to say that he was the second best pilot on the squadron! He'd certainly win the prize for the most laid-back character in 847, fazed by nothing and eternally optimistic even in the most unpromising or difficult circumstances. 'Don't worry, relax, everything's going to be just fine,' he would sigh if his helicopter was spinning out of control a few feet above the ground.

Spidey's a 'can do' person: if there's a problem, you don't flap, you fix it. If you want something done or you're in a predicament, you just go and find Spidey in his office in Yeovilton, padding around in his socks like it's Sunday morning at home, and he'll throw his head back, burst out laughing and sort your problem out there and then with some wise old words and a pat on the back. A solid family man in his early forties and a Somerset boy through and through, with old-fashioned values, the only thing Spidey loves more than flying is a good pint of real ale down his local.

After all the frenetic preparations over the previous few weeks, with the apprehension and tension mounting every day as we moved closer to war, it was a welcome relief to strap in alongside Spidey and spend an hour or so cruising and manoeuvring the little Gazelle through the bright blue morning sky. We spoke a little about what might be lying in store for us in Iraq, and although he didn't say 'Don't worry, Scooby' or 'I'm sure it'll all be fine', he was so unruffled and quietly positive that when I got out of the cab back on the flight deck, I felt more relaxed and reassured than at any time since we had set sail three weeks earlier. It was like therapy – and it was only when I noticed how much more at ease I felt when I returned to my cabin that I understood how stressed I had become.

It would certainly take some stretching of the word 'relaxed', however, to describe the state of my feelings at the end of that day when, returning in one of the Lynx to *Ocean* after a night sortie, we came within a few metres of instant death. It was the first of three alarming incidents, occurring on consecutive days, each serving as a chilling reminder that, if any of us were to die over the coming weeks, it was just as likely to happen in an accident as in contact with the enemy.

On this first occasion I was in the Lynx with Naphtha, a Royal Marine from Liverpool with a great sense of humour

– which was just as well in the circumstances. We were still in 'combat cruise' formation with the Gazelle, about 400 metres apart, flying at roughly 700 feet, heading home to Mum, looking down the toilet-roll tubes of our NVGs, when out of the pitch black in front of us a Sea King from 845 Squadron burst straight between the two of us, climbing from below. It all happened in a split second, but I could see the pilot's face as he hammered past our window at full pelt, totally oblivious to our presence. Being in a far heavier aircraft he wouldn't have felt us, but we certainly felt him; the Lynx jolted in his turbulent wake as he shot by. He can't have missed us by more than 100 metres, which in aviation terms is about as close as it gets. A few more metres to one side and five men, three in the Sea King and Naphtha and I in the Lynx, would have been pulverised. He was going at 90 knots, we were cruising at 100 knots, and at those speeds in the dark there is no warning of what's coming and no chance of taking evasive action. Just a single moment, lasting no longer than a heartbeat, can spell disaster.

We just didn't see each other and the radars on *Ocean* hadn't picked us up either, which can happen for a number of reasons – range or low height, for example, or the clutter of dots on the radar screens caused by increased sea state – but whatever the cause, that near-miss was a dramatic illustration of why night flying continued to be the greatest source of anxiety for all the pilots, even the most experienced. No matter how accomplished we were at flying our aircraft, no matter how much flying experience we had under our belts, at night our lives were out of our hands to some extent. Plain rank bad luck could kill us. My eyes almost popped out of the end of my goggles as the Sea King thundered past our right side, and my heart was still pumping wildly when we landed back on a few minutes later. Not that Naphtha seemed overly perturbed by our brush with death. He just said: 'I think the boy racers of 845 Squadron will be getting the pints in tonight, Scoobs.' Many a pilot, after such a close shave, would seek out the man flying the Sea King and have it out with him, but in truth, it was no more his fault than it was mine. It takes two to have a near-miss and we just didn't see each other. We were just two helicopters passing in the night, both holding on to the same hope in the back of our minds that the laws of probability – as well as a bloody good look out – would work in our favour. There's a whole sky in which to miss each other out there.

The next night was worse. The way you take off from and land on a ship is generally set in stone. You depart the ship from the port side and peel away; you arrive by the starboard side, hold the racetrack position if needed, before crossing the bow, then fly downwind on the port side and land on. If there are others waiting to land, you just join the queue until it's your turn. Only if your fuel's almost gone do you butt in. This is basic aviation procedure, but the etiquette appeared to be lost that night on the Chinook crew visiting from *Ark Royal*, who came within a whisker of killing me and my co-pilot, Hyena, as they bulldozed their way on to *Ocean*'s flight deck. It was lucky we weren't in one of the Gazelles, because there's no doubt that if we had been in a lighter aircraft I wouldn't be recounting this experience now.

I was at the controls of the Lynx about six miles away from Mum, having been out practising the new Hamster–Rat technique in an air patrol with a Gazelle, using our NVGs, and I needed to land quickly because we were very low on fuel. I radioed ahead to the ship to let them know that we had only a few minutes left and then immediately went into the holding pattern on the starboard, waiting for clearance from 'Flyco', the controller on the bridge, after the Gazelle had taken the first slot. We'd been circling at about sixty knots for nearly two minutes and the fuel alarms were telling us to get a move on when this bloody great bull of a Chinook came booming right over the top of us from behind. At this point we were about 200 feet above the sea and when I caught sight of the Chinook my stomach turned, because I knew exactly what was coming.

The huge downwash from the Chinook's two three-bladed rotors shoved the Lynx down towards the water's surface. It was a sharp, heavy drop, and although I couldn't see the water in the dark I knew it could only have been a few feet below us. As I wrestled with the controls to steady the aircraft, we then got hit by the vortices off the rotor blades, which flicked and rolled us on our side at about 120 degrees. Any further round and the Lynx would have ditched into the sea. I don't mind telling you that I almost shat my flying suit. There was no time to ponder what to do. The training just kicked in and I reacted instinctively. Having managed to bring the Lynx back under control and returned to the holding position off to *Ocean*'s starboard, I immediately got on the radio to unleash a good broadside of abuse.

The emergency wasn't over, however, because our fuel level was getting critical. There are only six landing spots on the bow of *Ocean*, plus an extra small one for a Gazelle at the bow, predictably known as the G-spot, and there was so much traffic coming and going between the ships by this time, as the flotilla began to congregate, that the flight deck party had to work very fast to clear the helicopters for others to land. Annoyingly for us – dangerously, in fact – this damned Chinook, in such a hurry to make its delivery, had just barged to the front of the queue, making himself number one and almost killing us in the process. He had failed the first time, but he came mighty close the second time by making us hold while he landed on. We are meant to land with at least 100kg of fuel on board, and we were very close to that minimum landing allowance (MLA) when the Chinook arrived. The orange fuel light in the control panel was flashing at us and the stress started to mount as we dipped closer to the 100kg point, known as the 'Hail Mary' mark because that's when you start saying your prayers.

We must have been circling for about three minutes in all

when the Chinook eventually took off (with a muttered 'Fuck off and good riddance' from our cockpit), but immediately *Ocean* went into a sharp manoeuvre, preventing us from landing. The situation was getting desperate now; again I radioed 'Flyco', who asked us to hang on for a minute until *Ocean* had come to rest. I could feel my pulse rising and my stomach knotting as the seconds ticked away and the last few kilos of fuel drained into the engine. The problem was that *Ocean* was carrying out a manoeuvre, simulating a scenario in which it had only one hydraulic ram moving the rudder, and so it was turning only half as fast as normal. The air traffic controllers were incredibly busy at that time, juggling a dozen balls at once, with so many different exercises taking place; but when it got to the point where we had no more than a minute to land or ditch in the sea, I got on the radio and said, 'I'm coming in whether you like it or not.' When the skids finally hit the deck and I shut the engines down, I sat back and exhaled in relief. Hyena just sat in the seat next to my left and laughed it off.

What is it with these marines? No matter how different they appear to be on the surface, and regardless of their social or regional background, they all react with the same ice-cool composure under pressure. It's partly the way they are trained, but I suspect it's more a question of character, as if they all emerged from the same gene pool, or swamp perhaps. You can teach a man to be cool up to a point – but only up to a point. At root, he either is or he isn't, and one of the main reasons these men succeed in qualifying as marines in the first instance is that they hold up so well in challenging circumstances. I'm not a panicker by any means, and I like to think I'm no coward. But I have to admit that I'm often flabbergasted by the almost cold-blooded self-control of my Royal Marine colleagues.

Hyena, 847's reconnaissance officer, was the giant version of Royal Marine and he had a brain built to size, with which he'd taken a first from Durham University. He often had the rest of us walking away from one of his briefings scratching our heads in bemusement. He uses words like 'bifurcating' and 'oleaginous' where the rest of us are happy to scratch along with their everyday equivalents, 'forked' and 'oily'. A top man and a good pilot, he was also one of the more eccentric characters in our midst, with some peculiar traits and habits which prompted an equal mixture of curiosity and amusement in his colleagues. For instance, Hyena has only one item of 'civvie clothes', an old T-shirt bearing the name of his favourite pub in Norfolk. If it happened to be in the wash whenever we went ashore, he just wore navy issue T-shirts and trousers. Once, when he lost his favourite T-shirt, he drove all the way from Yeovilton in Somerset to Norfolk to buy another, even though he could have bought ten others for the price of the fuel and saved himself a day's driving.

Hyena's house, by the same token, is said to have all the charm of a Northern Ireland safe house: that is, it has one telephone – 1970s dial-up variety – a bed, and a pile of unopened junk mail by the door. Material possessions, beyond a special T-shirt, hold no interest for Hyena, because his mind is constantly ruminating on subjects I couldn't even spell, let alone understand. Even so, I had to wonder, as we stepped out of the Lynx on to the flight deck that night, quite what had been going through that super-sized brain of his when, not once but twice, we came so close to ditching in the sea.

Hyena would have known as well as I did that if the helicopter had ditched we were as good as dead, even if we had hit the water right next to the ship and the crew had been able to see that we were down. There is a simple reason for this: helicopters are built to float in the air, not in the sea, and even though we couldn't ask for better safety kit and training from the navy and despite all the abandon aircraft drills (AAD) we carry out – when they try and drown you in the dreaded 'dunker' in an indoor pool – we all know that our chances of survival are in the balance once we hit the water. One piece of equipment known as STASS – short-term air supply system – has saved many lives, but overall the odds of getting out of the water alive are not great. (Those who have ditched and survived are welcomed into the exclusive 'Ditching Club' and get a badge to prove their membership of this elite group.)

If you do have to ditch, the procedure in a Lynx AH7 is to try and land on the crest of a wave with the engines running and then roll the aircraft on to its side. You keep the engines running if you can because you want to 'land' on the sea, not crash into it. You do have slightly more chance of surviving if you're in a Sea King because it has a boat-shaped hull designed to give it a short period of buoyancy as well as flotation cans on the side of the aircraft. The Lynx AH7 (the green, not grey, variety) has no flotation gear so it sinks like a boulder. I have lost a few friends in ditching incidents, but I also know a few men who have survived. One of them is my old pal Chapels, who was hovering in a grey Lynx just above the sea when he got 'run down' by an Omani gunboat from behind during an exercise a few years earlier. He sank to seven fathoms and his ears burst before he got out of his seat, but he managed to struggle free. He's one of the very few. (Losing 400 duty-free Marlboro Lights to the waves upset him more than anything else.)

If the pilots have a slim chance of getting out of a sinking green Lynx, the passengers in the back have virtually none, so we try not to carry any if we can help it. Strict conditions are imposed if we do carry passengers, taking into account the state of the sea and the number on board.

I have had a few near-death experiences in my career, but the worst of all happened in 1997. I was coming to the end of a two-year tour with 846 Squadron, one of the commando Sea King units involved in the handover of Hong Kong, and we were heading across the Indian Ocean to Brunei aboard the Royal Fleet Auxiliary ship *Fort Austin* for an important jungle training exercise with the marines. We had to carry out a check test flight, a procedure which required the helicopter to have a full tank of fuel, bringing the total weight of the aircraft to 21,000lb. It was only meant to be a short flight and it was just starting to get dark when I prepared for take-off, with Winters, a senior officer and highly experienced pilot, in the seat next to me and two flying maintainers (the engineers who fly as a passenger on 'check' flights) on seats in the back. When I launched the aircraft from the back of the ship and began to fly transition forward, almost immediately there was an enormous bang as one of the two engines blew. This is a critical moment for a helicopter that has been heavily weighed down by fuel, men or equipment, because if one engine fails the other engine is not powerful enough to keep it airborne – until more airspeed is achieved. The only way to stop the aircraft from ditching is to descend into what is called the 'ground cushion'. This involves flying as close to the ground or the water as possible, where the pressure of the air circulating below the blades means you need less power to keep you airborne.

On this occasion, the Sea King descended violently and we were only about ten feet above the sea when Winters grabbed the controls on his side. The light was fading but I could see the waves below almost lapping the hull of the aircraft as the water sprayed across the windscreen. I was still a fairly inexperienced pilot at that stage of my career, and it was just as well I had Winters in the other seat and not another rookie. The situation demanded not just a very high level of flying skills, but also an extremely cool head on the man at the controls – and Winters was just that: a cool head of the old school.

As the Sea King dropped sharply, I heard myself shouting the routine order: 'Torque split! Prepare for ditching!' over the intercom as the remaining engine screamed at maximum power. The rotors slowed and we flirted with the surface of the water for about three or four minutes as Winters battled to keep her in the air, skilfully coaxing the aircraft away from the surface. I can tell you now that the only truly cool person on that Sea King during those minutes was Winters. I was relying on my training and feeding off my sense of youthful invincibility to some extent, but the other two were virtually soiling themselves. Winters had saved us from ditching by a matter of feet and seconds, but the danger was still far from over because immediately we had to go into a pre-set drill, which I was reading from the flight reference cards, before we could attempt to land back on *Austin*. Still struggling to keep the aircraft airborne as he dragged every last bit of power out of the engine, Winters talked me through the procedure. I knew what to do in theory from training exercises and the simulator, but in this all too real situation it was good to have a quiet, methodical voice take me through it step by step.

The only way we were going to get the aircraft back to the deck was to dump fuel to lighten the load as quickly as possible. After running through all the safety procedures as quickly as I could, I flicked on the fuel-dump switches, but as I did so I felt a very fine jet of fuel squirt on to my neck and the unmistakable stench of avgas (aviation fuel) filled the aircraft. The fuel pipe, which runs through the cabin, had burst a tiny leak under the pressure of the evacuation and within seconds there was fuel everywhere.

It was sod's law that at that precise moment the fire caption signal on the central warning panel (CWP) lit up, indicating that the failed engine had caught fire. This is as bad as worst-case scenarios get: we were 200 feet above the sea, about three miles from *Austin*; it was almost dark and we had no NVGs; we were struggling to stay airborne, with the one remaining engine working at max power and almost at meltdown; we had a fuel leak in the cab, the CWP was telling us that one of the engines was now on fire, and the two engineers in the back were screaming at the top of their voices, convinced they were about to die in a ball of flame. I wasn't showing my panic, but I'm as convinced now as I was then that Winters wasn't even *feeling* any panic. He was so calm, I wouldn't have been surprised if he had taken out his baccy pouch and fired up a nice relaxing pipe.

It's very rare to get this kind of huge systemic failure in a Sea King, because they are superb aircraft – and as it turned out there was no fire after all, just what is known as a 'hot-gas' leak where the heat from the engine melted the fire indicator wire and set off the alarms. But we only found that out later. At the time, it was a race to get back to the ship before (a) we blew up or (b) the second engine packed up under the stress and we ditched. Winters pushed it to full speed as we made a straight dash for *Austin*, which was now barely visible as night descended over the Indian

Ocean. The wheels hit the deck with an unceremonious thud before I shut down the blades and the engine and we all piled out as fast as we could while the fire crew poured forward to make the aircraft safe.

I learnt two important lessons that night. One: if you develop one problem in the air, it is highly likely that another will soon follow. Two, and more importantly: stay calm at all costs, because only then will you be able to think clearly. We only survived that night because we stayed calm.

Although incidents of ditching are fairly rare these days, helicopter pilots in the services work with the risk every time they take to the air. It is part of the attraction of flying. Almost every time we fly, we push the aircraft's fuel to the limits of its MLA in order to try and squeeze every last minute we can out of a sortie. Every navy pilot will have his own bag of close-shave stories. They are not uncommon events, and most of the time we quickly forget about them, accepting them as an occupational hazard, and move on. Still, the two incidents I have just described en route to the Gulf, involving the Sea King and the Chinook, while not exceptional, were certainly more than just commonplace episodes, and they combined to blow away the brief half-day of peace I had felt following my leisurely flight with Spidey. We had an unofficial custom on *Ocean* that as soon as we had finished a night-flying mission we headed straight to the bar for a few beers, provided we weren't scheduled to fly again until the following evening. As the officer responsible for training, I was having to undertake a succession of night flights in order to give everyone the flying hours in the dark that they needed; and continuous night flying has a cumulative effect on the nerves after a while. Blowing the froth off a couple of midnight lagers proved an excellent sedative, a great way of coming down from the adrenaline-induced high I experienced every time I strapped on the NVGs.

I certainly needed a beer the following night, after a third drama in as many days. I was with Hyena again in a Lynx when the fuel light started flashing towards the end of our ninety-minute flight and we prepared to head back to Mum. There was just one small problem with that plan – we couldn't find her. This is not as daft as it sounds, because it is hard to navigate at night over the sea when you can no longer rely on features your eyes see to guide you, and we had been almost eighty miles away from her at one point. There was a system in place called 'Outhouse', whereby the ship will always be within ten miles of the position briefed at take-off. But at night, if there is a threat of attack, the ship will also turn off its external lights, and shortly after taking off it is impossible to see it in the dark. The air traffic controllers will sometimes turn off the radar as well so as not to give away the ship's position. *Ocean* at this point was not within ten miles of her original position, which meant it must have been under some form of threat.

At this point in the journey out to the Gulf we were not far from the coast of Yemen, where just over two years earlier the USS *Cole* had been hit by a suicide boat attack, killing seventeen men on board and injuring dozens more. We were in dangerous waters, and as a precaution *Ocean* had gone into defence mode. So that was the unpromising situation we found ourselves in: we had roughly ten minutes to find the ship, or ditch in the sea; we had no lights, no radar, no clue where Mum was or why she had moved, and next to no fuel. Even Hyena's two brains couldn't have worked this one out.

We were in an obvious spot of bother, and, realising the sudden gravity of the situation, I broke what is known as the 'Emcon silent' policy in order to speak to the ship. We had been briefed not to transmit to the ship, for security reasons, but such was the urgency of the situation we had no other option. I asked the ship to put its radar back on so that the operators could tell me where we were, but this was rejected, again for reasons of security, and so we were presented with two final alternatives. Either we tried to find another ship to land on (you don't need that much room) or we used a little gadget known as the RDF (radio direction finder), which is what we did. The RDF, a simple bit of kit built into the radio, is pretty basic, and unsophisticated, widely used in the Second World War (ours was built into our secure radio), but it was our only option right then. When we switch on the RDF and talk to the air traffic controllers in the ops room, the hand on the dial deflects; we have to move the helicopter around until the hand stops moving, which tells us that we are now on the ship's bearing. Mum agreed to transmit just twice, but that was all we needed to get a bearing, after which we were able to find her on the thermal sight and using our NVGs – our own 'mental plot' also helps.

If you are really lost, the only problem with the RDF system is that you have no idea, at first, whether the ship is behind you or in front: the device is only telling you that you are on the right bearing. You have to keep manoeuvring either side of the 180 degrees to work out the direction by seeing which way the hand was pointing. If you have all the time in the world, the RDF is useful, but when you are getting down to your last few kilos of fuel, as we were that night, the few minutes you spend moving around in the pitch dark are a little hairy, to say the least.

Having worked out which direction we needed to take, we sped back down our bearing as fast as the Lynx would carry us, and it was a huge relief, after a few minutes, to see *Ocean*'s shadowy form, starting as a small dot on the thermal sight, looming ever larger in our goggles as we approached. By the time we put the skids on the deck, we had no more than two minutes' worth of fuel left before we hit the MLA.

The 'lads' were there on deck as always, and as they began to fold away the blades and take the helicopter down to the hangar I made the now familiar descent down corridors and through the hatches to the wardroom at the end of deck two. Sweetcorn was there that evening and we exchanged a frosty nod as I bought Hyena and myself a beer and settled down at one of the tables. At that point I decided I'd had enough of our quarrel over training, and that it was time to bury our differences. Perhaps the three brushes with disaster I had suffered that week had put our squabble into perspective, or maybe I was just weary from two weeks of simmering confrontation, but it struck me as plain silly that two grown men, both experienced professionals fighting on the same side, heading into a war, had been unable to settle their professional differences.

So I asked Sweetcorn to join me for a smoke on the quarterdeck where, after cupping our hands for each other and sparking a couple of his full-strength Marlboro Reds, we got it all out in the open and agreed to sit down and plan any future training together. We don't really do hugging in 847 Squadron, nor do they go in for it in the marines, and you probably couldn't get your arms round Sweetcorn's giant frame even if he'd let you, but the mutual pat on the back we gave each other as we headed back to the wardroom to finish our beers was all it needed to put things right. It was a good moment.

CHAPTER FIVE

In the first few weeks after setting sail from Plymouth, I had spoken to Suzi about every five or six days. The tone of our conversations had, by and large, been civil; but there was, we discovered, increasingly little to talk about. Understandably, there was a limit to the interest she felt moved to express when I told her that I had spent the day, say, learning how to operate our new LTDRF laser system, or that I had attended a fascinating briefing about flight reference cards or authorisation guides, or that I had had an argument with Bunker, after inadvertently eating his lunch pack, that ended with him lifting me off my feet one-handed. Nor, having herself only a passing interest in military activities, was she going to be trans-fixed by the news that I had discovered during firing practice off the back of the ship that the sights on my assault rifle had been knocked out of kilter by six inches.

I certainly didn't want to tell her about the near-misses and the brushes with disaster, or about the mounting tension aboard *Ocean* as war loomed ever closer. What's the point in making a stressful situation even worse? Naturally, family and friends back home often go into denial about their loved ones, trying not to imagine the worst that might happen to them. So, as a general rule, servicemen on the phone to those back home try and affect a blasé attitude to what is happening, keeping them in the dark about the harsher realities and not letting on about anything that might be upsetting. Our phone chats, then, are often bland, contrived and forced, and after a while my conversations with Suzi started to dry up, so that I found myself repeating insincere reassurances that 'everything was going to be just fine' and that it was 'all pretty routine stuff out here really . . .' She, too, told me it was just boring business as usual at home and in the office where she worked and that I wasn't missing any fun. The daily accounts of our lives thus became about as interesting as the Features section of a North Korean newspaper.

Once *Ocean* had headed around the Arabian peninsula and moved into the Gulf, the tone of our conversations started to change, with a note of tension creeping in. It was perhaps just as well that by the time we arrived in the Gulf in mid-February there was very little space in the packed working schedule to work myself up into a great froth about whatever problems there might be back at home. I simply didn't have enough emotional spare capacity to deal with a domestic wrangle on top of the strain of preparing myself for my first experience of all-out military conflict.

At the UAE we went ashore to carry out desert flying and live-firing practice, in what we all knew would be our first and last stab at these exercises before the fighting began for real. The day we flew off from *Ocean* I was called in to see the Commanding Officer of the Commando Helicopter Force (COCHF), and I was a little nervous when I knocked on his door and he barked from under his massive tash, 'Ah, Jim! Come in!' I was expecting a bollocking of some sort, because in our business you don't get summoned to meet the top man unless it's a very serious matter, and so I was pleasantly surprised when he shook my hand and announced that he was promoting me from lieutenant to acting lieutenant commander, which, unless I made a major balls-up over the coming weeks, was as good as a full promotion. The news was a welcome boost to my confidence, and the higher rank was going to be helpful from a practical point of view because it would make it slightly easier to get my work done effectively. There would be a little less backchat and whingeing from the other pilots and a little more influence and authority with other squadrons and other bodies outside 847, including the Americans.

It's difficult to describe the excitement of live firing. It's very rare we are given the chance to practise it – the minimum requirement is every eighteen months – owing to the prohibitive cost of the TOW missiles, which retail at about £30,000 a throw. Although most of the forty or so pilots we took to the Gulf would have the chance to fly missions during the conflict, only twelve of us were listed to fire the TOW missiles: myself, Sweetcorn, Lush, Slaps, Cindy, Sonic, Cortez, Naphtha, Timex, Hovis, Two-Two (he's a small bore) and Mako, the American exchange Cobra pilot.

All twelve of us were given two shots each, at a total cost of well over half a million pounds to the taxpayer, but the exercise was worth every penny, even though some of the missiles failed to fire or 'rogued' and a few missed their targets. This was our only chance to learn from our mistakes, and the exercise was worthwhile if for nothing else than in reminding us of the potential problems and the possible unreliability of a missile system that was scheduled to be taken out of service, together with the army-owned Gazelle, when we returned home, to be replaced by a new generation of Apaches, which sadly would not be going to the Royal Navy.

Firing at old tank hulls in the distant sands, I couldn't get my missile away at the first attempt because the Lynx had moved out of constraints. I didn't need to be told that the seconds we lost might well have cost us our lives in the real event, but I felt reassured when I finally got it right and scored two direct hits. Lush was less fortunate, and I had great fun taking the mickey out of him back in the cabin that evening after his comedy effort in the desert. I say 'comedy' lightly now because he's still alive, but his practice session had very nearly ended in tragedy. When Lush pulled the trigger on his first attempt, his TOW popped out of the launcher but the motor failed to fire, and it just flopped into the sand a few dozen feet below him. When he took the Lynx back to get another missile, the 'lads' almost wet themselves with disbelief on seeing several miles of the thin copper guidance wire wrapped around the main and tail rotors in a thick bird's nest of metal. The automatic wire cutter had failed and Lush had unwittingly dragged the missile through the sand for several hundred metres on his return journey. He was lucky, because if it had detonated there was a good chance it would have brought down his Lynx.

We may have been the most experienced helicopter squadron ever to go to war in British uniform, but all of us were learning new lessons or old tricks during these final few days of preparation. Back on *Ocean*, we had live-firing practice with our personal weapons, aiming at cardboard targets positioned off the back of the ship. Timex, an ex-Falklands sniper, gave me some great advice about how to mix up my bullets when loading the assault rifle with live ammo. Normally you have a mixture of regular bullets and tracer rounds, the latter being bullets with a visible phosphorous tail which help you to pin down the target. There are thirty rounds in a magazine, which you are meant to count as you fire, but in the heat of a firefight this is not always practicable, and this old sweat showed me a clever way of loading the magazine.

His first three to five bullets, he told me, were always tracers, which helped him get his sights on the target. He'd then switch the gun to automatic, firing bursts of regular bullets, but he'd always slip in a tracer after fifteen rounds or so to tell him he was halfway through the mag and then add another tracer, one before the end, to give him a second's warning that he was almost out of ammo. I have always been a reasonably good shot, probably as a consequence of a childhood spent shooting pheasants, crows and rabbits in the woods and farmland up on Dartmoor, but all these little gobbets of advice from the old hands who had learned their knacks and techniques in the field were more than welcome. What's more, shooting game birds, vermin and small mammals was one thing, but killing other human beings was quite another. I had fired tens of thousands of rounds over the years in training, I had come under fire from Irish dissidents, Central American drug dealers and others besides, I had been at the scene of sectarian bombings in Ulster and seen my fair share of dead and dismembered bodies, but not once in twelve years in the navy had I ever fired a shot in anger myself.

Another slightly disconcerting thought in the final days of our preparations was the grim realisation, or acknowledgement, that some of us had next to no experience whatsoever of desert flying. I had flown just once in this uniquely difficult environment, but several others had never even set foot in a desert, let alone flown a helicopter or fought a war in one; and it was eating away at me, as the training officer, that this hole in our experience could prove costly. It was now that all the experience and know-how we had gained in Norway kicked in and proved its value, although it was difficult to convince ourselves at the time that training in the Arctic could have any relevance to fighting in a desert. Whenever the commando helicopter squadrons headed off to the camp at Bardufoss, 160 miles north of the Arctic Circle, for our annual Arctic warfare training, the joke among those who had never trained in Norway was that the exercises were about as useful to British warfare in the modern world as a sauna in the desert. Yes, the mock battles we enact with the Norwegian tanks are brilliant exercises for our general fighting and flying skills, but why the snow? Now that the Russians are no longer considered a significant threat to the West, who else might we find ourselves pitched against in the Arctic? The Canadians? The Swedes?

We knew differently, however. There is great method in the apparent madness, because snow actually has a great deal in common with sand when you're flying through it in a helicopter, odd as that may seem. At six pounds a pint, it may cost us the better part of a week's wages to go out on a Friday night in Norway, but the flying techniques we learned in the Arctic and the general all-round experience we gained as pilots were worth their weight in gold. If Northern Ireland at the height of the Troubles had taught us all we needed to know about operational flying, then Norway had given us a first-class education in technical flying. By some distance, Norway is the most dangerous environment and the harshest climate in which we fly, with its extreme and unpredictable weather conditions and its distinctive, difficult terrain with steep gullies, fjords, hills and mountains. The Norwegian tank crews and their mountain commandos (*jegerkommando*) are first-class operators, giving the commando helicopter squadrons, as well as the Royal Marine bootnecks on the ground, as good a workout as we could find anywhere in the world.

On a number of previous exercises, fighting in the familiar territory and conditions of their own backyard with state-of-the-art machines and equipment, the Norwegian tank squadrons had wiped the floor with us, but on my last visit there we positively annihilated them in a mock battle, taking out twelve of their Leopard tanks with the loss of just one Lynx. It's all about tactics and using our brains. We learned from past experience that if we hovered over fresh snow then the rotors would kick up a cloud that would give away our position and allow their gunners to spot and 'destroy' us. Sand is a similar giveaway. On that last visit we were cannier, being careful to hover higher or over rivers, snow-free trees and ice so as not to reveal ourselves. Little did we know at the time, operating at temperatures of thirty degrees below in the wooded ravines and mountain passes of northern Norway, that we were gaining superb experience for a conflict in the scorching deserts of the Middle East.

Some of that experience was nerve-wracking, some of it surreal. On one occasion, I was on exercise in a Sea King and had been airborne for over three hours. The tasking had been expected to last only two hours, and so we were getting low on fuel by the time we set off back for Bardufoss. At that time of year there are only about four hours of daylight up there, and with the sun already below the horizon it was starting to get dark very fast. We were just two or three miles from the camp when, as happens frequently in the Arctic Circle, the weather suddenly turned and we found ourselves in the thick of a ferocious snowstorm. We could barely see anything at all now, except for the odd patch of trees or rocks amid the swirling snow clouds. We weren't expecting to be airborne when night fell, but we had brought our NVGs with us just in case. Our situation was becoming critical as we strapped them on and began to search for a clear, flat area on which to land, squinting through the goggles at the forest and patches of ground just below us. We couldn't move too far for fear of crashing into the trees or hillside, and so we circled at a 45 degree angle of bank (AOB) at about fifty knots for what seemed like an eternity, desperately hoping for a break in the weather before the fading light turned to pitch black.

It was odds-on that we were going to crash when there was a momentary break in the blizzard and we spotted a tiny hunter's hut with a small open area in front of it. You can travel for a hundred miles in the Norwegian wilderness and not come across a single sign of human life, but there below us, as if sent by God, was an answer to our prayers and we made a dash for it. The snow quickly returned to close our window of vision, but every now and then we could get a glimpse of the hut and a possible landing area and I came down lower and lower, using the hut as our only reference point. The fuel warning light had now switched from flashing, indicating that we were very low, to steady, which told us that we were almost out and that we had about five minutes to get down. There was no choice but to put the aircraft on the ground now, praying that we hit the right spot or, as we say, 'happy with our reference' until we touched down.

We tried firing flares into the ground below to give us a landing marker as we descended, but the fresh snowdrifts extinguished them almost immediately. We overshot on our approach and, as we lifted away from the ground, I could see that our proposed landing spot was on quite a steep slope – so that even if we did manage to get her down, there was going to be a risk the aircraft might either topple over or slide down the hill. In a final desperate effort to make some kind of marker for me to aim for, the Royal Marine crewman in the back threw out a Bergen, which he would need to reclaim from the snow in order to survive the night if we made it out of the aircraft alive. But that failed as the dark form of the kitbag quickly disappeared from sight under the rapidly mounting drifts. We continued to circle for a minute and, for the first time in a Royal Navy helicopter, I braced myself for a crash landing.

We had been battling the snowstorm for about twenty minutes, and my aircraft commander and I had given up all hope of landing safely, when . . . Norway's answer to Miss Marple popped out of the woods to rescue us. Suddenly a light came on in the hut, casting out bright beams through the two windows and the open door and illuminating the open area in front like a runway. If she had been sitting in the cockpit I would have kissed that dear old lady there and then. We were so relieved we almost wept as I brought the Sea King down as fast as I possibly could. The wheels hit the snow and the helicopter was leaning at an alarming pitch as I shut her down and we jumped out into the freezing night air to find ourselves waist-deep in fresh snow. It took us about a quarter of an hour to wade the few yards to the hut through the drifts.

Our nerves had been utterly shredded by the experience, and we were still quaking when the lady invited us into her hut, sat us down and made us a cup of tea. Our escape turned out to be even more miraculous than we could have imagined, because it turned out to have been only by chance that our rescuer had been passing along the nearby track. The hut was not her house after all, just a lodge that she and her family used from time to time, mainly in the summer months. But as she drove by, she realised we were in trouble and had the presence of mind to park the skidoo and hurry as fast as her elderly legs would carry her up the hill to turn on the lights to help us.

The hour we then spent sitting in that single-room little hut, measuring no more than twenty feet square, was possibly the most embarrassing of my life. We had radioed the camp, asking them to deliver some more fuel once the weather broke, and then sat cupping our hands around mugs and trying to warm up. In an effort to break the awkward silence that followed, the Royal Marine crewman attempted to strike up a conversation with our elderly saviour. I was too frazzled to talk, and we were lost in our thoughts when the bootneck pointed to a picture on the wall showing the face of a burly-looking character with a hint of facial hair.

'Is that your husband?' he enquired politely.

'No, that's my daughter,' came the reply. We all immediately looked down at the floor and started frantically stirring our mugs of tea.

We had sat in silence for another minute or so when the crewman piped up again: 'Excuse me, love, do you have a toilet anywhere, or should I go outside?'

'*Ja*, certainly,' said the lady, and pointed to a pair of saloon-style doors in the wall, about five feet from where she was sitting.

The crewman got up a little sheepishly and we watched nervously, hoping he would head outside. Instead, he pulled an apologetic face, pushed open the small swinging doors, yanked down his trousers and sat down on the seat. We could see his boots under the door almost sticking back into the room. We looked at each other in horror and waited. There followed what surely must have been the loudest crap in the history of Scandinavia. It was just awful. The stench in that small room was appalling. The other three of us sat there in a stupefied silence, covering our noses and staring into our teas, as the bootneck farted, grunted and bombed the toilet with everything he had before emerging about five minutes later and sitting back down as if nothing had happened.

On 17 February, American and British jets started bombing a number of targets deep inside Iraq, concentrating on the country's air defence infrastructure. My emotions were mixed when I heard the news. On the one hand, as a helicopter pilot, I was happy that the Iraqis' air defence system had taken a pounding – the fewer surface-to-air missiles flying round our ears the better. On the other hand, there was clearly no turning back now. Any lingering, dim hopes that a last-minute deal with Saddam's regime might be struck had been blown into a shower of shrapnel overnight.

Two days later, after completing our desert training, we sailed further north up the Gulf towards the Al-Faw peninsula. We moved through the Strait of Hormuz, a narrow stretch of water separating Oman and the Emirates on the south-western side from Iran on the north-east, through which almost half the world's oil supply travels every day. Since leaving the Channel we had passed various staging posts on our journey – Gibraltar, Cyprus, Suez, the Red Sea – and the Strait of Hormuz was the final gateway. We had arrived.

The Gulf is just over 600 miles long, and as we

approached its northern end we could see dozens of small flares from the booms of the Iranian oil rigs and the trails of black smoke drifting skywards along the horizon. The tiny Al-Faw peninsula at the southern end of Iraq is a small strip of land providing the country with its only access to the sea, as well as a home to its only naval base at Umm-Qasr. It is here that the Shatt Al-Arab waterway, a confluence of the Tigris and Euphrates rivers, flows out into the Gulf, marking the border, at its southern end, between Iraq and Iran.

I was amazed by just how close we were to Iran, and there was a certain amount of confusion at first over where we could and couldn't fly. Normally, you are not allowed to fly within twelve nautical miles of a country, but with just a hundred yards or so separating Iraq and Iran, the situation was different and inevitably we would often be flying right up against the border. We were given strict warnings to be careful about our location at all times because the Iranians, who had gun positions lined up along the length of the coast and the Shatt Al-Arab, had their fingers on their triggers and would have no hesitation in giving them a quick squirt if we encroached. The dangers were highlighted the day after we arrived when two US jets accidentally crossed into Iranian airspace; fortunately they were immediately alerted by the air traffic controllers and turned round before the Iranians had a chance to lock on to them.

The waters of the northern Gulf were quite a sight when we arrived. The British task force may have been the largest assembled since the Falklands, but it looked like a bathtub toy navy next to the giant ships of the American fleet. Even HMS *Ocean* and *Ark Royal* were dwarfed by the colossal aircraft carriers the Americans had sent; and in addition to the carriers there were dozens of other ships spread out across the Gulf, including frigates, auxiliary supply vessels, minesweepers and floating hospitals. It was an awesome spectacle and a boost to morale to witness the sheer might of the coalition forces floating offshore.

As a helicopter pilot, though, I couldn't help but register, with a certain degree of concern, that there was going to be a huge amount of air traffic operating in a very tight space. The greater the congestion, the greater the risk of accidents, and the air traffic controllers back on the ships and up in the air were going to be under serious pressure to monitor and manage the hundreds of planes and helicopters that were starting to fill the skies as we arrived. Mid-air collisions were a grim and distinct possibility; and also, of course, with our cousins from across the pond in town, there was the additional and very real risk of friendly-fire incidents.

It was at this time, as we moved into artillery and missile range of the Iraqis, that the final details of the Royal Marines' planned assault on the peninsula were thrashed out, and we were all made aware of our specific roles. We knew already that there would be no significant pre-emptive bombing of the oil installations themselves, although there would be some directed at the areas surrounding them on the Al-Faw.

On 25 February, Clubs summoned all the pilots for a meeting to spell out the various phases of 847's role in what was dubbed Operation TELIC (also known on the mess decks as Tell Everyone Leave Is Cancelled). Our first task was to provide armed escort and support for the Chinooks and Sea Kings ferrying a brigade's worth of marines from 40 and 42 Commando ashore from *Ocean* and *Ark Royal*, both on the night of the landings and the following day, until all men and equipment had been dropped. Following the initial assault, we were to push north and west on the peninsula to protect the landing, while the marines battled the enemy positions in and around the oil installations they would be attempting to secure as quickly as possible.

Thereafter, assuming the assault was a success, we were to act as a screen, in conjunction with the Scimitar tank crews of the Queen's Dragoon Guards and the Royal Marine brigade recce force in their 'pinkie' Land Rovers, and together hold the line south of Basra as best we could until the US Marines and the heavyweights of the UK Armoured Division entered the fray. The first twenty-four hours would be crucial, Clubs concluded, but he didn't need to spell that out: it was plain to us all that if the Iraqis succeeded in repelling the assault and driving us back into the sea, and/or they torched the switching and pumping stations before the marines could seize them, then we would have failed in our mission. It was a very difficult challenge, whichever way you looked at it, and the margins for error were extremely fine. But the general feeling among the squadron when we discussed it over a beer in the wardroom that evening was that our mission was dangerous but achievable.

The question now was which of us would form the first wave of air patrols in the opening assault. Ordinarily, the first wave are the most vulnerable to being shot down, because during those opening salvoes the enemy are well dug in, their defences are still largely intact and they are likely to have the belly for a scrap. If ever they were going to have a go at us, it was at the outset when our first troops began pouring out of the helicopters. The joke in the wardroom that night, however, was that it was the second wave who would bear the brunt because, as the assault started in the dead of night, it was likely that the slumbering Iraqis would take a few minutes to raise the alarm and take up their positions; so it was the second wave that would get it in the neck. The proposed assault would surely present 847 Squadron with the most serious, sustained examination of its courage and skills for many years. But I'd rather have been in our flying boots than those of the Sea King pilots of 845 Squadron and the Chinook pilots of the RAF squadrons, who were assigned the task of landing right in the middle of the oil installations, under heavy fire, in order to disgorge the bootnecks on the ground.

Beneath all the gallows humour in the wardroom that night, we all knew there was a real possibility of getting shot down not just during the landings, but at any time from then onwards. The grim truth was brought home the following day when Clubs invited me out on to the quarterdeck for a smoke. As we leant on the railings, looking down on *Ocean*'s wake just a few metres below, he asked me if I had any thoughts about who would replace the various flight commanders in the event of any fatalities. The question hadn't even crossed my mind, probably because my mind didn't want to dwell on such a morbid prospect, and it was a sobering moment as I heard myself running through the possibilities.

On 1 March, 40 Commando together with 845 and 847 Squadrons were put on twenty-four hours' notice to go to war. After a flying visit from Chief of Defence Staff Admiral Sir Michael Boyce later in the day, word spread round the ship that the assault had been scheduled for the third week of the month. Most of us were disappointed by the news; we wanted to get stuck in and get it over and done with at the earliest opportunity. Hanging around, counting the days, did little to soothe the nerves. We'd been cooped up on *Ocean* for six weeks now: we were getting tired and a little ropey around the edges from the lack of sleep on board and the frenetic pace of training over the previous few weeks, all on top of two months of hard training and preparations back home. It didn't help that the final round of our Naps and Bats injections, to offset the effects of a biological or chemical attack, had triggered a spate of nausea and heavy colds throughout the ship.

On 5 March I stayed on board to complete a backlog of admin work while most of the squadron flew ashore into the Kuwaiti desert to set up Camp Viking, which would remain our flying base and home until we were able to move up into Iraq. On 13 March all of us back on *Ocean* were issued with our battle bags – an anti-flash suit and respirator – and ordered to wear them at all times, in case the ship was hit by a missile. It was a strange and mildly disturbing sight, like a scene from *Doctor Who*, to see hundreds of men going about their daily business dressed in identical overalls, gloves and hoods, with their breathing apparatus hooked to the waist. The ship's crockery was also safely stowed away and the paper mugs and plates were brought out.

The following evening I managed to make a quick call home before the phone systems were shut down until such time it was considered safe to turn them back on. It was an emotional conversation. There I was on a ship in the Gulf, standing in my anti-flash suit, holding the phone in one hand and my respirator in the other, talking to my wife lying on the sofa back at our home in the West Country. I felt a surge of . . . disappointment. Perhaps I was just tired and ill and nervous about the looming war but she had nothing to say and after a terse exchange of goodbyes, I hung up and went back to my cabin.

'Lush, I think Suzi fucking hates me,' I said, throwing myself down on my bed.

Lush stuck his great big nose over the side of his bunk, looked at me with a broad grin on his face, and said: 'Don't worry, Scoobs, she's not the only one. We all fucking hate you. Good night.'

There was friction at home, and there was more friction at

work. Tension within the squadron had inevitably been mounting by the day since we had sailed from Plymouth. It finally burst out into the open as the Iraqi coastline came into view. There were two main areas of dispute: (1) how the pilots were going to be paired off in the helicopters; and (2) who was going to be involved in the first missions and engagements when the war got under way.

There was a mixed bag of characters in 847, each with his different qualities and shortcomings. I had flown with and assessed every pilot on the squadron – I'd trained half of them – and I was in constant, daily contact with the other training officers concentrating on specialist areas of operation. In short, I knew the capabilities of all the pilots in 847 better than anyone; and it was my job as TO1 to sort out the crewing in the Gulf. One by one the pilots began to take me aside for a quiet word, and this threatened to develop into an unseemly scramble as everyone put in their requests to fly with Tom, Dick or Harry and not with Bob, Barry or Brian. The flight commanders, Sonic and Coco, an ex-Royal Marines colour-sergeant and veteran of the Falklands, also had a lot of input into the various discussions because they wanted the best for their boys.

As the personal demands started to mount, a kind of 'A' and 'B' team started to emerge. This was something that I was very keen to avoid, partly because it was a 'political' issue that needed careful diplomatic handling, but mainly because it had a potentially calamitous impact on the morale of half the squadron. Imagine a young pilot taking to the air and heading into battle, perhaps for the first time in his career, knowing that he's considered to be on the 'B team'. It was going to be stressful enough for him as it was, without his mind full of nagging doubts that he was considered not quite up to the task, in some way inferior to others in the squadron. The joke, tinged with bitterness, doing the rounds, was that the 'B' team was a 'suicide list' of expendable pilots who would fly the first assaults because it didn't really matter if they got shot down.

Such talk had a divisive, cancerous effect on morale, and I acted quickly to put a stop to it. The truth was that we all had our strengths and weaknesses: some were better pilots than others, some were better at night flying, some would be cooler under fire, some a little more reckless when prosecuting targets. All of us, though, were pretty good all-rounders with one or two special qualities to offer. There were no duffers. In 847 Squadron, with its multi-role capabilities, pilots were quickly moved 'sideways' or transferred if they didn't come up to scratch on all counts. In training, I had made it a policy to be as critical as possible of my fellow pilots, pushing them to the limits of their cap-abilities. But right then, standing on the brink of a conflict, with no time left to learn new tricks or improve skills, it was time to start slapping backs and 'bigging up' the younger, less experienced or less confident characters. Self-doubt is an occupational danger to be avoided at all costs in the cockpit of an attack helicopter heading into a combat zone.

Each 847 air patrol consists of one Lynx and one Gazelle

with two pilots in each and a door gunner in the Lynx, and there were some basic rules about who crewed with whom. For instance, it's not good practice to partner your CO and senior pilot or operations officer together on the first wave of assaults. They didn't do that in the Second World War and we weren't about to start doing it now. If they all get shot down in the opening exchanges, the squadron is in serious trouble. Nor do you want your ops officer flying too much, if at all: his place is back in camp, running operations. We had a problem in this respect because Sweetcorn, our ops officer, was desperate to get into the action. Many of us, myself included, tried without much success to persuade him it was important for 847 that he did his fighting in the ops tent, not in the air. We would have had more chance of finding Osama bin Laden at a Tel Aviv bar mitzvah.

I found myself having to rebut a similar line of argument when people began telling me that I shouldn't be flying either; that, as training officer, my place was back in the camp, preparing the crews to go into battle. I thought this was nonsense, for the simple reason that the training was over the day the fighting began. I was also a mission commander and one of the most experienced pilots – if not the most experienced – in both the Lynx and the Gazelle, and it was madness not to fly me ahead of a rookie when the war began. As I saw it, we all had to be flexible and adapt to different roles, and it was absurd to expect a small handful of guys to fly all the missions, day after day.

Continuous flying is exhausting in ordinary circumstances; in forty-degree heat, being shot at from all angles, it's even more draining, especially when you're not getting any sleep back in a noisy camp.

If you want anything done in the squadron, you need to get the CO on side; then he sits everyone down in a room and tells them to shut up and listen, and do what they're told. That, in the end, was precisely what I did with this crewing issue, and once Clubs had spoken that was the last we had ever heard of the matter. Talk of A and B lists was banished and the notion replaced with a fairer, more practical system. Rather than have one team flying all day and then having a day off to recuperate, I suggested we had one big team working over forty-eight hours, and that at the outset we established pairs of crew who would fly together, as much as possible, for the duration of the war. The rough rule of thumb was to crew a very experienced pilot with an inexperienced co-pilot, and at the same time to marry up the pilots' capabilities as best we could, so that each air patrol was the strongest possible all-round flying unit. For example, a strong pilot would team up with a comms expert or a weapons whizz-kid and great shot; perhaps a cool, steady hand would fly with a more fiery character; and so on.

I was to fly with Colour Sergeant Gizmo, one of the handful of NCOs on the squadron. He was a good pilot who never got flustered and I knew we would work well together. As for my skills, my role as training officer demanded that I know the aircraft inside out and to me flying the helicopters had become second nature, which had the benefit of freeing me up to concentrate on other areas of operation such as firing weapons, working the radios fast, observing targets, liaising with the Royal Marines and tank boys on the ground, coordinating the jets, calling in artillery strikes and talking to the other aircraft.

It's all very well, however, scoring top marks and having a cool head in training, but quite frankly I had no idea how I, and some of the other pilots, were going to perform in a real theatre of war. There was a nagging fear at the back of my mind that our professionalism and skills might desert us at a crucial moment under the weight of fire, stress and decision-making. Before heading out to the Gulf, therefore, and during training on the way out, I tried to put the boys under as much pressure as possible in a number of different ways, for instance by cutting the number of systems working for them in the cockpit, reducing the flying performance of the aircraft, and making them fly in appalling weather conditions on NVGs. No matter how stressful many of them found those exercises, we all knew they were a mid-air picnic compared to what lay in store for us in Iraq.

The plan was to have 'relief in place', with four aircraft in two patrols in the air at all times, and another four back in camp or aboard *Ocean* ready to take their place. We calculated that each air patrol had enough fuel to fly for a total of ninety minutes and that each crew would be flying about four patrols a day. It was a very intensive flying schedule when you consider we only had six Lynx and six Gazelles, and that both crew and aircraft needed downtime. The serviceability of the aircraft was going to be key to the whole operation and the role of the engineers was therefore crucial. To keep all twelve aircraft up in the air, working to maximum capability in searing hot conditions and with the floury sand getting into every part of the machines, was going to present the 'lads' with the biggest challenge of their careers. The success or otherwise of 847 Squadron to a large extent lay in their hands and toolboxes, because we had to be ready to respond immediately to any request from the marines. If the lightly armed troops on the ground suddenly came under heavy artillery or tank fire, they would call us in to take out the enemy positions. If we couldn't respond, lives and ground could be lost. We were all going to be stretched to the limit.

The other contentious issue centred on who was going to fly the first waves of the assault and who was going to be held back in reserve over the opening days. It was a strange debate in which I suspect none of us was being entirely honest with the others. When all the aircrew were called together to thrash out the issue, all the pilots, myself included, were putting our hands up in the air, like schoolboys bursting for the loo, claiming we were desperate to be part of the first missions into the fray. But that, I can tell you, was just complete bravado. There we all were, declaring our great bravery and selflessness, when a truly honest and brave man would have piped up: 'Actually, I'm slightly shitting it, and since you guys seem so keen to get blown up, I'm quite happy to hang loose on *Ocean* and watch *Shrek* in my cabin with a couple of beers.'

You just didn't say that, though. Everyone had to give the impression that only a team of wild horses could hold them back from jumping in those helicopters right there and then and flying straight into unknown enemy territory and a hellish storm of incoming fire. Human nature, however, just doesn't work like that; the survival instinct in all of us pulls heavily in the opposite direction. I may have got this completely wrong and I may just be a gutless coward, but as far as I understand it, no man in his right mind likes to walk or fly into a hail of bullets. (Unless, of course, you are Sweetcorn or Lush – men who would happily spend their summer leave leopard-crawling through a malarial swamp filled with crocodiles, if there was even an outside chance of finding an enemy of the British state to bayonet at the other end.)

If we had been an unhappy squadron, rife with in-fighting and personal ill-feeling, then perhaps there might have been a less impressive show of hands. To a man, however, we all felt a keen duty to push to the front of the queue, in spite of the gut feeling that we were volunteering ourselves for premature death. At the risk of sounding like a character in *Band of Brothers* (we watched the whole series on the way out to the Gulf!), it was a fact that we had built up a very strong sense of brotherhood in 847 over the years. Those bonds had begun to squeeze even tighter as we prepared to

Top left 'Procedure Alpha' leaving Plymouth. All eyes peeled for the ten foot poppy!; *Below Ark Royal* leads the way – HMS *Ocean* is to the right; *Above right Ocean*'s cavernous hangar – see how much difference folding the blades makes; *Above left* 'G spot' – six Sea Kings are folded alongside the island

Above Al Faw forms the backdrop to an 847 NAS Aviation Patrol (AP) protecting the vital oil installation, with Iran in the distance; *Middle* Training in Kuwait – the AP in the distance conducts a 'Relief in Place' with the oncoming patrol; *Right* An AP moves past a destroyed 23mm AAA gun

Above Two Royal Marines talk a Lynx on to a potential target; *Left* An AP flies past a bunker complex – Basra in the distance; *Below* The powdery sand reduces visibility to zero

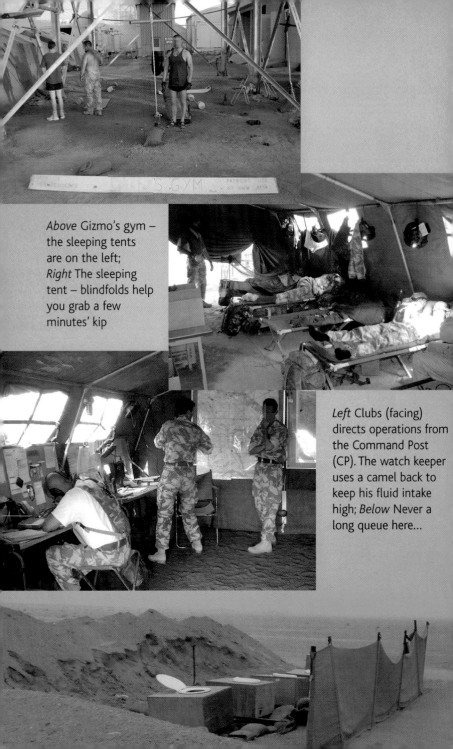

Above Gizmo's gym – the sleeping tents are on the left; *Right* The sleeping tent – blindfolds help you grab a few minutes' kip

Left Clubs (facing) directs operations from the Command Post (CP). The watch keeper uses a camel back to keep his fluid intake high; *Below* Never a long queue here...

Above Coco (back to camera), Gilbert (at the back) and I pass the situation on to Spidey (in the white T-shirt). Slaps gives his view on the day too; *Below* Outside the Ops building in Iraq and my face says it all – I'm off on the water treatments mission

Above With Guns and Gizmo – you can see the sand filters and exhaust diffusers on the engine; *Below left* Fully booted and spurred – and the Night Vision Goggles still need to be fitted on the helmet; *Below right* Hyena, Lush and Cindy fit another TOW

Middle The second tank – 10 degrees to go and the main gun would have been lined up; *Top* 24 March – the famous billboard with the first of the tanks in the foreground. The second tank is just out of sight in the top left-hand corner; *Bottom* Lush's MTLB behind the red gates – the street rubbish was everywhere

Above Home finally – the air crew were landing at Yeovilton as HMS *Ocean* arrived in Plymouth;

Below The CHF Tailored Air Group – not that many of us to do a massive job

fly into war together, but it wasn't something we acknowledged or discussed openly. Oprah Winfrey-style, public discussions about our intimacy as a squadron, our brotherhood or mutual respect and affection – call it what you will – do not sit comfortably with aircrew as a rule. The rude banter that we routinely exchanged with one another, laughing at each other's shortcomings and weaknesses, added a further layer of disguise to our true feelings. But once we had sifted our consciences and addressed our fears and anxieties, the bottom line was that we were all prepared to put ourselves on the line for each other.

It was interesting, too, that in the final couple of weeks before war erupted, when the schedule allowed, we relaxed as hard as we trained, enjoying every last minute of downtime, aware that there wasn't going to be much fun on the agenda over the coming weeks. Mindful of the growing tension aboard *Ocean*, the brass laid on a concert in the hangar, featuring a Royal Marines' rock band, and we also devised our own impromptu forms of entertainment.

On the Saturday night five days before we all knew the war was going to start, we staged a 'Forum of Fact' – a kind of mock trial – in the wardroom. The man in the dock was an Australian cameraman working for the BBC who made the mistake of casually dropping into conversation that, in his youth, he had once slept with the forces' pin-up, Kylie Minogue. Big mistake! There were a lot of angry, jealous men roaming the corridors of *Ocean* when news of his outrageous claim spread through the ship. I was assigned the role of lead counsel for the prosecution, with Naphtha, dressed as Freddie Mercury in leather chaps, struggling to mount a credible defence for his client.

None of us were in the mood or the right frame of mind for an evening of such low farce – it all seemed very silly and inappropriate, given the fact that we were going to war in a few days' time – but in the event, the Forum of Fact was a masterstroke of timing. You could see, hear and feel a gigantic, collective release of tension in the room as the beers flowed and we all roared with childish laughter. The cameraman, Kylie fans will be delighted to hear, was convicted of bullshitting and bragging, and sentenced to death by hanging. (We granted him a pardon in the end, on the condition that he got the beers in.)

The following night all the officers congregated in the wardroom and, a few beers down the line, some of the old boys broke into song. Soon we were all standing up, arms round each other's shoulders, booming out 'Father Abraham' ('Father Abraham had seven sons . . .') and the Luftwaffe song, a parody of the real version sung by German pilots in the war, poking fun at our colleagues in the RAF.

On Tuesday, we were put on two hours' notice. On Wednesday I sat down at the laptop in my cabin and wrote out a CV for a new job. On Thursday we went to war.

CHAPTER SIX

A weird silence had fallen over HMS *Ocean* as night enveloped the Gulf. The better part of 1,200 men and women were crammed into its vast network of cabins, decks and corridors, but the ship was as quiet as I had heard it since setting sail into the Channel over two months earlier. Through the darkness I could see the shadowy forms of six Sea Kings sitting in a neat line on their spots along the port side of the flight deck, their noses pointing towards the bow, ready for launching. Meanwhile, the hot, cavernous hangar below was a picture of business-like efficiency as the engineers and ground crew of 845 Naval Air Squadron made last-minute checks on the other half-dozen of their aircraft, waiting for the order to raise them on the hydraulic platform, one by one, into the cool, still air above.

Most of my colleagues on 847 Squadron at that moment

were in Camp Viking in Kuwait, making last minute-checks to the aircraft and packing their Bergens, priming their personal weapons, waiting for the order to go. To my frustration, I was held in reserve as the detachment commander for the remaining 847 pilots; for us, there was nothing for it but to sit and wait to be called forward, making ourselves as useful as possible in the meantime.

The amphibious operations room (AOR) was filled to capacity with the senior officers and other staff of all the units involved in the night's assault: about thirty men in total. This small room, located right in the heart of the ship, would be safe from all but the most catastrophic attacks. Brigadier Dutton, the commander of 3 Commando Brigade, was directing operations from *Ark Royal*, but Captain Johns, *Ocean*'s captain, was there, along with the CO of 845 Squadron and a bank of radio operators and 'watchkeepers' – men from each different component of the assault force, tasked with recording their unit's operations in the upcoming hours. Gordon Messenger, the CO of 40 Commando, was there at the beginning, looking every inch the warrior that his troops avowed him to be. When I walked into the room he was standing in full battle gear, hands on hips, his hard-set face covered in black camouflage paint, ready to join the fray after supervising the first wave of his troops to go in. If he was nervous, he certainly didn't look it.

Every desk in the room was manned, every radar screen was turned on, flashing, beeping, humming. The white noise from the many radios kept up a constant fizz and crackle in the background, like an untuned television someone had forgotten to turn off. The atmosphere was extremely tense, but for the time being at least it was fairly quiet as the clock ticked down to 'H' hour. This was the pre-designated time at which the first wave of helicopters were scheduled to touch down on the Al-Faw, having flown into the peninsula in long formation just above the waterline so as not to be detected by Iraqi radar systems. Almost exactly the same scene, only with a different set of characters, was being enacted a few miles across the water on *Ark Royal* as 42 Commando primed themselves for battle and the ship's company went into action stations.

After three months of intense planning, coordination and preparation, 1,500 Royal Marines of 40 and 42 Commando, together with a sizeable contingent from the Special Boat Service and the US Navy Seals (the American equivalent of the SBS), braced themselves for Operation Houghton – the first full-scale opposed landing undertaken by British forces in almost sixty years. Special forces and other commandos, meanwhile, were waiting offshore for the order to move in on the gas and oil platforms at sea. The gunners of 29 Royal Artillery, attached to 3 Commando Brigade, took up their positions on Bubiyan, a huge, flat, uninhabited island off the Kuwaiti coast reserved for the military. The men of the 16th Air Assault Brigade, under Brigadier 'Jacko' Page, readied themselves to storm the oil fields at Rumaila, while the fast jet crews went on standby, ready to strike at key facilities and to provide armed support for the troops as they were inserted in their drop zones.

Elsewhere, the full might of the American task force, totalling nearly a quarter of a million troops, went about its own final, last-minute preparations. On the ground, out in the Kuwaiti desert, the troops of 1 (UK) Armoured Division, including the 'Desert Rats' of the 7th Armoured Brigade, sat and waited for news from the front line and the order to storm into the demilitarised zone (DMZ) and up into enemy territory. The 30,000 British troops massed on the border included infantry, tank crews, engineers, logistics corps and medical units, bomb disposal teams, signallers and military police. The size of the British force was, give or take a thousand, roughly the same size as that which took part in the first Gulf War, making it the largest deployment of personnel since the Second World War, greater even than those sent to Suez and Korea.

The objectives of the operation were fourfold: military, environmental, humanitarian and economic – pretty well in that order. The immediate military aim sounded simple: defeat the enemy in the huge pumping and switching stations and secure a foothold on the Al-Faw peninsula. The fear was that if we failed to do this quickly then Saddam was going to repeat his environmental crimes of the first Gulf War, when he set fire to the oil fields and caused a massive ecological disaster in the region as millions of barrels of oil poured into the Gulf and huge clouds of tarry smoke filled the skies for weeks on end. Intelligence told us that once again his troops had laid explosives throughout the dozens of oil fields and installations in the region, and that these were set to be detonated as soon as the invasion got under way – or at least, as soon as it looked as if the Iraqi defences had collapsed.

By setting alight Iraq's most prized economic assets, Saddam wanted to cause as much havoc as possible, economically and environmentally, for the people deposing him from power. But he also hoped that the giant fires and billowing mountains of thick, acrid smoke would hamper the advances of the US and British troops, and give his own an outside chance of beating off the attack. What a propaganda prize it would be if he could appear on television the following day to announce to the world that his loyal troops had driven the armies of Bush and Blair back into the waters of the Gulf, even if that had meant sacrificing the oil fields for the greater good of keeping him on his throne for a short while longer.

The third objective was the urgent humanitarian priority of shipping in as much fresh water, food and aid to the people of south-eastern Iraq as quickly as possible. To do this effectively, coalition forces needed to secure the port of Umm-Qasr, the country's only deep-water harbour, in order to bring in those vital supplies for Iraqi citizens. It was also imperative to clear the waters, coasts and riverbanks of the hundreds of mines that had been laid over the weeks beforehand in anticipation of the invasion. Lastly, securing the entire oil industry infrastructure was vital to the economic health of the country. Destroy it, and the life-blood of the Iraq nation would be cut off at a stroke – and it would take months, years even, to restore. A country cannot survive on the export of dried dates alone.

As someone who has chosen to pursue a career in the armed forces, I have never seen it as my position to question, publicly at least, the moral rights and wrongs of a given conflict. If I am called upon to fight, then, like all but a wretched and contemptible handful of my comrades-in-arms, I will carry out my duty as requested, as best as I can, and without whingeing. It doesn't matter to us who the enemy is. We just fight. I am aware, of course, that the legitimacy of the war divided opinion across the world, even back at home. In all previous conflicts involving the deployment of the British services, the vast majority of the public gave the departing troops their unequivocal support and heartfelt wishes for a quick victory and a speedy return. That was not the case on this occasion, and we were keenly aware as we put on our helmets and zeroed our weapons that not everyone was rooting for us back in the shires and city boroughs.

Perhaps all soldiers, sailors and airmen feel this way when they stand on the cusp of a battle, but on the night of Thursday 20 March I couldn't help but believe that the cause for which we were about to put our lives on the line was a noble one. We were going to liberate an entire nation from a brutal tyrant and usher in a new, happier society for twenty-five million previously oppressed people. And then we would all go home for a pint and a fish supper and leave the Iraqis to run their own affairs with a proper government installed in Baghdad. That's what it felt like at the time, anyway, and I felt very proud to be a part of it.

That night a total of 46,000 servicemen and women of the British armed forces were spread out across the Gulf region, on land and sea and in the air, most of them poised to play a role of some description in the biggest war the world had witnessed since the first conflict in the Gulf twelve years earlier. On *Ocean*, I watched the 'guides' of the ship's company, holding their light-sticks in their hands, heading below to the various mess decks where the marines had congregated, ready to lead them up in 'sticks' of eight through the warren of corridors and hatches, out on to the flight decks and into the waiting helicopters.

There were just minutes to go now before they launched and I suddenly felt like a totally useless spare prick. I wasn't actually in my dressing gown and slippers, but it felt a bit like that as I watched the men alongside whom I had lived and trained over the previous decade or so steeling themselves for what would be the most momentous few hours and days of their lives. I wanted to be there at Camp Viking, with the boys chosen for the first wave, strapping on my chest armour and NVGs, not stuck here on the ship, wandering around like a lost spectator. It was a horrible feeling, being held in reserve, unable now to contribute anything to this massive effort, this key moment in British military history. People can say what they like about the politics and morality of it, but from a purely military point of view, a large-scale opposed landing, at night, into a heavily defended enemy position, with the risk of drastic human, strategic and political consequences if it went wrong, was a major operation by anyone's standards.

I followed the guides down to the mess decks below to wish the boys luck and felt a huge surge of adrenaline when I walked into the first room and saw all the bootnecks waiting for their turn to be called. They were all in full combat gear, faces blackened with camo paint, helmets on, Bergens and assault rifles at their sides – or, in Royal Marine slang, 'cammed up, Bergened up, bombed up, battle bowls on the bonce'. Some sat there in silence looking at the floor or staring into space, alone in their thoughts and prayers; others talked quietly to one another, the old sweats reassuring and talking up the younger lads, nervous before their first taste of battle. Others were pumping themselves up by pushing, chesting and even punching each other. It was an incredible atmosphere, a potent cocktail of tension, excitement, fear, determination and testosterone.

God only knew how they must have been feeling, but the hairs on the back of my neck stood on end as I wished them luck, and I felt a shudder of emotion all over my body as I headed back into the AOR. I'd been asked to be there in order to advise on any operational issues relating to the Commando Helicopter Force, and 847 Squadron in particular, and I was only too happy to oblige. Apart from getting a front-row seat on the action as it unfolded, it also meant that I would be able to contribute something, no matter how small and incidental, to the events about to unfold. Sleep was not an option that night. Over the radios I could now hear the American AC-130 gunships pounding the Iraqi defences on the Al-Faw peninsula. The Sea King pilots out on the flight deck had strapped in, started the engines and the rotor blades, and one by one were calling in to the AOR on tele brief – a telephone line from the aircraft to the ship. The crewmen of each helicopter waited by the open doors of the aircraft waiting for the men to emerge from below and to stow their Bergens in the back.

An aerial bombing operation had begun earlier in the day, targeting dozens of sites across Iraq. At one stage, news had swept around *Ocean* that one of the strikes had killed Saddam himself; but even if this had been true, it was too late to stop the invasion. The Iraqis had responded by firing a series of Scuds in the vague direction of the huge coalition encampments in Kuwait, and more towards the vast coalition fleet anchored offshore. The chemical attack sirens, meanwhile, had been wailing for most of the day in Kuwait City, with one missile landing smack in the middle of the harbour area. British Harriers, together with the jets of the US Air Force and Navy, flew mission after mission to seek out the Scud and Seersucker launchers across the south of the Iraq. Eight B52 bombers, meanwhile, had taken off from RAF Fairford in Gloucestershire.

As dusk settled over the region, US and British artillery opened up with huge bombardments into the Iraqi border zone, and the Iraqis returned fire from their own positions. The air-raid warning alarms were sounded across Baghdad, followed shortly afterwards by a series of huge explosions as the Tomahawk missiles and bombs from the coalition jets rained down on Saddam's palaces, the Iraqi intelligence headquarters and other key buildings. Pilots and special forces troops on the ground began sending back reports that several oil fields in the south had been set ablaze, but it was unclear exactly how many had been torched because the Iraqis were also setting fire to giant lakes and ditches of oil to fill the skies with as much smoke as possible.

I wanted to be out on the flight deck when the marines emerged – and what a breathtaking sound and spectacle it was when they began to stream out of the hatch into the open air. Up from the assault stations they came like a colony of ants, led by their guides, two abreast, Bergens on their backs, guns held out in front, the whites of their eyes under their helmets staring out from their dark, grim-set faces. The roar of the rotor blades from the six helicopters filled the air as hundreds of men poured out of the bowels of the ship, stick after stick, then disappeared into the dark interior of the Sea Kings and strapped themselves in. One by one, the pilots gave the thumbs-up sign to the flight-deck crew, the side doors were pulled shut and the aircraft lifted into the night sky, taking up a holding position in the racetrack pattern around the ship. When the first wave had launched from the flight deck, another six helicopters were brought up from the hangar, and the scene was repeated as a second group of marines streamed out on to the flight deck in a rapid but orderly fashion.

It's weird how life seems to imitate art sometimes: as I stood there watching the helicopters depart, I felt like I was watching a scene from the Vietnam film *Apocalypse Now*. All it needed was an orchestra to strike up Wagner's 'Ride of the Valkyries' as the first wave disappeared into the dark, flying very low and very fast, roughly thirty seconds apart, towards the Al-Faw. It was all beautifully choreographed and, thank God, there was only one small hiccough. A radalt – the radar altimeter for assessing the aircraft's height from the ground – had failed in one of the helicopters – but with amazing skill and speed, the engineers managed to replace it in a matter of minutes and the assault was able to continue as planned.

The AOR had been calm and quiet a few minutes earlier, but now it was a controlled, organised riot of noise as I hurried back to take my place and hear the assault unfold over the radio systems. I was nervous enough in the safety of the ship's heart, and I could only imagine how the boys in Camp Viking must have been feeling as they strapped into the Lynx and Gazelles and lifted off to link up with the Sea Kings and Chinooks from *Ocean* and *Ark Royal* and escort the troops into Iraq.

As soon as the helicopters were airborne the radios crackled with the voices of the pilots, checking in with *Ocean* and the air traffic controllers. The tension in the AOR was almost unbearable, and there was no disguising the strain etched on the faces of the commanding officers in the room. Intelligence from SAS and SBS units on the ground had indicated a large number of Iraqi troops inside the pumping and switching stations, and an even greater number dug in around the surrounding area. The X factor was the question of how hard the Iraqis were prepared to fight, but as a helicopter pilot all I needed to know of the dangers facing the troops being inserted was that a single burst of small-arms fire was sufficient to bring down one of the aircraft. As the Sea Kings and Chinooks were to be landing right in the middle of the installations, there was no doubt that they would come under close-range fire of some description. It's unlikely that any of the Sea King pilots who took to the air that night will fly a more dangerous mission in his career.

For the fifteen minutes it took the first wave of the helicopters to reach the oil stations, there was an incessant chatter over the radios, and you could also hear the guns of the Spectre gunships, still hammering away to keep the Iraqis' heads down. But when the first aircraft touched down and the pilot called in saying 'London' to confirm their arrival, there followed an awful silence. The gunships had stopped firing just seconds before the troops began to arrive, and all talk on the radio suddenly came to a halt. The silence on the airwaves was echoed in the operations room. For those few moments it was as if the world had stopped turning. The pause lasted for probably no more than five seconds, but the shock of the sudden stillness made it seem much, much longer. I distinctly remember looking around the room and seeing everyone frozen where they sat or stood; I watched a single sheet of A4 paper drifting off one of the controllers' desks and floating noiselessly to the floor. It was a terrible wait. For a moment I suspected the worst: that some or all of the first wave had been shot down as they came in to land.

And then merry hell broke loose.

The radios crackled back into life and all we could hear was a cacophony of shouting and a massive wall of gunfire as the troops poured out of the back and sides of their helicopters, blazing away as they sprinted to their pre-defined targets. One after another, every single unit landing on put out the same report: 'Contact! Wait Out!' which translates roughly as 'Fuck off, we're being vittled here, I'll call you later.'

Each of the helicopters was on the ground for no more than about twenty seconds, dumping its troops and lifting off as quickly as possible before the Iraqis had a chance to get their heads up and take a shot at it. At such range, the big, noisy, flashing lump of a helicopter presented a target that even an imbecile with a popgun would struggle to miss. Soon the crash and boom of mortar rounds, theirs and ours, could be heard clearly over the airwaves.

What we hadn't realised in the AOR until one of the returning pilots called in was that the weather ashore was absolutely appalling. Out in the Gulf it was calm and clear, but on the Al-Faw there were extremely strong winds and visibility was dreadful, made worse by the sand clouds being kicked up and the oil fires that had been ignited – a nightmare for helicopter pilots already labouring under the considerable flying difficulties presented by wearing NVGs, not to mention the strain of coming under heavy fire. There was one very narrow escape when one of the Sea Kings had dropped off a Land Rover and the pilot, concentrating on lowering the vehicle, hadn't realised that the aircraft had been swung round a full 180 degrees by the buffeting winds and lack of references. When he moved away from the drop zone he was completely disorientated and flew straight into the path of an incoming Sea King, the two missing each other by no more than a few dozen feet.

It was quickly realised, too, that under such heavy fire from the Iraqis it was too dangerous to land on the sites that had been originally earmarked in the planning. Following a rapid stream of reports from the pilots and the commanders on the ground, the decision was taken to seek out new landing sites as quickly as possible. This is where Jack, the man commanding the MAOT (mobile air operations team), stood up to the plate and earned himself an MID (mentioned in dispatches) for his efforts. The job of his team was to guide the helicopters into the landing sites, but such was the layout of the installations and the position of the enemy bunkers that there were no immediately obvious alternatives. They needed to create a new space, and so, under heavy fire, Jack and his team set about blowing up a series of telegraph poles to bring down the cables that were in the way of the helicopters.

Shortly after the first wave of helicopters had landed on the Al-Faw it was 'L' hour, the moment when the men of 539 Assault Squadron beached their landing craft and the marines stormed ashore. Their small boats, which can reach speeds of up to thirty knots, were put into the sea and the waiting marines rushed into them down the ramps protruding from *Ocean*. At roughly the same time more landing craft and helicopters, ferrying the men of 42 Commando, began to launch from *Ark Royal* as the assault quickly gathered in size, force and momentum.

The Iraqis, assuming that an opposed landing would have been considered too dangerous to attempt, must have been expecting the coalition to arrive by land from Kuwait, with the long drive up through the desert giving them plenty of warning of the attack that was coming. This rapid insertion of Royal Marines and special forces – almost 2,000 men in all – by air and sea appeared to have caught them with their trousers down, just as the planners had hoped. With fire raining down from the AC130s above, as well as from the frigates and destroyers out in the Gulf and the artillery batteries installed ashore, it was little wonder that by mid-morning Iraqis not under the command or influence of the Fedayeen, the chief whips of the Iraqi forces, were beginning to surrender in their hundreds.

That said, contrary to the media reports we watched on the news channels in the wardroom over the following days, and the newspaper reports we read a few weeks later, the assault was no cakewalk. The Iraqis were a stout foe and they defended their homeland with great courage until they were overwhelmed by superior fire and all hope of a surprise victory had been extinguished. The fighting that first night was incredibly intense, and though the marines suffered no combat fatalities there were casualties; the COs, to a man, later admitted they had been surprised by the ferocity of the resistance, particularly in the opening exchanges, as our lightly armed 'shock troops' took their positions and began the task of slowly flushing out the enemy. No one had openly said as much in the countdown to the battle, but most of the brass had been hoping for an almost instantaneous capitulation.

By dawn the marines had gained the upper hand, but it wasn't until the following afternoon that the final pockets of resistance were overrun and the switching and pumping stations were eventually secured without any significant damage to their infrastructure. While some marines dug in and others pushed beyond the oil stations to attack enemy positions out wider, the bomb disposal units were able to set about removing all the remaining explosive devices that had been laid throughout the structures, thus averting, once and for all, a huge environmental disaster. It was through this pumping station that all of Iraq's vast output passed from the oil fields out on to platforms in the Gulf where it was transferred into waiting tankers from around the world. I don't know this for certain, but I'd be very surprised if the

SBS boys, arriving by rigid raiders, hadn't got to the pumping stations before the marines in order to remove as many of the explosives as possible before the Iraqis had a chance to detonate them.

I have to admit to being gripped by events as they unfolded that night over the radios and the 'Link 16' pictures from the AWACS aircraft of 849 Naval Air Squadron. It was both stressful and exhilarating listening to my colleagues shouting and barking orders to one another, breathlessly sending in their reports of the battle status to the commanders back on ship, all the time against the background noise of heavy machine-gun fire and the explosions of grenades, mortars and missiles. *Ocean* herself was on full alert all night, and the air-raid sirens spent more time on than off as the Iraqis launched waves of Scuds and Seersuckers into the air – more, it has to be said, in hope than in genuine expectation of a hit. Next door to the AOR is the operations room – the hub of the ship's fighting and defence systems – and here the whole team were flat to the boards trying to pick out possible missile attacks heading our way from the mass of dots on their tactical display screens. The closest missile that night landed harmlessly about three miles away, but it would be many days, even weeks, before the ship could drop her guard and down her alert status.

At one point, as night slowly gave way to the first streaks of watery grey light over the Gulf, I went out on to the flight deck and watched the Sea Kings landing back on. The faces of the pilots told their own story about the ferocity of the fighting and the intensity of their own experiences. One by one, each of them having flown mission after mission into the combat zone, first dropping off the troops, then offloading the equipment, supplies and ammunition, they finally stepped out of their cabs. They looked completely shattered by their night's work, staring wide-eyed and vacant into the middle distance as they floated across the flight deck and back into the relative sanctuary of the ship. One pilot was so shaken up by his experience that when he handed over the aircraft to the next crew he slumped back in his seat in a state of catatonia, utterly incapable of moving, and had to be carried out of the helicopter by the ground crew.

I was dying to talk to the lads on 847 to hear their account of events. I knew that my old mates Sonic and Hovis were the first crew into the mix that night, and when I had spoken to them the day before they'd told me they'd found it really disconcerting in the days leading up to the assault that they couldn't walk past anyone in camp without that person shaking their hands, patting them on the back, looking at them soulfully and wishing them all the best. It was as if people were telling them it had been nice knowing them and were saying farewell for a final time. They're a cool pair of cats, though, those two, perfect characters to lead the squadron's way, and from what I could tell from the chatter, they and the others seemed to have acquitted themselves admirably in the hideous conditions. At daybreak, 847 had fired its first missile in anger in heaven knows how many years, when Mako, our American exchange pilot, took out the door of a bunker with a TOW. We liked Mako by now – he had chilled a bit since we had managed to persuade him of the virtues of a few pints of Old Speckled Hen – but for some reason I felt a little disappointed that it hadn't been one of the British boys, perhaps one of the older hands like Slaps or Sonic, who had got the opening shot away.

As the marines launched their assault, British and American tanks and troops, including the Black Watch and the Royal Fusiliers of the 7th Armoured Brigade, poured over the border from Kuwait and raced up through the DMZ and the pock-marked wastelands of south-eastern Iraq towards Basra. At the same time, the US Marines laid siege to the port of Umm-Qasr while minesweepers started to move in to clear the shores and waterways of hundreds of explosive devices laid by Iraqi boats.

I spent most of the night standing behind the controllers on the HELO (helicopter control) desk providing answers to questions about 847. As the assault unfolded through the night, the commanders and controllers needed to know, for instance, how long 847 could sustain their missions in the weather conditions . . . Was the Lynx capable of taking out such and such a target? . . . How many casualties could the Lynx lift? . . . and so on. Compared to what the pilots were doing out there in the battle, my contribution to the assault is barely worth mentioning, but I was glad to be putting something into the mix, no matter how small. It was just good to be involved. Something inside me would have died if I had spent the opening night of the war sitting on my bunk watching a film.

The operation was running almost exactly to plan – almost too well, you couldn't help feeling. The most dangerous element, inserting the troops under fire, was successfully completed and the troops had settled into the battle. Then – I can't recall the precise time, but it must have been about four in the morning local time – the news arrived like a bombshell in the operations room. An American CH46 troop-carrier helicopter had crashed in the Kuwaiti desert, not far south of Umm-Qasr, killing eight Royal Marines and the four US aircrew. All eight marines were part of 3 Commando Brigade on a special mission and they had been living among us over the past two months; they were all familiar faces to me, and close friends to many others.

For the first time in roughly six hours, not a single person in that room said a word as we took in the news. Some stopped what they were doing and put their heads in their hands; others looked away or down at the floor, blowing out their cheeks as they exhaled heavily. The cruel truth, though, was that there was no time to stop and reflect because the battles and engagements up on the Al-Faw were still raging. Within a minute the whole room was back to business, working the radios and tactical displays, studying the maps, issuing orders, relaying information. If anything, the atmosphere was electrified by an even greater sense of purpose. We would mourn their loss later.

I didn't go back to the cabin that night, and it was only once the sun was high in the eastern sky over Iran and the intensity of the firing began to diminish that I finally slipped off to my pit, still buzzing with adrenaline but sick at the news of the crash, my head swimming with a thousand thoughts.

On the following two days, Friday 21 and Saturday 22 March, the battles continued across the Al-Faw as the Americans tried to subdue the Iraqis in fierce exchanges in and around Umm-Qasr. The British, meanwhile, were engaged in sporadic fighting throughout the peninsula as the line of advance pushed north from its tip. The US forces who had bypassed the fighting in the south, continued to push ahead up a direct route to Baghdad, but were slowed by major resistance near Najaf and Nasirayah. The aerial bombardment of key sites and installations continued without pause. Casualties started to mount on both sides, but there was so much activity it was difficult to get a completely clear picture of what was happening on the ground. (Watching the news reports on the television was next to useless because the reporters just regurgitated the limited accounts fed to them by the military spokesmen. The reports told us much less than we already knew, and we might just as well have been watching John Craven's Newsround.) Black smoke from the oil fires and the bombardments hung heavily over the horizon, and the skies roared with the noise of jets and helicopters coming and going from the ships in the Gulf.

As for me, I was hard at work on *Ocean*, wandering the ship's corridors, admiring the grey paintwork, lying on my bunk, staring out to sea from the flight deck, and occasionally popping my head around the door of the operations room to offer help: 'Can I get anyone anything? Tea? Coffee? I can get you biscuits too, if you want. Ginger Snaps. They're delicious. I've had a whole packet already today . . . Oh, OK, right, you're busy, are you? All right, there's no need to swear. Well, I'll be off then. Perhaps I'll pop in later. Bye now . . .'

Imagine going to the pub for a drink with your family and best mates when a huge fight breaks out at the bar and you're stuck in the toilet. That's a little like how I felt back on *Ocean* as the war got under way, and the sense of uselessness and frustration got worse with every Ginger Snap consumed and every twiddle of the thumbs. I'm only slightly joking when I say that if I had had to endure another day of it, I think I would have stolen a helicopter or dived off the side of the ship and swum ashore to join the boys at Viking. I'd never been to war, and I had been feeling a little apprehensive about the prospect of fighting in one, but once it began I quickly discovered that being held back in reserve while your colleagues are flying into the flak is a far more trying condition. When I was finally called forward for Sunday morning, odd as it may sound, I felt a huge sense of relief that finally – Hallelujah! Thank the Lord! – people were going to be firing real bullets and tank rounds at me.

On Saturday morning, the day before I flew to Viking, I

was shaken awake at six in the morning by one of the ship's stewards and told to go and see Wings, the ship's senior air officer and the man in overall charge of aircraft operations on board *Ocean*, as quickly as possible.

'Thank God you're alive, Scoobs,' said Wings as I arrived, rubbing the sleep from my eyes. 'Something awful's happened. I think Clubs is dead, maybe other 847 too. Two Sea Kings have just collided off *Ark Royal*.'

I felt like vomiting. The crash had happened no more than half an hour earlier and the first snippets of information coming in were confusing. There were so many missions, so many aircraft up in the air at any one time, and so much else going on up on the peninsula that for thirty minutes we thought that our commanding officer had been killed. Apart from the loss of a close friend and colleague, there was also the question, which had to be addressed immediately, of reordering the squadron's chain of command.

Once the fog of misunderstanding began to lift later that morning, the true facts of the accident were established. Clubs, it turned out, wasn't aboard one of the flights after all, and was safe in the operations tent at Camp Viking, as yet unaware of the tragedy. The two helicopters involved were both airborne early warning (AEW) Sea Kings from 849 Squadron, based at Culdrose in Cornwall. In the original flight programme, I had been scheduled to be on one of these helicopters, 849 squadron having requested that, when possible, an 847 pilot join them on some of their missions over the first few days of the war (849 were radar and surveillance experts, who generally worked with jets over the sea, but we had greater experience of working over land, coordinating with the various troops units on the ground); but, unknown to Wings, that plan had been changed two days earlier.

The AEW aircraft and their pilots are known as 'baggers' in the services because the radar hanging off their side looks like a large bag. One was taking off from *Ark Royal*, one was coming back into land. What made the collision incomprehensible to us at first was that both aircraft were fitted with the most powerful radars in the business, capable of homing in on a man walking his dog forty miles away, so picking out another helicopter right under their noses shouldn't have been a problem. How the hell, we wondered, had these experts in the arts of detection failed to spot each other and take diversionary action?

The incident is still under investigation. The only good news was that it happened in an instant and the impact was so great that none of the seven who lost their lives would have known it was coming. They would have felt nothing. Six of them were British and the seventh was an American exchange pilot.

The crew of HMS *Liverpool*, the ship closest to the crash, spotted the giant orange fireball that lit up the sky and immediately put out the alert. Needless to say, the search and rescue teams in the air and on the water found no survivors, just debris, even though they were on the scene within minutes. Four of the bodies were recovered over the following week.

Royal Navy helicopter pilots are a small, tight community. We all know each other by name, and most of us have flown with one another at some point in our careers. I knew all the dead, except the American. I would be claiming a false intimacy if I said I was close friends with any one of them, but they were more than just work colleagues. I had shared a few pints with all of them, and I had flown with two of them just the week before. Their deaths sent shock waves through all the helicopter Naval Air Squadrons, as well as the crew of the *Ark Royal*, where they had been living for the previous eight weeks.

Once we had established the rough facts of the accident, I went out on to the quarterdeck for a smoke, and my hand was quivering as I lit up and leant on the railings. When I walked back to the wardroom, a handful of other pilots were watching the reports of the crash on one of the major television channels, and there was a collective uproar when a picture of the wrong type of Sea King was flashed up on the screen: it was a 'Junglie' green one without a radar, not a grey one with the unmistakable 'bag' of the AEW helicopter. At this stage, the details handed to the media were still sketchy, so no one back home knew to which squadron the destroyed Sea Kings belonged. The families of all the Sea King squadrons out in the Gulf, watching the reports back in Yeovilton and Culdrose, saw the archive pictures of the wrong Sea King and assumed that the dead were from 845 Squadron, who are based at Yeovilton. As no one was allowed to call home at this stage of the war for security reasons, everyone back in Yeovilton went berserk with worry while everyone down at Culdrose, though sad, breathed a sigh of relief that it was not their men who had died.

Several hours later the truth came out and it was Culdrose that was plunged into despair. (When I arrived home a few months later, I discovered that, when the news of the crash first broke in the UK, the television station flashed up an archive picture of a Lynx, sending my family – and those of the other 847 pilots – into a paddy of anxiety before the MoD press office quickly alerted the broadcasters to their mistake. Perhaps it was then, in their haste to correct the error, that they put out the picture of the wrong Sea King.)

I can only imagine, with dread, what the families in Culdrose must have been going through over the days that followed, because by all accounts the atmosphere was bad enough on the *Ark Royal* as colleagues of the dead packed up the personal belongings of our friends for sending home, and closed up their cabins. The crews of the squadron's remaining state-of-the-art aircraft were stood down for the rest of the day in respect, and, in an old navy tradition, they retired to the wardroom and drank on the mess bills of our lost friends.

The worst aspect of those deaths was that they were the result of an accident, not enemy action. The human cost of the losses was immeasurable, but on a much less important level the crash was also an enormous waste of assets. When you factor in the cost of training these expert pilots and observers with the value of the aircraft and the radar systems, the total figure was not far short of £100 million. Again, it's a minor consideration when seven good men have just died, but it was a fact that had to be addressed that the tragedy also undermined our ability to plot the air/land picture and our general operational capability. Unlike the Americans, we cannot replace specialist pilots and cutting-edge equipment with a quick phone call the morning after a crash.

If the Sea King collision had occurred at home during an exercise, then our reaction to the deaths would have been one of shock and pure sadness. Out in the Gulf, however, in a war setting, it was slightly different: the disbelief and the grief were mixed up with a sense of anger and an even greater feeling of resolve that our friends weren't going to have died in vain.

That night, almost exactly twenty-four hours after the crash had happened, when I took off for Viking with Gizmo alongside me in the Lynx, I felt more steeled than sad. The flight into the Kuwaiti desert took no more than about fifteen minutes, and when we brought the aircraft down through a great cloud of whirling sand the sun was just starting to poke its head over the waters of the Gulf. It was still cool, but in an hour or so the sweat would start to run, and by mid-morning the atmosphere would be an open-air sauna. Camp Viking was slowly coming to life after a short night's sleep, and the aircrew, engineers and marines, most of them in regulation beige T-shirts and combat trousers, were starting to emerge from their tents, yawning and stretching as the first weak rays of light began to filter through the thin haze blanketing the desert sands.

When I first saw my old chum Hovis stumbling out into the open air, I didn't recognise him. He looked like a tramp. His face was unshaven and his hair was sticking up on one side. He looked filthy and he smelt even worse, and if I had had a pound coin on me I would have flicked it in his direction. Most of the boys, in fact, looked as though they had been through the grinder over the previous seventy-two hours. They had been flying from dawn to dusk up at the battlefront, and there had been little respite back in the camp after packing away the helicopters for the night. The air-raid sirens had been wailing nearly constantly through the small hours as the Iraqis, positioned a long way north of Basra, continued to fire dozens of Scuds and Seersuckers in the rough direction of the coalition troops and camps. None, as yet, had found its target, but they had been effective in another way by depriving the invading forces of anything resembling a proper night's sleep since the conflict had erupted.

The boys were so tired, they didn't even have the energy to take the piss out of me. I was expecting a barrage of jokes and abuse about me spending the war drinking beer, sleeping in late and watching football on the telly, but mostly they just stood around grunting and farting as they tried to shake the fatigue out of their heads and bodies. Some of them were crouching down out in the sand, unloading their rations; others stood naked, showering themselves under the hand-held water-bags with which we were issued. The bags have roughly three minutes of water in them, and you warmed them up a little by lying them down in the sun for a few hours. Later in the day, however, when the sun was high in the sky, you'd want them as cool as possible and you'd leave them in the shade.

Ablutions over, the camp began to gravitate towards the supplies tent where the ration packs were kept. Silver bags full of indeterminate food, they are prepared simply by dunking them into a pan of hot water. I have to admit that the British rations are very good, even though most of the time you have no idea what's actually in them. It's not just that they're rammed with calories to keep our energy levels high, they taste OK, too, and they're far better than the ones issued to the Americans. (This is one area of equipment and supplies where the British can still hold their own with our cousins from across the pond.) When I say they're good, though, I don't mean you'd be happy to be served them in a restaurant, and after a few days you do start to tire of them and begin to crave real food.

The boys out at Camp Viking had reached that difficult point in their relationship with their ration packs when, out of the back of the Lynx, I took a tray of sausage sandwiches smothered in HP sauce, each individually wrapped in tin foil by the stewards back on *Ocean* and, incredibly, still warm when we arrived. As I carried them towards the tents, the look of curiosity on the boys' faces soon turned to one of mounting hope and they quickly began to encircle me like a pack of wolves. Within seconds I was at the centre of a small ruck as everyone dived into the tray and ravenously ripped open the foil wrappings. Not since I had been on my E&E exercise about ten years earlier had I seen hunger and gluttony like it. If I had also brought a full troupe of naked dancing girls from the Moulin Rouge, I don't think any of the boys would have taken a blind bit of notice of them, so busy were they piling into their 'bag rats' with an almost obscene, animal relish. It was a very odd moment, but I was soon to learn that the smallest, most humble items which we took for granted back home, or even on board *Ocean*, became luxury goods out there in the field. Anything that brought comfort or respite was welcomed with open arms. I can't imagine the scene if I had brought a pile of hot plates loaded with full English breakfasts.

I had last seen most of the squadron the week before, when the mood on board had been almost joyful as we tried to rest and relax a little with a few beers, the odd sing-song in the wardroom and a mock trial for the Kylie-defiler. Now, though, the mood was serious and businesslike, and there wasn't much banter flying around. It had been reasonably calm up on the Al-Faw, the others told me, but this was likely to change dramatically the following day when another major operation, the battle for the southern suburbs of Basra, was to be launched. In a concerted push by the 7th Armoured Brigade, the Royal Marines and the Paras, the British were to launch an all-out assault on the Iraqi defences dug in around the country's second largest city.

The hope was that the predominantly Shia people of Basra, with a little encouragement from our friends in MI6 on the ground, would rise up as they had done twelve years earlier and expel the Fedayeen and any regular forces remaining loyal to Saddam's Sunni-dominated regime. There was a strong reluctance on the part of Brigadier-General Brims, commander of the 7th Armoured Brigade, and the other British planners, to storm Basra itself for fear of causing a civilian bloodbath – a caution that allegedly didn't sit too comfortably with the top brass of our American allies, although they were eventually persuaded of our strategy's virtues. Better, the British argued, to close off the city, allowing the citizens to come and go while slowly, methodically picking off the Iraqi tanks and troops that remained, and isolating the Fedayeen paramilitaries and the diehard loyalists of Saddam's Ba'athist party.

The battle for Umm-Qasr was an instructive case in point, highlighting the difference between the American and British approaches. When the assault on the Al-Faw got under way, the US Marines laid siege to the small port, bringing to bear a vast amount of heavy fire in an effort to overwhelm the enemy spread out in different locations across the town. Bombing wasn't perhaps the best way to win over the 'hearts and minds' of the people there. The day before I arrived in Kuwait the Royal Marines of 42 Commando took over from their US counterparts; adopting a less belligerent, explosive approach, they were out patrolling the streets within twenty-four hours, handing out sweets and shaking hands with the locals, showing them they had nothing to fear from the invading forces so long as they weren't firing guns.

For the remainder of our deployment in the Gulf I was detailed to fly missions in the Lynx as a mission commander, with Gizmo flying the aircraft and me 'fighting' it, but for my first mission I went up with my cabin mate Lush. I took the flying controls in the right-hand seat, with Lush on the left working the missiles, sights and radios. I was more than happy to go through my first experience of war with Lush alongside me in the cab, partly because he was a good friend and, like Gizmo, a cool head in a crisis, but also because he was a good pilot and a highly experienced marine. He had flown a number of missions over the Al-Faw already, had studied the terrain and was alive to all the dangers that lurked there in the desert sands, the drained marshes, the date palms and the scruffy shanty towns and buildings that spread out from Basra towards Kuwait in the south.

The sky was completely clear when we went through the nerve-shredding procedure of checking in with the American AWACS controllers and moved up through the mini-sandstorm we had created and into the clear blue sky. The visibility was perfect, but there wasn't a breath of wind up there as we headed out over the Gulf before turning north towards the Al-Faw. Ideally, we wanted wind because (a) it gave us a bit more power and (b) it helped to smother the noise of the rotors and allowed us (flying below Iraqi radar) to get right up close to the enemy before they were aware of our presence.

As we drew ever closer to the coastline, my heart started to pound harder and harder. I had no idea what to expect from my first combat zone. I could see clouds of black smoke sitting like solid objects in the perfectly still air. Lush scanned the horizon through the sight, his finger on the grip of the TOW missiles, ready to launch at the first sign of danger. Behind us, Geek and Doormouse in the Gazelle, the other half of our patrol, watched our six o'clock, occasionally pushing out in front of us over to our left. The landscape of southern Iraq is so flat and featureless that there is virtually nothing to see or identify until you are almost on top of the place.

Cruising at about 100 knots, 80 feet above the surface of the sea, it was a grim scene that greeted us as we hit the shoreline. This was a landscape without a single redeeming feature to offset its incredible ugliness and desolation. The sands of the coastline were black with oil residue and littered with junk and the rusting hulls of boats; what vegetation existed appeared to be in the advanced stages of decomposition, and the hideous stench it gave off made me gag. Deeper into the desert and drained marshlands, the prospect looked more like a closing-down sale at a metal breakers' scrapyard, with the scorched remains of tanks, trucks and MTLBs (motor transport long bodies) scattered randomly across the wasteland, grim reminders of past struggles in these troubled sands. Black patches of oil leaks and bomb craters gave the land a pockmarked, moon-like appearance.

'It's just like Cindy said. It looks like one of those crap black-and-white Atari video games from the 1970s,' said Lush, staring down the sight for possible targets up ahead. We were motoring at almost full speed and the images below rushed past me in a crazy, dream-like stream, one on top of another, so that I could barely take one scene in before another filled my vision.

I saw an observation tower with a white flag hanging limply from the top of it; below there were two Iraqis crouched in its shade waiting to hand themselves over to the coalition forces. A little further along, the remains of another observation tower lay in a pile of charred wood and metal. Just outside the small fishing town of Al-Faw, sitting at the mouth of the Shatt Al-Arab on the tip of the peninsula, I saw three Iraqi regular soldiers waving white flags as two marines motioned to them with their weapons to sit down with their hands on their heads. Not far away, I saw my first dead person of the war, lying spread-eagled over the lip of a trench, his face blackened by the burning sun.

I could see British forces everywhere as Land Rovers criss-crossed the featureless expanse while Sea Kings and

Chinooks arrived with reinforcements and supplies. It was midday and the sun was high in the sky to the south behind us, which perhaps explained why the battle front seemed eerily quiet. But for the odd explosion in the shimmering, hazy distance and the smouldering oil fires a little further away on the horizon, there was little evidence of concerted fighting. The Iraqis had gone to ground, waiting, nervously you'd presume, for the British forces to launch the big push towards Basra that everyone knew was coming. We knew it was to start the following morning, but did they?

It took some time for my eyes to adjust to this flat, drab, colourless environment, but Lush began to point out a number of smashed troop bunkers and tanks, half buried in their sand revetments. From a purely operational point of view, what I was seeing confirmed everything we'd been warned about, namely, that this was going to be very difficult terrain for us to work in. It was a helicopter pilot's worst nightmare. There was simply nowhere to hide; no hills, forests, ravines or large structures to conceal our approach or to take cover behind. Throughout the fighting we would be constantly visible to the enemy; and if you're visible, you're vulnerable.

It was the same problem for the lightly armed recon-naissance vehicles of the Queen's Dragoon Guards on the ground. As we approached the tank troop, I counted their little Scimitars spread out across the desert: six little pinpricks wobbling in the heat haze. Our mission was to team up with them in a joint patrol, each doing roughly the same as the other, one in the air and one on the ground. Our main role was to observe the enemy dug in on the outer perimeters of the scruffy towns that sprawled out towards the desert. After checking in with the QDG commander, the tanks fanned out in an arc and we pushed the screen a little closer towards the enemy. Within minutes the tanks came under a barrage of fire from the Iraqi T55s hiding in the lines of date palms in the distance, and a volley of PD shells threw up columns of sand. That's as far as you go, my little British friends, seemed to be the message.

The door gunner, 'Guns', was kneeling down in the back, poised over his mounted GPMG with its bullet belt trailing into the carrier. As the odd shell rained in, Lush, finger still poised on the trigger of the TOWs, immediately got on the radio and asked the QDG if they wanted us to start engaging the enemy with missiles. My adrenaline levels, which had been rising steadily since leaving Viking, now hit the roof as I experienced my first ever salvoes of my first ever war. I was more excited than scared.

'Thanks, but don't worry. I'd save your assets if I were you,' replied the QDG commander in his cool, cut-glass tone, like he was handing around sherry before luncheon. 'We might need you later.' He was right, too, because if the T55s suddenly broke cover en masse to take on the Scimitars, the four TOWS on the Lynx were the only protection the QDG had against heavy armour. For the time being, his six gunners contented themselves with bursts of fire from their 30mm Rarden cannons. Over the radios we could hear the curiously satisfying 'rat-a-tat-tat' of the rounds hammering back at the enemy positions within range, and we could see the small flashes of fire spitting out from the end of their muzzles. This is called 'recce by fire' and it was an impressive sight.

We left the QDG to it and pushed out a bit wider along the front to see what might be lurking there on the fringes. Up in the air we had a certain amount of freedom because, at 120 knots or so, we could get from one side of the Al-Faw peninsula to the other, a mere thirty-mile stretch, in a matter of minutes. This wasn't a luxury available to the QDG in their Scimitars, who had to be careful about getting stranded in hostile territory, short of fuel or ammunition. Out to the west, the sprawl of buildings, roads and palm trees gave way to open desert. It was possible that there were enemy encampments dug into the sand, hidden beneath camouflage netting, but we couldn't spot a thing and so we headed back east towards Al-Faw town.

Below us on the roads there was a great deal of activity, military and civilian, taking place. It was a slightly confusing scene as two enemy forces went about their separate tasks within a mile or two of each other while, in between them, most of the ordinary people of Iraq seemed to be going about their business as if tanks, gunfire, helicopters and jets were just a part of everyday life in this corner of the world. If it had been Taunton or Basingstoke, the civilian population would all be locked up indoors, keeping their heads down for fear of getting caught in the crossfire or by an ill-directed bomb. I couldn't help smile in admiration as the Iraqis tried to go about their normal lives as best they could in the middle of a war zone. Some could be seen heading back from the markets with bags of shopping, while young kids ran along the roadsides, apparently without a care in the world. It reminded me a little of that famous picture from the Second World War of the London milkman, in his smart white coat, stepping over the rubble of a bombed-out building, holding a carrier of milk bottles, utterly indifferent to the smouldering carnage surrounding him.

The other peculiar aspect of the scene was that just a few miles down the road from where the QDG were coming under intense fire from an Iraqi tank division, pick-up trucks were openly driving around the streets, with white flags fluttering in the wind, often right past British troops on the ground. On the front of these vehicles there were soldiers still carrying their weapons – but they were waving, not firing, at the British guys, who returned the greetings by raising their hands in friendly acknowledgement as they sped by. Can there ever have been a major war like this? It was downright weird.

It was heartening that many Iraqis seemed to be surrendering, or at least refusing to fight, but it was disconcerting at the same time, for a number of reasons. First, were they truly surrendering or refusing to fight, or were they just taking the mickey, waving the white flags to protect themselves before regrouping on a newly defined battle front and taking up positions elsewhere? Second, if they were genuine about not fighting, how would their driving around brazenly advertising their peaceful capitulation to the invaders go down with the thousands of diehard, brutal Fedayeen characters whom, we knew from a stream of reports, were busily trying to galvanise or 'browbeat' the regular forces into standing their ground? Like a hole in the head, you couldn't help think. Third, for as long as it took to subdue the peninsula and seal Basra, it was going to be very difficult and dangerous for us to distinguish between the real foes and those who just wanted to slip out of their combat gear and quietly go home. We knew that the Fedayeen and their cohorts, faced with an enemy better equipped and better trained than their own troops, were prepared to try any dark trick in the book to try and outwit us, and there was a great risk that we might be lulled into a false sense of security and find ourselves in the middle of an ambush.

After an hour and fifteen minutes we headed back to Camp Viking, handing over to the follow-up air patrol as we crossed paths over the Gulf, waving at each other like lorry drivers on the M4, and passed on what we had seen to them. That first mission was what we call a 'famil flight', one in which we make ourselves 'familiar' with the conditions and landmarks of our area of operations. It was just about perfect for me, a war rookie, and provided me with a relatively soft intro to the hard world of combat. While we were never in obvious danger ourselves, I got a good view of the whole battlefield and I got my navigation bearings by making a mental note of different landmarks. The mission also rammed home a number of potential difficulties and hazards to be faced over the coming days.

It was clear that the Iraqis weren't going to come out into the open to challenge us. To do so would be suicide, given our air supremacy. That meant that they were going to stick inside or close to the towns and villages, where they were protected to some extent from all but the most precise bombardments. When it came to firing our weapons, or calling in artillery and air strikes, we were going to have to proceed very carefully.

I circled the tented desert village that was Camp Viking a couple of times, checking for possible enemy soldiers or insurgents, and below I could see the tiny figures of our engineers and ground handlers, scurrying around like so many camouflaged ants, working away on the other four aircraft in the blazing midday sun (we always held two air patrols – that is, two Lynx and two Gazelles – in reserve back on *Ocean*). The various tents were spread out around the camp, covered with camouflage netting: five for sleeping, each accommodating about ten men; a galley tent, where we fed and watered, next to the quartermaster's tent where all the provisions were kept; the largest, Operations HQ, from where our war was controlled and commanded; and next to that a smaller tent where we held our briefings. Dotted throughout the makeshift compound were half a dozen Land Rovers, a number of fuel storage balls (or 'bollocks' as they were known), brought in daily by Sea King and Chinook, and two Hagglund BV vehicles, the tank-tracked personnel and cargo carriers that were designed for shifting heavy equipment in the snow, but proved equally effective in sand. A sand berm demarcated the perimeter to the camp, and bunker positions in each corner, manned by marines and squadron personnel around the clock to guard against a surprise attack. We were only twelve miles from the Iraqi border, and on clear nights you could see the lights of Umm-Qasr twinkling on the horizon.

Landing in the desert presented the same difficulties as taking off, with billowing sand obscuring our vision as we approached the ground. At the start of the campaign there were no air traffic controllers or MAOT to guide us in, as they were needed more urgently elsewhere; instead, there was just a single oil barrel standing in the sand. I aimed the nose of the aircraft at the drum and, as the sand whipped up around us, it was all I could see as I brought the Lynx in at a 45 degree angle, lowered her gently on to the ground below and shut down the rotors.

I was drenched in sweat from head to foot as I stepped out of the cab and peeled off my heavy chest plate. The heat was astonishing. I dreamed of stepping under a freezing cold shower. One of the ground handlers was passing out our weapons and rucksacks from the back of the aircraft when the relative quiet hanging over the camp was interrupted by the blare of the chemical air raid siren. When I say 'air raid siren' I'm talking about a Royal Marine pressing the horn of one of the Land Rovers: the sound is regular and monotonous if the suspected incoming missile is thought to be only a conventional weapon; sharp and irregular if biochemical attack is feared. The Iraqis fired hundreds of missiles in the opening days of the war from positions north of Basra, without any real idea where they were going to land. Either these missiles were picked up by the radar operators, who were alert to any blip on their screen heading south, or the air traffic controllers were informed by the special forces on the ground, who had been sent deep into enemy territory to seek and destroy the missiles at their mobile launch sites. If the missile was fired from a previously unknown site, the controllers erred on the side of caution and assumed that it was a biochemical attack.

Immediately the Land Rover horn sounded, all sixty or so men ran to their tents, grabbed their helmets, gas masks and assault rifles, and jumped into one of the four sandbagged bunkers that had been dug into the ground at various locations across the camp.

All except Lush, that is.

As I broke into a jog towards one of the bunkers, Lush exclaimed: 'Well, fuck that. I'm off to bed. Saddam can fuck off. I need my kip.' And with that, he calmly ambled across the sand and disappeared inside his sleeping quarters.

The rest of us settled down in the bunkers, staring at each other through our big-eyed, sinister-looking masks – and sat there, sweating buckets under the sun directly above our heads, waiting for the all-clear. Saddam may not have been able to get his hands on us, but he could still torture us. In midday temperatures reaching the mid-thirties Celsius the heat was incredibly debilitating, and after fifteen minutes or so I could feel myself swooning, like a drunk. A full forty-five minutes later the welcome continuous sound of the all-clear siren was given and we all began to stagger out of the ground, pouring water over our heads as we made a beeline for the shade of the tents. No more than a minute can have passed when the sound of alarms filled the air again, and there was a collective groan of anguish and a tirade of expletives across the camp. 'For fuck's sake . . .!' Wearily we put our masks back on, picked up our weapons and helmets, and trudged back to the burning hellholes from where we had just come. Then we sat and sweated for two hours, almost delirious in the unforgiving heat.

CHAPTER SEVEN

'Trust you to sleep through a fucking war, Newton! You better get your arse out of your pit because you've got ten minutes to launch.' It was Spidey, the senior pilot, and he was shining a torch right in my face. My eyes felt like they were stuck together with superglue as I leapt out of my sleeping bag and reeled out of the tent, my legs wobbling beneath me, still full of sleep. It was 0230 Zulu time – i.e. UK time – and 0530 Iraq time, and I was scheduled to have been airborne at first light in the first air patrol of the day.

My rude awakening was the perfect start, or at least the most apposite start, for a day packed with nasty surprises and sudden shocking surges of adrenaline. Monday, 24 March 2003 was the most momentous day in my life, and every last detail of it, every graphic image, is still seared on my mind like a cattle brand. It wasn't an extraordinary date just for me, either. It was one hell of a day for the entire 847 Naval Air Squadron, probably the most eventful in its long history, stretching back to the end of the Second World War. Two 847 air patrols were operated at all times from dawn to dusk and every airman of the squadron who had been called forward from *Ocean* was engaged in constant, heavy fighting. Never, moreover, had the engineers and ground crew had to work harder as they battled the scorching desert heat to refuel, rearm and patch up the aircraft before sending them racing back out into the field.

The battle was concentrated around the southern Basra suburb of Abu Al Khasib, where an entire Iraqi tank division was dug in among the buildings and the date palms, alongside thousands of regular troops under the whip of the Fedayeen. The Iraqis came out to fight with such ferocity that day you couldn't help wondering whether they had got hold of intelligence telling them that the heavy armour of the 7th Armoured Brigade was still not yet ready to join battle, and that only the thin line of the little, lightly armed recce vehicles of the QDG and the brigade recce force (BRF) stood in their way on the ground. If the Iraqis had one chance of repelling the invading forces and scoring a major victory, then, whether they knew it or not at the time, it was that fourth day of the campaign before the full might of the task force was in position to roll into action.

I suspect they did have intelligence, because 24 March was also the one day of the entire conflict when the QDG and 847 Squadron were as good as left to fend for themselves. With the Americans focusing on Baghdad, and encountering stout resistance on their path to the capital, back in the south there was little air support allocated to back up the thin 'screen' of two reconnaissance units, one on the ground and one in the air, standing between the Iraqis and the Kuwaiti border. While the jets were too busy bombing Baghdad and supporting the Americans racing up country to help out, the big guns of the ships at sea and the artillery on Bubiyan Island were out of range. In short, there was only one small unit of support protecting the beachhead, the QDG and the BRF from the heavy armour of the Iraqis tanks: the four Lynx and four Gazelle helicopters of 847 Squadron.

The sun was still low in the morning sky when Gizmo and I took to the air for the first mission of the day, and the battle began almost immediately as the QDG started to come under sustained attack from the Iraqi T55s, a couple of miles north of the screen they had laid out across the desert. The chaotic scenes of the exchanges were played out on the radio airwaves, which crackled and boomed to the sound of explosions and gunfire, both incoming and outgoing, with barely any remission from first to last light.

One by one the QDG boys called in to report they were being shelled: 'Victor One Zero, contact, wait out . . .' Seconds later, we heard: 'Victor Two Zero, contact, wait out . . . Victor Three Zero, contact, wait out . . . Victor Four Zero, contact, wait out . . .'. As 847 raced to the scene to help them out, the Welsh boys had a lucky stroke when they succeeded in calling in an American F16 on its way up north to support the advancing US troops. The QDG confirmed a sighting of troops at a major bunker complex, close to the tank revetments, and the F16 checked in with a J-Dam strike on the target that sent a huge orange fireball climbing high into the sky and caused bedlam on the ground.

I had never seen a J-Dam strike but I was in pole position on the battle front to watch this go in. Packed with 2,000lb of explosives and accurate to within ten yards of its target, the J-Dam is a truly awesome and destructive weapon. The explosion, when it struck, was enormous. It was like a volcano, an eruption of earth, fire and thick smoke bursting out of the ground and billowing high and wide for hundreds of yards from the target. Luckily for the Iraqis – and I found myself almost breathing a sigh of relief on their behalf – the 'smart bomb', as it is also known, had missed the target by a couple of hundred yards, thus saving God only knows how many troops from instant death. Instead, it sparked a scene of pandemonium, like someone had poured boiling water into an anthill, as dozens of troops, hundreds perhaps, started running in every direction in shock and terror. It was unlikely those troops returned to fight another day. In its way, it was the perfect result for all concerned: casualties were kept to a minimum but the bunker was effectively eliminated from the battle front.

As I scanned the enemy lines through the roof sight I kept noticing several red-and-white 4 x 4 taxis, hammering east and west down the E6 motorway below Basra. The drivers were not your average cabbies. These guys were all kitted out from head to foot in black uniforms, like martial arts experts, and they were carrying AK47s. The day before, tank crews had reported seeing a group of similar-looking characters battering a young kid and then hanging him from a lamp post. These 'taxis', moreover, were stopping every kilometre or so to allow the men in black to run out of them and into the long rows of date palms and low-rise buildings strung out along the road where we knew there were columns of tanks as well as mortar and rocket positions, communication centres and command posts.

My suspicions increased when I got 'visual' on a pair of the cabbies browbeating a unit of regular forces, waving their arms and guns around. You could bet a week's rations that they weren't complaining about the miserly tip they had just received. These were Saddam's notorious Fedayeen, some of the 40,000 local toughs and thugs operating outside the military command structure and feared throughout Iraq, who posed a much greater threat to our advance than any conventional forces that lay in our way.

One of the big problems facing us over those coming days and weeks was the challenge of working out who or what was a legitimate target. It was often difficult to tell the difference between civilians going about their daily lives – which many of them were, in spite of the war raging around them – and the undercover bastards, hiding behind civilian fronts, directing operations and ready to blow us out of the air and the QDG out of the sand at the first opportunity.

They knew we were going to play it by the book and stick to our rules of engagement.

It seemed as plain as the nose on my face that what these 'cabbies' were doing was 'rallying' – intimidating – the regular forces that had been thrown across the southern suburbs of Basra to try and halt our progress up to the city itself. It was no coincidence that, within minutes of these men in black arriving at a location, the handful of QDG Scimitars holding the thin screen below us would start to receive a pile of incoming fire from that position. A lot of Iraqis had already surrendered, and the Fedayeen were bullying the rest of them to stand their ground – or else. The logic was simple enough: get rid of the Fedayeen and you get rid of the regular army, saving possibly thousands of their lives, and however many of ours, at a stroke.

As soon we'd touched down I leapt out of the Lynx and ran to see Clubs, to report what I had seen. Exhilaration and fear were still coursing through me when I started jabbering away at him about all the dodgy 'taxis' I had spotted over the previous hour. Was it the adrenaline and the nerves talking? Was I just getting overexcited in the early days of my first ever war? And why hadn't one of the old sweats on the squadron already spotted what I thought I had? We may have been several kilometres away, moving at speeds of up to 120 knots, but through the TOW roof sight with its x14 magnification, it all seemed as clear as a bell to me.

That was my interpretation, anyway, and Clubs seemed to

agree, so he put me straight into one of the Land Rovers with Spidey at the wheel, and dispatched us to see Brigadier Dutton, the commander of 3 Commando Brigade, at the brigade HQ about three kilometres from 847's camp across the Kuwaiti desert. Brigadier Dutton was leading the Royal Marine assault to secure the peninsula, and I was just about to put him right on the spot, forcing him to make a huge military and political call. If any shit was to go down back home, it would be on his head. He's an impressive, mildly scary character, Dutton, as good a soldier as you'll find in the British forces, but the politicians would hang him out to dry if I'd cocked this one up.

Brigadier Dutton was in no mood for small talk, and I wasn't exactly feeling like Ken Dodd myself as we walked out into the baking desert and sat cross-legged in the sand. I told him what I had seen, and he put his chin in his hand and stared out across the endless expanse, the desert stillness broken only by the sound of muffled explosions in the distance.

'So, Lieutenant Newton, you are a hundred per cent convinced that these taxis are being used by the Fedayeen on the battlefield?'

'Yes, sir,' I replied.

'Well then, I'm trusting your judgement on this and we will put the order out that they are now legitimate targets under our normal rules of engagement,' he said. 'This may well save a lot of lives. But if you're wrong . . .'

And with that he rose to his feet and walked quickly back

into the command tent to pass on the information to his team.

It was perhaps the biggest decision I had made in my twelve-year career in the Fleet Air Arm, and if I, or one of the other boys, ended up mistakenly obliterating a taxi full of women and children, we would have to live with the horror of having killed innocent people for the rest of our lives. It would also be a PR disaster for the 'liberating' US and British troops, as pictures of the carnage would surely be transmitted all round the world as evidence of our alleged barbarism. The Iraqis were just waiting for us to slip up, because they knew as well as we did that they had more chance of winning the war on television than on the battlefield. If we had ever been in any doubt about this, then we'd been set right two days earlier when one of 847's air patrols had returned to camp with reports of these black-clad characters pouring out of the back of an ambulance, one of them carrying a video camera, daring us to take a shot at them. You can just imagine the footage handed over to the media: a burning ambulance, followed by pictures of bandaged children in a hospital, allegedly maimed in our brutal attack.

The temperature was already topping thirty-five degrees Celsius when I saluted the Brigadier and turned to leave. The sweat was clinging to my combat fatigues, mainly as a result of the blistering heat, but the anxiety was eating away at me too. Had I done the right thing? Or had I just single-handedly compromised Britain's war effort, a mere three days after the boys from 40 and 42 Commando had smashed their way on to the Al-Faw peninsula?

Now, though, wasn't the time to ask searching questions about whether I had made the right call. I was scheduled to be back in the air on the second of my two back-to-back missions that morning. The other patrol would be starting to head back to camp to refuel, and so I jogged across the sand and jumped into the passenger seat of the Land Rover as Spidey released the handbrake and we sped back across the desert, leaving a long trail of billowing sand in our wake.

When we raced into Camp Viking Gizmo was already sitting in the cab of the Lynx ready to get going. 'Guns' was standing under the stationary blades, adjusting his knee pads and checking that his mounted GPMG and magazine belts were all in good order before we took to the skies again.

I needed a long drink before I got back in the Lynx. We were all downing between ten and fifteen litres of water a day in the desert. You had to or you'd go wibble and pass out, which wouldn't be too clever in the middle of a tank engagement. Nor did we piss the water out either: it just fell from us in torrents of sweat.

''Obnobbing with the top brass these days, are we, Scooby?' said Lush, twitching his big regulation marine's tash as I poured some of the water over my head and then drank the rest of the two-litre bottle without pausing for breath.

'Do some work, you lazy Cockney,' I smiled back at him.

You needed the banter as much as you needed the water out there. They were the two things that kept you going. And if it was banter you were after, there was no one better equipped to provide it than Lush, the original diamond geezer.

I could feel my heart starting to pound again as I quickly ran about getting ready to return to the battlefield. I went into the operations tent, where radios crackled with the sound of voices, gunfire and explosions, computer screens flashed and flickered with incoming data, and several of the men in Clubs's team were consulting the walls of maps that had been stuck on boards and desks around the room. Jets roared past overhead as they hurried to and from the fleet of ships anchored a few kilometres off the coast in the Gulf. It had been reasonably quiet on our patch during my first mission of the day, but you could tell from the noise on the radios, the traffic in the air and the tension in the room that it was getting a bit lively out there now. We had trade. I could feel my breathing getting deeper and faster as I swallowed down the catarrh rising to the back of my parched throat.

I tried not to let my nerves show as I picked up my tasking sheets, including the 'smart pack', handed out before each mission, telling us, among other directives, where we could and couldn't fly, at what speed and at what height, the radio frequencies and call signs, and so on. Our mission on this occasion was to head straight up along the pre-set route known as 'Hammersmith', which was designated as safe from enemy and friendly fire, to go and support the QDG, who were involved in an engagement with some T55s. The Iraqis' old Russian-made tanks may have lacked the pace and manoeuvrability of the QDG machines, but they packed a far mightier punch. Their guns also had a much longer reach than those of their adversaries in the Scimitars, which, strictly speaking, were not tanks at all, but lightly armoured reconnaissance vehicles.

Most of the Iraqi T55s had been upgraded with thicker armour and 105mm or 125mm guns, so that, while they were no match for the American M1 Abrams or our own Challengers waiting offshore, they posed a considerable danger to the Scimitar with only its 30mm Rarden gun and a GPMG to protect itself. The violence the Lynx brings to the battlefield would be gratefully received by the Welsh lads sweating their nuts off inside their little iron tanks.

'Good job this morning. Look after yourselves out there now, Scoobs,' said Clubs, patting me on the back as I left the tent. 'See you back in about an hour and fifteen.' He was good like that, Clubs. If we cocked up, he'd give us a proper ear-bashing, but he was the first to congratulate us if he thought we'd performed well. What I particularly liked about him was he also went out of his way to thank or praise not just the pilots but also the ground crew, even the teenage lad cleaning the windscreens and changing the oil. Clubs, who'd worked his way up through the ranks of the marines after starting among other things, as a PT instructor, understood better than anyone the importance of treating every member of the team with respect.

I had sanitised myself earlier in the morning, removing my wallet, my watch and any evidence that gave away that I was an officer. All the squadron's pilots are either officers, colour sergeants or sergeants, and our captors were sure to know that, but if it did happen that we were shot down and then somehow managed to evade the Iraqis for a few hours or so, there was a slim chance we might be able to convince whoever did pick us up that we were just Ordinary Joes who had got disorientated during a battle and had nothing of significance to tell them. Like the other pilots, I was wearing the uniform of a grunt, a regular soldier, so that if we were captured I might escape the more rigorous lines of interrogation that are reserved for officers carrying valuable operational or strategic knowledge.

Our 'day sacks' (field rucksacks) had already been stowed, together with our SA80 assault rifles, gas masks, NVGs and spare ammunition. The rucksacks contained emergency clothes, rations, water and the phosphorous grenades, which burn hotter than magma, for blowing up the aircraft if we were forced to abandon it. Unfortunately, flying into a combat zone stark bollock naked was not considered sound aviation practice and we were forced to pile on layer after layer of gear before setting off.

I pulled on a fresh T-shirt and shirt with a 'sweat rag' round my neck, strapped on my shoulder holster with its 9mm Browning pistol, and then attached my LCJ (load-carrying jerkin), which is where we kept our Combi-pens with the anti-nerve agent and morphine injections as well as our Downbird radios to use if we were on the run and needed picking up. Finally – just in case I caught a chill – I put on my helmet and slotted my armoured chest plate into the LCJ. I felt like an overdone boil-in-the-bag chicken even before I had stepped into the cab of the aircraft.

'You're good to go, Lieutenant,' said Deps, the second-in-command of the engineers. I walked around the aircraft for a final check, wiping the salty sweat from my eyes, climbed into the left-hand side of the helicopter and strapped myself in. Gizmo, on the right, would be doing the flying. I was to 'fight' the aircraft, which meant firing the TOW missiles, as well as working the various radios, using the TOW roof observation sights and plotting grid positions with my hand-held GPS and a bundle of maps on my knees. Guns, the poor sod, strapped himself into the little seat in the cramped area at the back of the aircraft where there's barely enough room for a Bergen, let alone a Royal Marine the size of a house.

Gizmo fired up the first engine and quickly followed up with the second; then, with the generators now on-line, I turned on all systems. My heart was pounding against my chest plate as a mixture of intense excitement and enormous fear stirred both body and mind. It was the same every time, even when we went out on exercise over Salisbury Plain, but in the Gulf, in a real war, the feeling was multiplied tenfold. You assume you'll come back from Salisbury Plain.

I checked all my systems, punched the info from my smart

pack into the GPS, and ran a check on all the radio channels. I nodded to Gizmo, and as he released the rotor brake the blades began to circle overhead, first with a couple of gentle rotations and then with a furious, noisy whirl. The sand immediately kicked up all around us and we couldn't see more than a yard beyond the windscreen. It was like taking off in the dark or in a snowstorm. The engines behind us were now running at 450 degrees Celsius, the gunner's door had been shut for take-off and, without any air conditioning, it was truly stifling in our body armour and flying gear.

I checked in with Chainsaw (he snores like one) and Geek (he's clever) in the Gazelle that made up the other half of our air patrol. Although the Gazelle can call in 'fire' in the form of the fast jets or artillery, in rough terms this little unarmed helicopter was the eyes of the patrol, while the Lynx was the fist.

As Gizmo gently lifted the skids off the ground, I waited for the dreaded moment that always followed when the radar warning receiver (RWR) panel lit up like a Christmas tree, telling us that every fucking radar system in the Arabian Gulf was now locked on to us. We had just appeared as a little blip on a dozen AWACS screens in the Gulf, and for those few seconds nobody knew if we were coalition or what is known to the air controllers as a 'pop-up unfriendly'. I called in on the radio as quickly as possible to identify ourselves to the American electronic warfare controllers back on the ships, who by now had switched their systems to the fire control radar (FCR), just in case we did turn out to be an enemy aircraft.

The FCR, an intense pencil beam of radio waves, homed in on my helicopter to get all the info it needed about my aircraft's height and speed. I hated that moment more than any other, because the beam was effectively telling my aircraft that we had been locked on to and were about to be shot down. The Lynx started going nuts as it tried to tell us to take evasive action. All the RWR lights started flashing, and frenetic warning signals bombarded my eardrums through my headset. Then we just waited, holding close to the camp. *Flash! Flash! Flash! Trim! Trim! Trim!* We had all suffered this alarming experience about half a dozen times since arriving in the Gulf, but it didn't get any easier, especially when the conflict began in earnest and everyone, including the controllers, was on edge and on the alert for missile attacks. I'd like to say that deep down I knew everything was going to be fine, but there had been enough 'blue-on-blue' friendly fire incidents involving the Americans in recent years that I just couldn't relax. You never knew.

In normal conditions, Gizmo would lift the helicopter vertically to clear the dust cloud and then move forward, but this wasn't possible in the Gulf, owing to the exertions the engines were already having to make as a result of the intense heat and the heavier weight of the aircraft, which was carrying four TOW missiles, three crew, a mounted machine gun and a pile of extra equipment. (It had been fitted with sand filters, as well as exhauster defusers and flare dispensing systems which aim to confuse missiles with infra-red capabilities trying to lock on to our heat source.) In short, we didn't have enough power to clear the sand cloud, so we had to use one of the take-off techniques we had developed during our annual Arctic training in Norway, where snow presents exactly the same problems to the helicopter pilot as sand.

We had created a kind of helicopter runway inside Camp Viking by clearing a strip of land of all possible obstacles, and we had been hovering a few feet above the ground at one end of the 'runway'. Clouds of powdery sand were still swirling around the aircraft as Gizmo tilted the nose of the Lynx forward before accelerating as quickly as possible up to about fifty knots. The Lynx, straining to its limits as it hit max power, shuddered and shook violently as we sped blindly through the giant dustbowl, and then suddenly we burst into beautiful sunshine and a cloudless blue sky as it cleared the perimeter of the camp and headed into the desert. Seconds later I heard the welcome sound of the American controller: 'Hello, Cravat 33, you're sweet, sweet, cleared to proceed. You go have a nice day now.' I relaxed a little, knowing that the Americans had acknowledged me as a friendly. But only a little.

We needed to fly as low as possible out there to avoid being seen, so as soon as we were out of the camp Gizmo brought us down to about thirty feet above the ground and upped the speed to about 100 knots. We were so low I felt as if I could almost reach out and touch the ground as the landscape shot past in a blur of beige beneath our feet.

The Gazelle began to catch up with us, Chainsaw and Geek moving up alongside in a well-rehearsed procedure, and as we sped over the Iraqi border we took it in turns to cover each other's six o'clock and look out for enemy. Without having to consult the map, we knew we had arrived, first in the DMZ on the border, and moments later inside Iraq itself.

By the time I flew back out for that second mission, the order had been given by Dutton to fire at the taxis under our normal rules of engagement and the 847 boys were quickly into the breach, harrying the taxis as they sped east and west along the E6 main road. Flicking through the radio channels, all I could hear was a barrage of fire and different call signs as the battle intensified up and down the front. Slaps, Lush, Cindy, Hyena, Naphtha, Sweetcorn, Mako, Sonic, Timex, Vatman, Fingers, Bunker, John Boy and Suicide, supported by the rest of the boys in the Gazelles, were in the thick of the action that morning as, among other tasks, they hunted the Fedayeen taxis to distraction with the aim of severing their contact with the regular forces and thus breaking the chain of command at its head.

Fittingly, it was our warfare instructor Cindy, our hippy guru in the ancient arts of bringing violence to the battlefield, to whom the honour fell of engaging the first Fedayeen people-carrier with a TOW missile. It was clear from the outset that there was one particular taxi, careering up and down the road all morning, that was doing most of the 'rallying' or intimidating. It was the occupants of this vehicle who had been seen by the tank crew beating a young civilian boy and then hanging him from a lamp post in view of the regular forces, presumably as a warning that none of their own families would be safe unless they stood and fought. Destroying that taxi became the focus of 847's attention that morning.

Cindy's patrol was one of the first into the fray, and as his first missile streaked earthwards the taxi swerved at the last moment, evading the explosion by a matter of yards. TOWs are designed for piercing armour and causing explosive mayhem within, and they aren't very effective against much else unless you score a direct hit; so the taxi was able to continue on its way, shaken but largely intact. Lush soon joined the fight with Geek in the Gazelle. His first missile missed due to range and the second missile rogued after its trailing copper wire hit some power cables, and the third was heading for the target when someone inside the taxi must have screeched 'Brake!' because the car went from 90 mph to a standstill in a few seconds as the TOW exploded right in front of it – that is, exactly where it would have been had they not braked. Lush's patrol returned to refuel.

Enter stage left Slaps – a Royal Marine old sweat, a cool-headed pilot, my right-hand man in training and one of the most important and respected members of the squadron.

He was a good shot with a TOW as well, but he also missed his target by a matter of yards with his first effort as the taxi hit max speed again along the E6. The occupants of the vehicle could be in no doubt by now that we had rumbled the taxi ruse and were on their case. Immediately the taxi came to an abrupt halt and half a dozen men in black piled out and opened up on the Lynx and Gazelle with their AK47s. The Lynx quickly swung round into a side-on position so that the door-gunner could return fire with the GPMG. As the rounds burst all around them, the Fedayeen jumped for cover and the air patrol was able to move south to regroup, just as his gun jammed. When they returned five minutes later the taxi was still in play and Slaps immediately re-engaged it with two missiles, but both of them rogued and they were forced to retreat, cursing their bad luck. It was just as well they weren't locked in an engagement with one of the tanks.

Slaps then did an extraordinary and brave thing: he landed the Lynx in the battlefield and got out of the aircraft to swap over the misfiring missile stations in order to give his final TOW a better chance of staying true. He then calmly climbed back into the cab and off they went again. When the air patrol reached the front, both aircraft came under heavy artillery fire, the delay in the engagement having given the Fedayeen time to call in their big guns. One shell landed slap between the Lynx and Gazelle, sending heavy shock waves through both. Three times, Slaps tried to get his fourth missile away at the taxi, but the launcher was jammed and the frustrated patrol was forced to return to Viking.

The taxi disappeared under the cover of the date palms, its occupants no doubt laughing in relief at their lucky escape. Our identification of the taxis as military vehicles was a breakthrough, but unfortunately it spawned a secondary problem. Aware that we were going to target them from then on, the Fedayeen changed tactics and started also using ambulances to carry out their business, hanging out of the back of them as they sped down the road, taunting us and waving their AK47s, ecstatic in the knowledge that we were never going to fire on them in those vehicles.

Cindy had no luck with his missiles either, try as he did to blow every hostile 4 x 4 taxi in southern Iraq to kingdom come. He was chased south by incoming Arty rounds, closely followed by the QDG. Once out of range, he set about calling 'fast air' to take on the guns. When Lush returned after refuelling, he found the artillery batteries that had been busy shelling the QDG all morning but none of our own artillery were in a position to help. Incredibly, he managed to find a jet to call in to do the business, but the ground controller would not authorise the use of 'close air support', so the F16 fucked off up north, low on fuel . . . seen off with a sarcastic 'Lovely, cheers my friend,' from Lush. The whole front was alive with Arty rounds.

While the others busied themselves with the Fedayeen, I was a mile or two further west along the battle front with

Gizmo, Geek and Chainsaw, battling the tank outside the abandoned school, as described earlier. I'll never forget the look on the faces of the ground crew and engineers when I came back in to land, still buzzing and shaking with the fear and excitement of my first real taste of a real war. They could see that I only had two TOWs left and they were all pointing, wide-eyed with disbelief, aware that every empty launcher carried a little story of its own. As we stepped out of the cab, they crowded around us excitedly, probing for details. 'Fucking hell, boss, what happened? What happened?' They could hear from the noise in the distance that a battle was raging, but to see that their own aircraft had obviously been right in the thick of it had filled them with an almost childlike awe and excitement.

For Sweetcorn, a man who had been straining to fire missiles at people he doesn't like from the day his mother first laid him down in a crib, it had been an especially frustrating day. After a fruitless ninety minutes trying to raise jets to take out a number of targets he had done well to find, not a single one was available to help out and he returned to camp, effing and blinding and kicking the shit out of the sand as he stormed back into the operations tent. On a later patrol that afternoon he was no luckier, and when he handed over to me for the final patrol of the day he was not in the best of moods at missing out on the main action.

If only he had come with me.

The sun, growing ever larger and weaker, was sliding

towards the horizon to our left when Gizmo and I in the Lynx, alongside Coco and Gilbert in the Gazelle, routed north from camp before turning west to take up position at the far end of the main battle front, where the QDG were still stoically holding the line under a bombardment that had barely ceased all day. It was the fourth mission of the day for all of us, the maximum that daylight allowed us to fly, and the fatigue had started to seep into our bodies and minds. It's easy to make mistakes when the brain has started to slow, and as we raced through the drifting smoke into the setting sun I kept shaking my head to wake myself up and muttering to myself: 'Come on, Jim. Come on, boy. Just ninety minutes to go now.' I needn't have bothered, though, because my adrenal glands needed no prompting to take over the role of rousing me into action. No sooner had we arrived in our designated 'battle position' (BP) than the first artillery and tank shells began to crash around us as we sped low across the desert floor in search of the QDG's tormentors. And what an array of targets we had to choose from!

Following up QDG reports of enemy tanks in this vicinity, Coco, the mission commander on this particular patrol, spotted a tank soon after we arrived on scene. When he called me on the radio to alert me to their position, he was, at this stage, a model of calm professionalism. 'Just there, Scooby,' he said. 'About two thousand six hundred metres away, twelve o'clock. From that taller building, two hundred metres right, low building, T55 next to the billboard with the small picture of Saddam Hussein . . .' I looked down the sight but could see nothing, even though the bombardment around us told me it must have been there or thereabouts. While scanning the featureless landscape in front of us, and the treeline slightly beyond, I quickly switched radio channels to check in with the QDG commanders. As they came back over the airwaves to acknowledge, the first thing I heard was the sound of rounds bouncing off the turret of the Scimitar against a background rattle of outgoing machine-gun fire. 'It's a bit lively at the minute, sir,' the commander said. 'Can I get back to you in a moment?' I loved the QDG boys. So cool, even with shells bouncing off their heads.

It *was* a bit fucking sharp too, as sharp as anything we had experienced all day, all war even. It was as if all units at the battle front were aware that the fighting was almost over for the day, and everyone was making one final concerted push, unloading all the ammo they had left before retiring for the night. As the fire rained in on us, Gizmo and Gilbert, driving the two helicopters, constantly kept the aircraft on the move, ducking and weaving between the shells so that the tanks and enemy were unable to bracket us.

At this point I had no idea quite how close the tank was. Coco, however, was very obviously aware of its proximity and he repeated his talk on to me. 'About two thousand six hundred metres away, twelve o'clock. From that taller building, two hundred metres right, low building, T55 next to the billboard with the picture of Saddam Hussein . . .'

Hearing the increasing urgency in his voice, I desperately scanned the date palms with my sight, switching back and forth from the high-magnification mode to thermal imaging, looking for the heat of the tank's exhaust fumes. I scanned and I scanned, but still I could see nothing and still the shells continued to pour out of the skies, sending files of sand and smoke high above the ground and filling the air with the stench of explosive. Several minutes went by, and Coco was starting to lose his patience with me, his annoyance obvious as he repeated the talk-on. I could hear the beginning of a quiet 'Oh for fuck's sake!' as his voice trailed off.

Though I was calmer than I had been during the morning's tank engagement, the tension mounted with every second that I was unable to spot the tank. It was as if I had been put into a small room, blindfolded, while strangers punched me. If this tank was so fucking obvious, why the hell couldn't I spot it? And what was all that spiel about the Saddam Hussein billboard? I just didn't get it. I could see nothing but sand and smoke and date palms and a few buildings. I was meant to be good at 'obs and recce', too. It was starting to get dark now, but if anything that should have been a help because there was a greater chance of spotting the muzzle flashes in the fading light. The problem for Coco was that I was the one with the missiles. The Gazelle has no weapons; it can only ask others to bring in fire. I was their only defence. Aware that we were running out of time, Coco gave up on me, switched radio channels and started desperately trying to raise a jet to take out the tank.

While he was doing that, I switched to my thermal imaging sight and almost immediately locked on to a large group of enemy troops concealed beneath the trees. When I switched back to the high-magnification sight I saw roughly two dozen soldiers, some towards the front, dug in and firing machine guns at us, with others moving in and out of a lean-to tent. I could see aerials emerging from the tent and the vehicles of high-ranking officers, and I knew instantly what I had stumbled upon. It was a command post (CP), from where the enemy commanders were controlling the battle along their section of the front. They were so close. This was a major find and I immediately called in to HQ to report it.

In a textbook battle, you want a jet to drop a bomb or Forward Observation Officer (FOO) to send in an artillery strike to take out this kind of target: something big and heavy which would kill everyone instantly before they knew what had hit them. But this wasn't an ideal battle, given the lack of resources on the day, and so when I switched channels again and tried to raise Toffee 45, the call sign of the A10 gunships, to come in and to do the job, I did so more in hope than expectation of getting a response. I knew Coco had been trying to raise them too. All this was happening at breakneck speed because we were still under heavy fire, and Coco was virtually soiling himself with desperation over the tank he quite rightly wanted me to destroy as a matter of urgency. At this point the two of us might just as well have been fighting two different wars on opposite sides of the world for all the success we were having in communicating with each other. I was concentrating on a CP firing at us, which he couldn't see, while he was concentrating on the tank, which I couldn't see and against which he couldn't defend us. We were, so to speak, two helicopters passing in the fast descending night.

I told HQ that I was reluctant to launch a TOW into the CP on the grounds that that type of missile was totally inappropriate for the task, but I was told that in the absence of artillery and fast jet support we couldn't be fussy and ordered to engage. 'If there are senior commanders in there, you have to fire,' came the reply. 'Cut off the head of the snake, Scooby . . .'

Gizmo was doing an incredible job keeping the Lynx in constraints, given the mayhem of fire going on around us, as I took aim and put the CP into the crosshairs of the graticule. The thermal imaging sights had picked up a strong source of heat next to the tent – probably a generator for their comms network – and it was at that that I aimed the TOW, squeezing the trigger while Coco continued to yell at me to take out the tank.

I felt my stomach tighten as the trigger yielded under my hand. This was going to be horrible. At any moment one of the dozens of shells filling the air and ground around us might have crashed through the windscreen and condemned us to our own horrific deaths, but I couldn't help feel a powerful sense of sympathy for those men on the ground, even though they were firing at us. Like us, they were just brothers, sons or fathers, asked by their political masters to kill strangers. I had never properly understood what ex-soldiers, particularly those who had served in the trenches of the First World War, had meant when they said they often felt a greater sense of kinship with the enemy they were firing at than with their own countrymen who had sent them off to fight. But as I pulled that trigger, I understood perfectly.

I watched the TOW hovering outside the aircraft for a second or so after launching from its tube before it screeched away like a giant, angry firework towards the date palms. Gizmo began to count the seconds as I kept the crosshairs firmly positioned over the heat source – and then I recoiled sharply as a giant fireball filled my sights: the TOW must have hit some kind of fuel tank. Wet flames burst in all directions, quickly turning the CP into an inferno as men scattered any which way they could to escape. It was bedlam down there, and suddenly those still standing started firing manically, left, right and centre, up, down and sideways. I saw two men run out of the burning tent; one of them was on fire, and he fell to the ground and started crawling. I thought I was going to be sick. Was it really I who had done that? I had never knowingly killed anyone until that moment, and I was shocked at the horror of the scene below. Quickly, desperately, I cut the wires from the launcher and loaded a second missile.

'Hurry the effffff up, Scooby!' shouted Coco as another massive PD round burst below us, shaking the Lynx out of position. He repeated the talk-on for the umpteenth time, this time ending it with a 'For God's bloody sake, Scooby!'

In all the pandemonium I don't think I was really listening at that point. Hearing but not listening. All I could think about was getting a second missile away into the CP where the Iraqis were still busy firing at us. A few were lying around, clearly dead, probably killed by the compression of the explosion, and some had fled the scene; but there were still half a dozen of them firing through our left flank. They were all fairly close together, and so I aimed the second missile for the middle of the heat source and squeezed. As I continued to stare down the sight, I saw a man try to stand up, then collapse to the ground. His colleagues ignoring his plight. It was at that moment that I saw his hand reach out in my direction, a split second before the second TOW impacted right behind him in a sharp flash. They died where they lay.

Barely had the second missile hit home when a fucking great big PD explosion erupted right between us and the Gazelle, making both aircraft shudder once again as the shock waves crashed against the frames. The tank, or tanks, had obviously witnessed the missile strikes on their CP, which had given them the time to adjust their fire on us. The sympathy and horror I had been feeling a few seconds earlier were instantly replaced by fear and aggression as I turned my attention to finding the T55 which had been so exercising Coco for the past five minutes.

We flew closer to the Gazelle, and Coco could barely contain his frustration now as the tank began to fire everything it had at us: PD shells, airburst, 12.7mm ack-ack from the heavy Dushka gun and stream after stream of machine-gun fire. Coco was now virtually hoarse with repeating and half-shouting the talk-on to me over the radio as I continued to struggle to find the tank until, finally, he said: 'Right, Scooby, come over to me and I'll point them out for you with my own finger.' It was a shock, too, as Gizmo manoeuvred the Lynx even closer to the Gazelle and I kept my eyes stuck in the sight. I was on x14 magnification, and that turned out to be part of the problem, because when I switched to low magnification there it was, so bloody close it seemed as if it was sitting on the nose of the aircraft. Coco had told me the tank was about two and a half kilometres away, but in fact it wasn't much more than 1,500 metres, which is way, way closer than you ever want to be in a tank engagement. Ideally, in these situations, we'd be about four or five kilometres in the distance, hovering behind a hill, popping up every now and then to seek out the target and then to fire.

The reason why I had been unable to spot the T55 became immediately obvious when we arrived alongside the Gazelle. In the Lynx we had been side-on to a billboard, at a roughly 30–45 degree angle; so unlike Coco in the Gazelle, square on to the board, we hadn't seen the painting of a smiling Saddam Hussein, holding out his hands as if welcoming visitors to the Al-Faw peninsula. (In other circumstances this would have been funny, but right then I wasn't really responding to the humour of the occasion.) Once we had moved around, I instantly understood Coco's almost hysterical pleas for me to find the tank, which had been walking its shells ever closer to both aircraft since we had come into contact. The tank was sitting on the other side of the billboard. Nor was our little engagement happening in quiet isolation, either. It was total chaos up and down the front: the desert was dancing with eruptions of sand while great clouds of smoke drifted and hung over both lines, and there was a riot of noise inside the aircraft and over the radio channels as the day's fighting reached a hellish climax.

Through the sight I could see the gunner on his Dushka unleashing a continuous volley of heavy fire at us, sending streams of flashing light right past our windows. For a second I could see right down the dark opening of the barrel before a bright flash filled my sights and the gunner started walking a rapid succession of shells towards us, each one kicking up a plume of sand. Under different circumstances, I'd have said that there was something lovely about the pretty symmetrical pattern he was making in the sand, but right now I was more concerned with returning his fire with a nice fat TOW missile as quickly as I possibly could.

We had only seconds to fire – to live, perhaps – but in spite of this very great urgency, and in spite of the great haste in which we were working, it was curious how the whole scene appeared to be unfolding in slow motion. It was odd, too, that I was now feeling very calm. Perhaps I was still in shock from the strike on the CP, perhaps it was the training kicking in, perhaps Coco had been doing my urgency for me or maybe it was just a kind of fatalistic resignation to my fate – whatever the reason, I was acutely aware of an other-worldly serenity suffusing me at that moment. It seemed as if I was there for minutes on end, slowly loading the TOW, the shells slowly marching forwards to the nose of the Lynx, Gizmo slowly – and superbly, I should add – manoeuvring the helicopter up and down, left and right, to avoid the incoming fire. The Lynx felt like the animal whose name it had been given. It was all lithe grace and stealth as it moved around the field and began to corner the bigger beasts that had been tormenting it, and prepared to pounce.

In truth, all this happened in a matter of seconds.

I wanted Guns to put some GPMG into the tanks to break their fire and get their heads down while I lined up the missile. But we were moving around far too much for that, and there was no let-up in the incoming fire.

The battle was now a straight knife-fight between the Lynx and the T55, and I closed out the din of the rest of the battle front and concentrated on what was probably the most important half a minute of my life. So far that day I had fired four missiles, none of which had rogued and only one of which had missed the target, and that by a mere matter of yards. I was aware as I lined up the turret of the nearest tank in my crosshairs that by the law of averages I was well overdue a misfire. The other boys had had terrible luck with their TOWs all day long, but I prayed that this would not be the moment when mine decided to flop on me. I had a tank in front of me and I had two missiles left. The maths was simple.

The first TOW – the third of that mission – flew as a true as an arrow, impacting right on the button. There followed what felt like a long pause; and then, a second or two later, the tank exploded in a massive fireball, sending shrapnel flying in all directions as the fuel tank and the remaining shells and magazines ignited. A column of black smoke, visible for miles around, shot into the late afternoon sky.

I exhaled a huge sigh of relief – but the breath was barely out of my body when I caught sight of a second tank, moving into a fire position; the barrel of its main armament motored around to line us up. I could see its goggled commander sticking out of the turret, stabbing his finger in our direction and screaming at his machine gunner. The blazing tank to his right was no more than 150 yards away and the explosion would have given him the shock of his life. For fifteen minutes or so, they had had the upper hand on us, firing on us at will, while receiving nothing in return. Now it was their turn to shit themselves. I had only one TOW left, but my target didn't look like he was feeling lucky. He was a brave bugger, though, because he could have turned and fled for the cover of the date palms, and yet he didn't budge an inch. In my head I saluted in respect, which was strange considering I had to destroy him.

It was like *Star Wars* now outside our windows, as streaks of laser-like light from the heavy machine-gun fire whizzed, flashed and whistled into the air. I couldn't see the rounds of the small mounted machine gun, but I saw its muzzle flickering like a sparkler on bonfire night as the gunner pumped hundreds of bullets in our direction, while a cocktail of airburst and PD shells shook and stirred the earth and air around us.

It took me about five seconds in total to turn the rotary knob on the missile select function, press the button to cut the wire off the old missile, get back into the sight, fix the tank in the crosshairs and pull the trigger. Suddenly, the tank's heavy machine gun just stopped firing. It must have jammed as his last round erupted beneath us. There was no time to bless our incredible good fortune. Gizmo did an amazing job in keeping the bucking Lynx in constraints as our final TOW raced towards the tank. In the seven or eight seconds it took to arrive while I held the crosshairs firmly on the centre of the target, we all knew what was about to happen. His big barrel turret was now one second, maybe two, from lining us up as the TOW screeched away. As with the first tank, there was a monumental explosion, but this time no pause; it just went straight up, followed a few seconds later by a second explosion as the tank erupted like an overheated pressure cooker. At the moment of impact, the turret had stopped motoring into position and his main armament was ready to fire. He was just seconds from taking us out.

Coco was still shouting over the radio, but now it was with the joy of a man who has just won the Lottery, married Claudia Schiffer and been awarded the Nobel Prize, all in the space of about ten seconds. 'Move!' I said forcefully over the radio, interrupting Coco's celebrations, and as I turned the radio dial I could see and feel my hand quivering.

'Not so fast, my hasty little friend,' said Coco. 'Take a closer look in those date palms and you'll see half the Basra tank division parked up in there.'

He was right. There were six of them, all turning on their engines, belching out plumes of exhaust fumes and preparing to break cover to come and engage us and the QDG. They had sensed their opportunity. They'd have seen me fire all four of my missiles and known that I was now 'Winchester' (completely out of ammo), except for the GPMG in the back, which was next to useless in a tank engagement. This, the commander must have felt, was the moment to reveal themselves. Major mistake. If they had just kept their heads down and their engines off and stayed concealed in the ground beneath their camouflage meshing, then we would never have spotted them and would just have gone home. You could see what the commander was thinking, however: there's been next to no coalition jets to worry about all day, Mr Newton's dumped all his missiles in the Lynx, it's almost dark, so let's get out there, show them that there's still plenty of us left to come out to play tomorrow and maybe stick a few shells up the bastards' arses on their way home.

I probably would have done the same; but what this commander didn't know was that circling about 15,000 feet above us was a dirty great big American A10 'Warthog' gunship, groaning with bombs and cannon fire and now desperate for a piece of the action. He hadn't been so keen a few minutes earlier when Coco was desperately trying to persuade him to drop down a few thousand metres to join the party. But now, seeing the smoke from the second tank I had destroyed, he immediately checked in with us and was back to the battle like flies on a turd. It is a little galling, I have to admit, when we're right down in the maelstrom of the action in our plastic bubbles, involved in a firefight with tanks no more than a block away, to know that these big, heavily armed jets, protected from small-arms fire by their titanium shells, are virtually in outer space, roughly six or seven times further away from the action than us.

'So you can see the tanks now?' said Coco, mischievously, but clearly annoyed that only now were the Americans prepared to play. 'See those two columns of black smoke? Well, in that row of date palms next to them, you'll find about half a dozen more. I'll talk you on to them.'

'Right, I see what you mean, this place is crawling with tanks,' said the American pilot as he flew over to identify the target.

'That's what I've been trying to tell you for the past half

an hour, my friend, but you're not interested in the little people down here until you see a nice, fat slice of the action to get stuck into, eh?' Coco then delivered a brief historical summary of the achievements of 847 Squadron and their predecessors in 3 BAS before he started talking them on to the tanks.

It's called a 'nine-line brief' when you manually steer another aircraft on to a target, and Coco, an expert in this art, went straight into pointing out the landmarks as the A10 began its descent from on high. 'Follow that road west, past the waterworks, head for the two columns of smoke . . .'

Halfway through this performance Coco was interrupted by his co-pilot Gilbert, reminding him that it wasn't for fun that the engineers had spent half the journey down to the Gulf fitting 847's aircraft with the state-of-the-art LTDRF, and that he no longer had to use the old-fashioned nine-line brief – or at least, not all of it. The laser target designator and range finder, to give it its full title, makes target identification much simpler: one aircraft simply 'paints' the target with a laser beam and the other aircraft can see the reflected laser energy and come in and bomb the target.

Within seconds of Coco painting the first T55, the first of two Warthogs came rumbling out of the distance and dropped a 500lb bomb, obliterating the first tank where it sat. It was unlikely that the tank crew had any idea what was coming because the Warthog was still fairly high in the sky when it struck, coming at them from a ninety-degree angle along the date palms before banking away to the left and making a return run to drop a second bomb. It was an awesome, terrifying sight to behold, each consecutive eruption on the ground making our TOWs look like mere homemade devices by comparison.

A second Warthog followed up with two bombs of its own, pulverising two more tanks, before the first came back in for a final run, this time just a few hundred feet above the ground. It was a breathtaking sight, this ugly, evil-looking bastard of a machine, with its snarling teeth painted on the nose and its two big, cumbersome-looking engines sitting on its back spitting out exhaust fumes, lumbering towards the date palms at about 300 mph. Watching it approach that low, although I knew what was coming, I was still stunned by the ensuing spectacle. When it got within 600 metres of the date palms, the gunner opened up with his 30mm cannons, spewing up a 100 foot wall of sand into the air as hundreds of rounds strafed the tanks and the date palms. The intensity of the fire and the almost artistic impression it created in the sand made the spectacle horrifying and beautiful all at once. As we turned for camp, a long, high drape of dark smoke hung over the line of tanks and trees, like the final curtain had come down. It had been a truly painful and dramatic performance in this little sideshow in the wider theatre of war.

From the moment we came under a heavy barrage from the tanks to that last run made by the Warthog, the entire engagement hadn't lasted much over twenty minutes; and yet, on that short flight back to Viking, I felt as if I had just exhausted a whole lifetime of emotions. I exhaled heavily, over and over again, desperately trying to compose myself, as a huge sense of relief that I was still alive began to sweep over me. The terror and revulsion I had felt were still plain to see in the quivering of my hands. Just as I had done that morning, I sat on my hands so that Gizmo couldn't see them.

It was a bloody miracle that not one of the several hundred rounds that were unleashed at us during that engagement managed to hit either the Lynx or the Gazelle. Hundreds of them missed us by a matter of feet, and at times I felt as if I could have put my hand out of the window and touched them. What made it all the more remarkable was that we were so close to the tanks, virtually sitting on them. Even young Guns was shitting himself. You could put a great deal of our lucky escape down to the incredible flying performances of Gizmo and Gilbert, but there was also a substantial element of sheer good fortune to it. Even more incredibly, all four of my TOWs had hit their targets. When you consider that not all of the TOWS fired by 847 Squadron that day had hit their targets, then our escape seems even more remarkable. Furthermore, retreating was never an option – and for that Coco, our mission commander, deserved a mighty slap on the back for encouraging us to stand and fight. If we had cut and run after taking out the CP post it would have taken about four or five minutes to get out of the tanks' range, and that was all the time in the world the two commanders between them would have needed to adjust fire and bring down one or both of us. Coco didn't know it at the time, of course, but his actions that afternoon earned him an MID. It was an especially impressive effort.

As we landed on in the near-darkness back at Viking, I felt faint as I stepped out of the cab. The young Royal Marine machine gunner was still wide-eyed as I slapped him on the shoulder.

'We're all still alive, thanks to you and Gizmo, boss,' he said. 'I won't forget that. Cheers.' When Royal Marines start getting choked up, you know you've been in the thick of it. I'm glad he was shaken up, too. I would have begun to question my suitability for the job if everyone else around me sailed through engagements of such ferocity like they were enjoying a summer's day out on the Solent. 'It was our turn to step up today,' I replied, 'but you'd better say thanks to the boys in the Gazelle too.'

I took three sharp, deep breaths to try and clear my head as I walked, a little stiffly and unsteadily, towards the ops tent to see Clubs, and then write up the details of my mission report, or 'misrep' as we call them. The following half-hour or so was something of a blur as I ghosted through the various routines and procedures that follow a mission. I remember Sweetcorn seeking me out to congratulate me on my afternoon's efforts. I appreciated his gesture as much as any in the days that followed. We might have had our differences over the past few months, but he's not a man to

251

bear grudges and I wasn't surprised he was the first out of the blocks to come and have a word.

As I tried to describe the details of the engagement to the CO, I heard myself talking at a rate of knots as the adrenaline carried on raging round my body. Then, slowly, it began to drain away, to be replaced by a feeling of listlessness and exhaustion. Images and noises from the day flashed and erupted in my mind: explosions, fire, smoke, bodies, burning tanks, crosshairs, all in my high-magnification sights, the surreal sight of Saddam Hussein's smiling, friendly face . . . As I floated around the camp, I was aware that the day's experiences had had a huge psychological and emotional impact on me, as powerful in their way as all the missiles and shells that had erupted during the engagements. I knew it would be many months before I could bury those images once and for all. It was post-traumatic stress without the 'post'.

One other image from that day will remain with me until my dying day: the sight of a vast sandstorm rolling towards us across the desert. I had never seen a natural phenomenon like it, and that includes Hurricane Mitch, one of the deadliest tropical storms in history. I was on tour with the Army Air Corps in Belize, taking part, among other things, in operations against drug-running cartels, when Mitch struck the region with devastating consequences. We were immediately diverted to bring humanitarian assistance to the Central American countries worst affected. I was battened down when the hurricane struck, and saw only the tail-end of it as the centre landed further up the coast.

For sheer, awe-inspiring spectacle that giant wall of sand in Iraq was the most breathtaking display of extreme nature I have ever seen. There was something almost biblical about this tsunami of sand, appearing first as a dark line on the horizon and then just rising higher and higher and higher as it rolled ever closer to our camp. Any chance of getting our heads down after the most shattering day of my life was blown away by the first gusts of the storm as we scrambled into the helicopters to fly them back to the safety of *Ocean*.

Some of our colleagues in other helicopter units and forces in the Gulf tried to sit out the storm, but they were quick to regret the decision once the tempest had passed through and they ventured out of their tents to inspect the aircraft. Even in normal circumstances the floury sand finds a way of infiltrating every nook and cranny of the machines; in this raging storm, the aircraft were completely choked and mashed with billions of microscopic glassy grains. The engineers subsequently had a nightmare trying to clean them out, racing against the clock to get them serviceable again.

As we flew back to Mum, I had time to reflect on the day's action. From a purely military point of view, I felt immensely proud of what 847 Naval Air Squadron had achieved on 24 March 2003. It was truly remarkable. We had punched a massive hole in the Iraqis' offensive capability by destroying so many tanks, but an even bigger psychological one by doing it with such limited resources and with so little back-up. Perhaps even more significantly, by destroying the CP we had also disrupted the crucial connection between the Fedayeen and the regular forces, dislocating the chain of command, thus giving the real Iraqi soldiers the opportunity to melt away from the battlefield. The fewer of the regulars we slotted the better, as far as we were concerned. We had nothing against them. They were just soldiers doing their jobs like us. It was the child-hanging bastards in black we wanted to nail.

In our less modest moments, perhaps, if you caught us after a few pints of cheap lager in the wardroom, the men and women of 847 might like to think that, together with the almost unnaturally courageous tank crews of the QDG and the marines of the BRF and 3 CDO Brigade, we had stymied a major Iraqi counterattack that day – and, in doing so, had saved the coalition not just from a significant military setback but also from a public relations disaster of the first order. All day the Basra tank division had tried to break out and overrun the QDG, but between us, and helped by the last-minute intervention of the American Warthogs, we had kept them at bay. The Iraqis, we felt, had had their chance to push us back into the sea; now that chance was all but gone as the heavyweights of the 7th Armoured Brigade began to rev their engines over the Kuwaiti border, finally ready to roll into the battle.

Or so we thought.

It wasn't until we arrived back on *Ocean* in the pitch dark that I realised quite how I exhausted I was. I had left the last dregs of my spare capacity out there on the battlefield. Back at Viking, all I wanted to do was get my head down, and I was virtually hallucinating with fatigue as I strapped on the dreaded NVGs and lifted into the air for the fifth time that day. It took only about fifteen minutes to find *Ocean*, and I began to relax a little as Flyco gave us clearance to land. It was a lovely feeling as the skids of the Lynx gently touched down on the flight deck. I was dreaming of a hot shower, a plate of proper food, a couple of pints in the wardroom and a nice, relaxing smoke out on the cool of the quarterdeck.

Perhaps it was the fatigue, but for some daft reason I had been expecting *Ocean* to be an oasis of soothing calm and home comforts, a quiet retreat from the shocking violence of the battlefront. How wrong I was – and how stupid I was to think the ship would be anything but a hive of frantic, heightened activity. The war was only four days old, after all, and battles were still being fought just a few miles away; jets and helicopters had been roaring and screaming overhead all day and night, and you could see the giant fires burning wildly in the dark distance.

The ship was just as much at war as we were, and the first duty of the crew was to protect her. They were fighting a different type of battle from ours, because they couldn't see their enemy. The only visual of an attack they'd get would be the small blip on the radar screen indicating the imminent arrival of an incoming missile. At this stage of the war, anything was still possible. The full capability of Saddam's forces was still an unknown quantity – and quality – and the ship was vulnerable to all manner of attacks, including mines (of which there were hundreds floating about), missiles (likewise) and maybe even suicide boats, similar to the one that had maimed USS *Cole*.

When we stepped from the cockpit on to the flight deck it was like walking straight back into the front line. *Ocean* was at action stations, and so far 'up threat', as the crew put it, they thought *they* were in the thick of the battle. If we'd flown another twenty miles south and boarded a ship of the Royal Fleet Auxiliary, who supply the warships of the Royal Navy with fuel, food, stores and ammunition, we'd have found all on board there too thinking and behaving as if they were at the front line. At the other end of the scale, miles in the opposite direction, the SBS were crawling their way through the marshes and deserts of southern Iraq and into the suburbs of Basra, deep behind enemy lines. Although we were a combined force working as one, each constituent part operated to some extent in its own hermetically sealed world. Each of these domains has its own specific roles and responsibilities in a war situation, with its own attendant pressures and stresses. Everyone felt under threat of attack.

It was a strange feeling, then, to return from what for me was the most terrifying and frenetic day of my life, desperate for some kind of break from the mayhem, only to find another atmosphere electrified by the business of war.

The whole crew, kitted out in white anti-flash, flame-resistant body suits, was rushing to and fro, up and down corridors, in and out of the various operations rooms. The ship's warfare operations room was buzzing with talk about possible enemy contact. The air was alive with aggression, manic purpose and a fear that at any moment the ship might be struck by one of the Seersuckers that the Iraqis were still lobbing randomly into the mix by the dozen. These missiles are designed to destroy or incapacitate large ships. They have a range of eighty miles and so they could be launched from miles behind the battlefront. They are so big and cumbersome, and they move so slowly, that you might mistake one for a flying bus. Their great danger is that they can fly at very low altitude – i.e. below radar – and though pretty unsophisticated they are capable of inflicting massive damage, especially if they strike a ship just above the waterline.

Just after we landed on *Ocean*, I gave an interview to a British television news crew while sitting in the cab of my Lynx, but to this day I have not even the faintest memory of it, let alone the details of what I said. I only found out about it when a few weeks later I received a letter from my Mum, telling me how proud she was to have seen me on the telly that night. (Her postscript added: 'But you did look terribly tired, darling. You really must try and get some decent sleep. Are you eating properly!?!' Dear Mum, she was probably still holding her giant plastic poppy.) My brother later told me that he had dropped his dinner on the floor when I appeared in the main evening news, sandwiched between a piece on Saddam Hussein and an interview with Donald Rumsfeld!

Mum will have been pleased to know that I did get a good night's sleep that night – curled up on the floor in a quiet room, about twenty feet above the waterline, still in my flying gear. I must have stretched out in the first empty space I found.

CHAPTER EIGHT

The war ground to a halt on 25 March as combatants on both sides bowed to the superior force of Mother Nature and retreated behind closed doors, waiting for the winds to subside and the swirling fog of sand to settle. Leaving behind a small group of men to defend the camp, all the pilots of 847 Squadron returned to *Ocean*, gratefully seizing the opportunity to do all the things that were impossible out in the desert, namely, washing properly, eating properly, sleeping properly, drinking beer and watching television. It may not sound that exciting or glamorous, but out in the Gulf it felt like a luxury weekend break in the Caribbean. Within twenty-four hours, however, a general restlessness kicked in again and all of us were itching to get back into Iraq before the momentum we had worked up began to drain away.

The mood of the squadron and the wider atmosphere of the ship had shifted significantly since the beginning of the conflict. To a man, we were all doubly tired, fractious and stressed. This was partly down to the combat fatigue coming on top of the long weeks of intense preparations, but it had also been an unpleasant surprise to us that the Iraqis were putting up such fierce resistance. I don't think I was alone in clinging to the hope that within a few days of the opening assault the Iraqis would roll over and let us tickle their tummies. The events of the day before had proved emphatically that that was not going to be the case. There was plenty of hard fighting to be done. On the twenty-sixth a rumour swept the ship that the uprising in Basra we had been praying for was now under way. The news had an electric effect on all of us, but it quickly turned out to be a false hope. Quite the opposite had happened, in fact. A major fight had erupted.

It turned out to be the largest tank battle involving British forces since the Second World War. Fourteen Iraqi T55s broke out of southern Basra into the Al-Faw peninsula. You wondered whether they had any idea that waiting for them a few miles south was a similar number of Challenger tanks of the Royal Scots Dragoon Guards. All fourteen Iraqi tanks were destroyed with no losses on the British side. A huge column of roughly 100 vehicles carrying infantry troops also came out in a major counterattack, but they were quickly beaten back by our warplanes and artillery. If they had attempted the breakout just twenty-four hours earlier, the result might have been very different. As it was, from that day on it was no longer a question of 'if' but 'when' we secured the peninsula and then turned our attention to Basra, which we planned to squeeze until the pips squeaked, flushing out the Fedayeen bastards and the Ba'ath Party hard-liners by the sheer pressure of our presence on the outskirts of the city.

From the moment the conflict began, the coalition had been desperately trying to secure Umm-Qasr in order to bring in humanitarian assistance and basic provisions, especially water, for the local people. Apart from the real need for these supplies, the war planners were also keen to show the ordinary Iraqis that we were there to help them. The marines of 42 Commando had done a superb job after taking over from the Americans to secure and settle the town of Umm-Qasr, but the discovery of several mines at the entrance to the port delayed the arrival of supply vessels while our minesweepers cleared the waterways as quickly as they could.

Back on board *Ocean*, the strain of the conflict was starting to tell in our behaviour. Part of the mounting irritability could be put down to a suffocating feeling of overfamiliarity with the people alongside whom we were living and working, day in, day out. We were becoming stir crazy. Even close friends can annoy you after a while – just as wives or husbands would. Imagine having to go to a small pub every night and talk to the same people about the same subject (i.e. war) for half a year. Imagine, too, that you have to eat your breakfast, lunch and dinner and take your coffee with those same people. You go for a shower and there they are again. You go to work and, surprise, surprise, guess who's there? There comes a time when you crave your own space, and it was a craving that somehow wasn't fully satisfied by sitting in a tiny windowless cabin below the waterline with the ship at action stations in anticipation of an enemy attack. Compounding the sense of isolation from the outside world, there was no Internet connection and no phone calls could be made while the security restrictions remained in place. The newspapers lying around were three weeks old, and the news channels we watched appeared to be covering a different war from the one we were fighting. Needless to say, we couldn't just pop out for a walk.

Lots of the men took up smoking during this period – or started again after years of abstinence – and the existing smokers significantly upped their daily intake. A small handful started drinking more too. The vast majority of us didn't want to drink more than about three cans in a sitting – our bodies simply didn't want alcohol – but the tiny handful of heavy drinkers among us welcomed the break from operations to sink into a fuzzy haze of false happiness in the evening, perhaps blotting out their experiences over the previous few days. Inevitably, however, the booze buzz turned to bad temper and we had a couple of ugly scenes in the wardroom.

These eruptions were inevitable – they happened every time we went on a deployment – and it was no surprise that the first one of significance involved our old friend Bozo. After a couple too many beers in the wardroom, Bozo fell into an argument with Naphtha – whose call sign refers to the flammable liquid which, like his temper, has a very low flashpoint. The argument, predictably, was about nothing of any great consequence, but it soon flared into an aggressive stand-off between the two men. It went from chat to disagreement to argument to heated discussion to the brink of violence in under a minute. We heard it escalating, and the chat in the room had already died down to a low hum when Bozo ripped a wall light out of its fittings and we all quickly leapt to our feet, ready to intervene. We then froze where we stood until Bozo finally dropped the light to the floor and sat back down. This was dealt with very quickly by command – help is always on hand.

Hovis was another who found himself in a spot of bother back on *Ocean* during this lull in the fighting. Like many of us, our electronics warfare officer had flown a number of hair-raising missions over the previous days and, in between, he had been working around the clock on various technical issues. He hadn't slept much for three nights and he looked extremely ragged around the edges when he ghosted into the wardroom one evening.

Hovis was desperate for a cigarette, which was strange because he doesn't normally smoke. At this stage of the war there was a strict ban on smoking at night out on the quarterdeck and the cross-deck passage out on top. The ship was still in her aggressive, highly defensive posture, and the heightened alert level had started to grate on one or two of the boys – mainly the smokers, it has to be said – who felt that the security restrictions imposed were disproportionate to the real threat. We all had great admiration for the XO and the ship's company for the way they ran their ship and looked after us, but after a few days of flying through a barrage of artillery, tank shells and machine-gun fire, it was difficult for some of the pilots to understand why there was such a fuss about security out there in the calm waters of the Gulf. This, in a roundabout kind of way, is what Hovis, squinting through his puffy, exhausted eyes, tried to explain to the XO after being told he couldn't go outside for a smoke until the morning. Only it didn't *quite* come out like that.

'Sir, your ship is rubbish,' said Hovis.

One of those terrible silences then filled the room. The last time I had witnessed a single comment cause such astonishment was during an evening out in Belfast a few years earlier. We had been having a conversation about the most embarrassing things we had ever done in our lives, when one of the boys piped up that he had once given his room-mate at university a blow job. One of the boys dropped his pint in disbelief, and I'm surprised no glasses hit the floor in the wardroom that night, in amazement at Hovis's brazen disrespect for one of the most senior and respected officers in the British armed forces. If Hovis had kicked Her Majesty The Queen up the backside during Trooping the Colour I don't think the onlookers could have looked any more stunned than they did at that moment. I've witnessed Hovis say and do some remarkable things in his time, but he had just massively raised the bar of his own outrageousness with those five jaw-dropping words. What made it all the more remarkable was the casual way the comment just plopped out over his pint glass, and the fact that Clubs, his boss, was standing right next to him at the time.

The XO, to his enormous credit, barely twitched. He proceeded to explain to Hovis, very calmly, that of all the British and US ships in the Gulf, *Ocean* was the closest to the fighting on shore. Clearly, the XO had picked up on Hovis's stress and exhaustion, and, rather than berate him, had decided to gloss over the remark. But before Hovis had a chance to reply to the explanation, Clubs quickly jumped into the conversation, saying firmly, 'I think it's time for our electronics warfare instructor to retire to his cabin.' As he spoke, he looked at me and flicked his head towards the door, telling me as clearly as if he had spoken aloud to escort Hovis from the room before he personally threw him out on his arse.

While some drank a little too much and others told commanders where to get off, most filled their downtime from combat by going to the gym and working out manically. More people started writing their wills, too, and another two of the boys gave me letters to deliver to their wives and families in the event of their deaths. Death, or the fear of it, was hanging around the ship like a brewing sandstorm now. We had witnessed it with our own eyes, and delivered it with our own hands. We had all seen corpses lying in the sand and floating in the waters. We had watched it flash past the windows of our aircraft. The horrible reality of war enveloped us. There was no escaping it, even on board *Ocean*.

Adding a surreal twist to the atmosphere was the sight of injured Iraqi troops in our midst. Many of them had been flown here from the battlefield by our casualty evacuation teams so that they could undergo surgery by our doctors. It was a strange feeling when, on the odd occasion, I found myself walking past and exchanging nods of acknowledgement with a man I might have been shooting at a few days, or even hours, earlier. War, I was quickly discovering, was one very weird business – a fact that was brought home to me once again when, twenty-four hours after returning from the front, I found myself sitting in my cabin, squeezed between two eighteen-stone marines, watching *Shrek* again on my laptop, all three of us giggling like little children at the animated adventures of an ugly green troll with funny, sticky-outy ears.

I was forced to spend four days back aboard *Ocean* as the fighting continued ashore. After two days in the air I was due two days to recuperate, and having lost twenty-four hours of flying time to the storm, the squadron's mission schedule was simply shunted forward and my downtime was prolonged. While my body appreciated the respite from the exertions of close combat, my mind and heart were tugging hard to get back to the front. I could see and hear the fighting from the flight deck as multiple explosions rose up across the horizon, the smoke drifted out across the Gulf and the jets and helicopters tore back and forth from the front. The war was now moving at a great pace as the main bulk of the coalition forces brought their mighty weight to bear on the conflict, and the Iraqis, still battling manfully after a week of fighting and sustained bombardment, dug in around Basra and endeavoured to thwart the advancing line of armour and infantry.

The Black Watch, quickly into the action after pushing up from Kuwait, laid on a small but daring show of strength and bravado for the residents of Basra. A raiding party of tanks and troop carriers drove straight into the centre of the city, where they destroyed a television mast and two statues of Saddam Hussein before withdrawing to the British camps encircling the city. It was a particularly audacious move, considering that no British forces had entered Basra up to that point and that the battle to secure the region was continuing unabated around the city. At the same time, air and ground forces stepped up their attacks on the Ba'ath Party buildings. The message they were sending to the Iraqi public was clear: we have no argument with you, only with the people who have been oppressing you for so many decades . . . and if you fancy rising up and having a pop at them yourselves we'll be right there to back you up at a moment's notice.

Meanwhile, a Seersucker strike on a shopping mall in

Kuwait reminded Hovis and the rest of us that Captain Johns and every other ship's commander in the Gulf was right to maintain the highest threat level; the first bodies of British servicemen killed in the conflict were flown home to Brize Norton; and a raiding party into an Iraqi position by the marines discovered a huge stash of biochemical suits, reviving those fears, buried shallowly in the backs of our minds, that so long as the war continued we remained at risk of a particularly hideous form of attack. More positively, a fresh-water pipeline from Kuwait to Umm-Qasr was completed, beginning a daily flow of 600,000 gallons of water into the region.

When I was finally called forward again on 29 March, it was on to Iraqi soil that I brought down the skids of the Lynx. The squadron had struck camp at Viking a couple of days earlier and moved up to a new base, dubbed Camp Bonzai, just south of Umm-Qasr. This place, which was what we would call 'home' until we were finally stood down, was situated in the middle of a giant industrial complex, and the first thing I noticed about it was that it was littered with the turds of the US marines who had passed through there in a great rush a few days earlier.

There were turds everywhere you turned. Turds on the ground, turds in the warehouses, turds in the offices, turds in the cupboards, turds in a kettle and turds on the conveyor belts. They had even made improvised toilets by shooting holes in the seat of plastic chairs. You wondered quite how the Americans had found any time to do any fighting in between relieving themselves all over the complex during their brief stopover. It was like one of those giant sandpits laid on for dogs you find in public parks. Just sand and turds.

Some of the boys felt that the Americans had shat everywhere deliberately, knowing that we were moving in after them, because they were angry and embarrassed that the Brits had managed to quell Umm-Qasr within a few hours of taking over from them, and were making us clear up their shit as a punishment. There is great respect between the two forces as a whole, but there is also a great rivalry, and I think this is particularly true of our respective marine corps. We rated them, and they rated us; but, as with two football teams from the same city, a powerful tension exists between the two. We also went about our business in completely different manners, with the British adopting a less belligerent approach. By and large, the Americans prefer to chain-gun a place first, then hand out the sweets. Perhaps it's the Northern Ireland factor, but the British have learned from experience that the scorch-and-burn policy generally serves only to inflame situations, creating more problems than existed in the first place.

Whether or not the Americans had wanted us to clear up their dung, Bonzai was truly disgusting, and the smell of the place wasn't exactly freshened up by the stench of the fetid water in the crane-lined docks that ran alongside it. Within twenty minutes of arriving in Bonzai, I saw two dead Fedayeen agents in black clothing float past, drifting out to the Gulf on the tide. A few yards away, three smiling Iraqi boys hung homemade fishing lines into the dank, oily water.

Three sides of Camp Bonzai were flanked by giant warehouses while the fourth faced out on to the waterway. The marines had dug themselves in all around the camp in a string of sandbagged revetments, slowly swivelling their mounted heavy machine guns as they scanned the area for enemy. They'd also taken up positions in the high towers in each corner, providing us with superb observation platforms over the surrounding area. Dozens more marines patrolled the area immediately around the camp. At Viking, twelve miles or so from the Iraqi border, we needed only a handful of men to keep a lookout, but here at Bonzai we were camped right in the middle of the Iraqi population, and the locals were going about their lives as best they could just a hundred yards or so from the camp's perimeter – with the Fedayeen lurking in their midst.

The 847 boys had wasted no time in settling into their new accommodation. The sleeping tents had been pitched in a wide-open space at the centre of the complex, with all the aircraft and heavy equipment set off to one side. Four air-raid bunkers, reinforced with sandbag walls, had been built at various locations around the complex, all easily accessible for us to run into at the first sound of the Land Rover siren. The operations room had been set up inside the largest of the offices, and a tented radio shack with dozens of aerials had been constructed against one of the warehouse walls; the galley area, just as it had been at

Viking, was no more than an open-sided tent with a table, a small tank of boiling water and a few boxes of provisions. The shower area, if you can call it anything as fancy as that, was an open stretch of ground where you stood naked and opened a bag on your head. (The women used the shower area too, but wore swimsuits.) The washroom was a tanker lorry full of water with a tap off the back for brushing our teeth. The toilet, for the time being, was just a big hole in the ground, positioned as far from the living areas as possible, with some planks laid across it for us to stand on. (After a week or so, Iraqi contractors arrived to install some mobile loos.) Gizmo, ever resourceful, had even built a small open-air gym for the squadron's use – and this wasn't the end of his creativity: when I arrived I found him down on his hands and knees putting the finishing touches to a tiny little garden he had built in one corner, complete with surrounding brick wall and a border of live 23mm ZSU rounds, providing more evidence, as if we needed any, of the weirdness of war.

Some of the pilots opted to set up their sleeping quarters in the abandoned office buildings on the site, partly because the rooms were a little cooler than the tents but also because they afforded better protection against the compression and flying shrapnel of a Scud strike. I found my own space in a small corner office, which was piled high with a random selection of goods in bundles and boxes. There were stashes of UN clothes, left over from the aftermath of the last Gulf War, and there were several boxes of cheap car radios, presumably smuggled into the port as a nice little income supplement for whoever used to work there.

There was, naturally, a turd in one of the filing cabinets and the place was crawling with cockroaches, but after a quick spring-clean the room was just about habitable, if not exactly homely. For a bed, I used one of the fold-down 'cots' that were issued to us, which were just military versions of the sun-loungers you find on beaches in cheap holiday resorts. By my bed I kept a radio, my Bergen, my diary and my gas mask, and I hung my SA80 assault rifle on a quick-release cord above my head. It wouldn't have won any AA rosettes for excellence, but at least it was a space I could call my own.

Later that evening in Bonzai I met my first US soldiers – not including Mako, our exchange pilot – since arriving in the Gulf. I don't have strong feelings about Americans as a whole one way or the other, and most of the ones I've got to know, I've liked; but this brief meeting provided a perfect illustration of the difference between our two forces. They arrived through the camp gates, roaring into the concourse in a Humvee jeep, blaring the Queen song 'We Are The Champions' from a portable boogie box. Like so many US soldiers, the three of them had heavily worked-out upper bodies with tiny little pin legs holding them up. They had all the gear, too: goggled helmets, M16 Armalite assault rifles, knives, laser wands, grenades, ammo belts – and a bagload of attitude to boot.

To be honest, I can't remember the nicknames or call signs by which they introduced themselves, but like so many of the Yank guys they were along the lines of 'Thunder', 'Lightning', 'Tomcat', 'Wolf', 'Jaws', 'Hitman' and so on, and it was with perverse pleasure that I put out my hand and said: 'Hi, I'm Scooby and this is Cindy, our warfare instructor. Can we get you a cup of tea?' I know they like to think of us as their quaint, slightly peculiar relations from across the pond, and we were only too happy to make a little game out of it. Their faces were a picture as they shook hands with Cindy while looking up, down and across at his colossal frame. They couldn't quite square the 'Cindy' with the muscles, and it was as amusing as ever to see them stop and pause briefly as they tried to work out if we were being serious.

I spent the rest of my first day back in camp readying myself for what was shaping up to be another momentous battle: preparing my 'smart pack' information bundle, checking my personal weapons, packing my field rucksack, reading up on the latest battle reports and intelligence dispatches, and studying the maps and landmarks of the area. Operation James (as in James Bond) was to be launched at first light on 30 March, the following day.

Six hundred Royal Marines from 40 Commando, backed up by 847 Squadron, two tank squadrons (the QDG and the Black Watch) and a unit of commando-trained Royal Engineers, were to lay siege to the Iraqi defences embedded around the Basra suburb of Abu Al Khasib. If we could break the Iraqi resistance there, then we could press right up to Basra city limits while taking control of the last stretch of the Shatt Al-Arab waterway. The Iraqi forces would then be forced either to surrender or to retreat inside the city, where it was hoped most of the regular forces, now away from the battlefront and the zealous scrutiny of the Fedayeen bullies, would take the opportunity to give up the fight and melt back into the safety of the civilian population.

From talking to the other guys on the squadron that day it was clear that the cracks that had started to open in one or two people's behaviour back on *Ocean* had widened that much further after another three days of fighting and another three largely sleepless nights in our noisy new home. Fuses had shortened, and petty squabbles that in ordinary circumstances would have been resolved calmly and quickly had escalated into slightly sharper exchanges. Morale was still incredibly buoyant, but, although help was never far away, some whinged and moaned that little bit more than normal as the physical and mental pressure, not to mention the sleep deprivation, began to take their toll.

There were rumblings of irritation, for instance, about one of the pilots, who had an unwelcome tendency to take his aggression out on the battlefield by heading too far north in search of a fight, thus endangering the crews of both aircraft in his patrol. He was a senior officer, too, which made it more difficult for the others to voice their frustration, to his face at least. Mako, the American, had also come in for a few sharp words, in his case about flying technique. As a Cobra pilot for most of his career Mako had been accustomed to flying much higher than us, safe in the knowledge that his helicopter's titanium shell made him almost invulnerable to small-arms fire. This instinct to climb high in order to get a better look at the battlefield had been ingrained in him by his training, but out in Iraq, in the Lynx and Gazelles, it put him, and his co-pilot, at much greater risk of being shot down. The British pilots had always been taught to stay low, completely out of sight if possible, and one or two of them had complained that Mako was taking unnecessary risks. What may have been second nature to Mako went against all the unwritten rules in 847's modus operandi, and a few words had been exchanged.

Part of our problem out in the Gulf was that 847, faced with possible swingeing cuts, even liquidation, by the many proposed changes to the Fleet Air Arm, stretched itself to the very limit in the field in order to prove its operational value to the services. We put our hand up for everything and it was fascinating to see how we coped, in our different ways, with the extra demands we piled on to an already stressful situation by our eagerness to please. The majority of us just fought, ate, shat, slept, did our weights in Gizmo's makeshift gym and generally got on with the job in a no-nonsense fashion. Some, even the normally outgoing types, retreated into their shells and became introspective and quiet. Others, including some who were usually quieter, sought out company and became more outgoing and chatty. For most of us the stress manifested itself in a loss of energy, combined with an increase in banter. My mood tended to be a little lighter in the evening because I was able to tick off another day, happier that I was twenty-four hours closer to surviving the war and getting home. I was at my grimmest in the mornings, because what little energy I had I put into concentrating on performing out in the field.

I just wanted the bloody fighting over as quickly as possible, and I guess that was partly the reason behind my eagerness to prosecute targets as aggressively as I did. If I had spent my missions finding targets and then simply reporting their location to HQ for the fast jets and artillery to go and bomb, then I would have done no more and no less than our general working brief required us to do. As it was I fired eleven TOW missiles, and I ended up in the thick of the fiercest engagements experienced by the squadron. My thinking was this: someone was going to take out the targets we found, so why shouldn't I just cut to the chase and do it myself?

I looked upon the Al-Faw as a boxing match, with us in one corner and the Iraqi's armour in the other, and I didn't want to prolong the fight by hanging around for a points victory after twelve rounds. I wanted to pile in with a flurry of punches, floor my opponent and get out of the ring as fast as possible. Kiss, kiss, bang, bang, thanks very much, I'm off home now.

The worst manifestation of combat stress I witnessed out in the Gulf happened at Bonzai, and it was no surprise to any of us that it was Bozo. He had been under considerable pressure even before setting out for the Gulf, and with hindsight perhaps it was inevitable that the accumulated fatigue and the strain of combat would combine to tip him over the edge. Perhaps we were guilty of indulging him a little; but that was understandable because he was a good pilot and a brave, experienced marine with over twenty years of experience under his belt: nobody could question his general competence, commitment or loyalty. Everyone, moreover, is entitled to a difficult period in their lives, and it was just an ugly coincidence that Bozo's tough time came when the squadron happened to find itself at war. Back on *Ocean*, Bozo was able to find short-term relief from the stress in a few pints and getting a half-decent night's sleep, but in Iraq there was no beer and next to no sleep. Bonzai was strictly non-alcoholic territory, for obvious reasons.

Two weeks after we'd arrived, Bozo was among a small group of officers sitting around outside one of the abandoned offices, chatting and resting between missions. He was busy cleaning his 9mm Browning pistol, which was something he had started to do quite obsessively since we arrived in Bonzai. On this occasion he seemed especially agitated, and the rest of the boys started casting mildly anxious glances at one another as he continued to break the pistol down into its constituent parts and then put it back together, over and over again. As he fiddled with the weapon in an increasingly frantic manner, the boys snapped at him, 'Can you put that bloody thing down and stop fucking about?'

Bozo's magazine was still in the pistol, and they watched in horror as he pulled the working parts back, released them and then pulled the trigger. Sitting in a chair opposite Bozo, minding his own business was a Royal Marine captain. The pistol was pointing straight at him. There was a loud crack as the bullet flew straight between his legs, missing his genitals by a matter of centimetres. As it ricocheted around the walls two of the boys instantly piled on top of Bozo, pinning him to the floor and wrestling the pistol off him amid a flurry of swear words. Others burst outside after hearing the commotion. Once Bozo had calmed down he was called in to see the CO, who promptly removed him from all flying duties for the rest of the duty and sent him straight to bed. The fact that he slept for eighteen hours solid, through a constant barrage of noise of helicopters landing on and taking off, tells its own story about the fatigue he had been experiencing. He didn't even wake up during the air-raid sirens. Clubs dealt with the episode superbly. A negligent discharge (ND), as it is known, is a very serious offence and carries severe penalties. Bozo was suffering from a form of combat stress, had made a terrible mistake and we treated him gently. However, the appropriate action was taken – it had to be. But the Royal Navy looked after its own and help was quickly on hand.

Indeed, Clubs handled all the men of the squadron impressively during those demanding few weeks when the conflict was at its most intense and exhausting. Every evening he would call us together in a circle and stride around, briefing us all on what we had achieved, or failed to achieve, that day. He knew all our birthdays and he made a point of singling people out for a cheer and a slap on the back if it happened to be their day. That may seem like a small gesture, but it was a clever bit of man management, momentarily diverting our minds from the business of conflict, reminding us that ordinary life was still continuing in spite of the extraordinary circumstances in which we were living and working. In every meeting he would single out a couple of characters for special praise, dividing the plaudits equally among pilots, engineers and the lowest-ranking members of the ground crew. Nobody was left out and the democratic approach had a uniting effect on the squadron.

The only criticism I heard of Clubs's performance was that he didn't get involved as deeply as he might have done with the day-to-day operations. Most of us, though, welcomed the way he trusted us to get on with business. We were, after all, highly trained and experienced pilots. There's nothing worse than a boss with a 'long screw driver', constantly interfering in every area of operations. The fact was, too, that such was the range of his commitments he simply didn't have the time to stick his spanner into the works. He had less sleep than anyone else in the squadron, and during the opening days of the assault on the Al-Faw he never went to bed at all, getting by on the odd hour's snooze here and there. He had Sweetcorn, the operations officer, and Spidey, the senior pilot, to oversee the daily running of the squadron.

If there was any problem, it was that Sweetcorn wanted to fly as many missions as possible when most of us felt that the squadron would have been better served if he had stayed in camp more and conducted and coordinated the operations from there. You couldn't but admire Sweetcorn's eagerness to lead from the front, but his frequent absences from the operations HQ tended to leave a power vacuum. As a result, Spidey ended up taking on additional responsibilities – and he also bore the brunt of our whingeing about the occasional lack of direction, particularly on the more chaotic days when the fighting was nearly constant and the shape and the focus of the battles were constantly changing.

These, however, are small gripes. Considering the intensity of the fighting, the number of missions flown and targets prosecuted, as well as the steadily growing quantity of troops in theatre and the inevitable chaos of the battles, we thought the senior officers tasked with running the squadron acquitted themselves with great distinction – which was just as well, in view of the mayhem that was unleashed on 30 March.

CHAPTER NINE

The skyline above Basra was turning a dirty grey as night gave way to the dim light of a new day. Alpha, Bravo and Delta rifle companies of 40 Commando were just beginning their advance on foot towards the fortified Iraqi positions around Abu Al Khasib in the first infantry-style assault by an entire commando since the Falklands War. Back at Bonzai, Gizmo, our door-gunner for the day and I were once again going through the now familiar but no less harrowing procedure of checking in with the AWACS teams.

'Hello, Zero, this is Cravat 21,' I said over the radio as we swept out of the dust cloud and over the desert. 'I'm airborne from Bonzai with three POB [personnel on board], four TOW missiles and six hundred rounds of 7.62 ammunition and I'm on Task 062.' We nervously awaited clearance, with the Lynx RWR frantically flashing its lights at us, warning of a possible incoming missile attack, before my new best friend, the John Wayne sound-alike, came over the airwaves. 'Cravat 21, sweet, sweet to proceed. You be sure y'all have yir'selves a nass day out there now.' We immediately swept out of the camp and headed north from Umm-Qasr along our pre-designated 'safe' route, alongside Bunker and John Boy, the two largest marines in the squadron, who had somehow squeezed their giant frames into the little Gazelle.

Bunker and I had long since made up following our little spat over that lunch of his I'd accidentally eaten in Oman. John Boy was one of the more inexperienced pilots we had on the squadron, a humorous Welshman who does a highly amusing but disturbing dance routine with Leatherman to a drum and bass rap song called 'Painted Cow', dressed only in a small pair of briefs. An archetypal marine, John Boy was having an excellent war: he appeared to be having a genuinely good time, not just getting by, but loving it.

Bunker and John Boy were top operators in the field and I was glad to be flying in the same patrol as them on what we could tell from our briefing the night before was promising, or threatening, to be quite a day.

This was the eighth mission I had flown since arriving in the Gulf, but my heart was pumping as hard as it had when I'd first entered Iraqi air space with Lush a week earlier. As we flew north towards Basra I could see the smoke from the early morning engagements starting to billow in the distance, with the odd explosion breaking the skyline every now and then. Flicking through the radio frequencies, above the roar of the engine and the rotor blades I could hear the tank commanders barking orders, with the sound of rapid gunfire and shelling in the background. We were roughly fifty feet above the desert, cruising at about a hundred knots, which feels at least twice as fast when you are flying that low.

Our mission on this occasion was to head straight up to Abu Al Khasib, where the most ferocious battle of the war, involving British troops, was now in full cry. The marines of 40 Commando were fighting inside the town itself, flushing out the enemy street by street as they tried to squeeze them up against the Shatt Al-Arab waterway a couple of kilometres to the north. Only lightly armed themselves, the marines were receiving solid support from the Challenger 2 tanks of the Royal Scots Dragoon Guards and the recce vehicles of the ever-present QDG. Earlier, the 105mm light guns of 29 Commando (Royal Artillery) had unleashed a huge barrage of shells on the Iraqi defences in an effort to soften them up before the marines arrived.

The noise over the radios was a cacophony of shouting, machine-gun fire and shell explosions as the battle intensified. There had been reports of some small groups of Iraqis surrendering, but by late morning the majority of the Iraqi forces were still dug in and they were putting up a stout fight.

As we approached the front, looking down the high-magnification sight I could see what looked like three

MTLB armoured troop carriers, hull down at the side of the road at the very southern limits of the suburbs where the buildings end and the desert begins. It was difficult to be entirely sure that these were indeed armoured troop carriers; and, hull down, American Bradleys look broadly similar at that distance, so it was also hard to be sure they were enemy vehicles at all. So we crept a little closer, sticking as close to the desert as possible without going so low as to kick up a sand cloud that would betray our presence and location to the enemy.

As we crawled nearer it became obvious to both Bunker and me that the three vehicles were indeed Iraqi armoured personnel carriers. We could see the turrets with the heavy machine guns on their swivel plates, and we could see men standing on two of the machines scanning the southern horizon through their hand-held binoculars. As we stared at each other down our tubes, I could see one of those men shout at his gunner while pointing in our direction. A second later the muzzle of his heavy machine gun was flashing away. We were about four kilometres away at that point and in no danger of being brought down by small-arms fire, but we knew it wouldn't be long before the MTLB troops sent word and grid references to nearby tanks or artillery positions.

Sure enough, no more than half a minute later a single PD round from an unseen artillery battery landed nearby. The Gazelle bore the brunt of the explosion, with the compression waves from two rounds close enough to buck the little aircraft. I quickly contacted Nomad Bravo, the ground controller in charge of supervising the jets and the artillery, for permission to fire on the target, but it seemed to take an eternity for them to reply. Both pilots weaved and wriggled the aircraft around the battle position as the Iraqi gunners adjusted their sights and launched fresh volleys of rounds. It had almost got to the point where we'd have to cut and run when the reply came back: 'Cravat 21, you're cleared hot' – that is, I was permitted to engage the targets.

Gizmo put the Lynx in constraints as I lined up the most easterly of the three MTLBs and launched the TOW. Such was our distance from the target that it took about twenty seconds for the TOW to impact, and when it did I thought I had had a direct hit because all I could see through the sight was smoke and Iraqi troops running out of the back of the vehicles and taking up firing positions in the junk-filled ditch by the side of the road. But as the smoke cleared and the sand settled, I saw that the TOW had missed, belly-flopping about 100 yards short, its motor apparently having run out of puff. I had kept the crosshairs steady on the MTLB throughout the missile's flight, so it can only have been a mechanical failure, or range, which prevented it from reaching its target.

The explosion had sent shards of shrapnel somersaulting over the MTLBs and there was no doubt that the troops had felt its compression waves. They were running all over the place now, emptying their machine guns indiscriminately at the southern skyline. Gizmo moved us forward another kilometre or so, brought the Lynx into the hover and put her into constraints again. As soon as the aircraft was steady and I had fixed the MTLB in my graticule I launched the second TOW, keeping my finger tight on the trigger as it streaked towards the MTLB, now frozen solid in my crosshairs. Suddenly, for no obvious reason, the missile changed course dramatically and flew off at a crazy angle before erupting in the sands over to the right. It was my first and only 'rogue' of the war.

'Bollocks!' Gizmo and I spat simultaneously as the TOW wobbled off into nowhere. Frustration, mixed with mounting panic, welled up in my stomach. We were rapidly running out of time before the artillery gunners – whoever and wherever the hell they were – finally caught us with one of the dozens of shells they had been launching, one after the other, every four or five seconds, each of them exploding long – to the rear of us – but in the air now as well as on the ground.

My heart was pumping like a piston engine, and at the back of my mind there lurked the lingering fear that one of the MTLBs, or indeed all of them, might be carrying a fitted or portable missile system known as a Sagger, which is similar to the TOW in that it is guided on to the target by a trailing wire. They were so well dug in, it was difficult to know for sure exactly what weapons they had at their disposal. If it was a portable Sagger, it would take a few minutes to set it up on the MTLB before they could fire at us, and so, erring on the side of caution, I told Gizmo that we were going to attempt a running shot, rather than risk staying put in the hover and giving them the opportunity to adjust fire on us. I cut the wires of the rogued missile and lined up another as we flew at speed towards the low-rise suburbs and straight at the MTLBs, coming at them now on the diagonal. Through the sights, I could just see two Iraqis lying on top of the MTLB, firing rapidly as we bore down on them.

We were roughly two kilometres away when I squeezed the trigger and watched my third missile tear away into the distance, burning furiously as it shot on an almost flat trajectory over the desert just a few feet below. About twelve seconds later it arrived on target, piercing the right-hand shoulder of the vehicle. The impact sent the two men on top flying off to the sides as the vehicle lifted into the air and, although they probably would have survived the blast, anyone still inside would not have been so fortunate. The small explosion was quickly followed by shooting flames and plumes of smoke pouring out of the back of the carrier. The Iraqis had ceased firing at the moment of impact and as we turned away I could see the rest of them scrambling for cover in the long ditch and the nearby buildings while the other two MTLBs reversed as fast as they could and sped towards the cover offered by the buildings behind them.

We had just one missile left so, as we made our way back to Bonzai to refuel and rearm, we flew past the commando siege of Abu Al Khasib to see if we could offer any passing assistance on the way. Heading into the thick of the fighting, my eyes were glued to the sight and very soon I spotted an armoured vehicle pulling up at a bridge along one of the main roads, a couple of kilometres south of the battle where, very strangely, there was still some semblance of everyday life in evidence despite the ferocious exchanges taking place a little further up the road. Throughout my entire deployment I never overcame my amazement at the stoicism of the ordinary Iraqi people who had found themselves caught up in a war for which the vast majority of them had little or no enthusiasm. Shops continued to open and many locals showed their defiance by walking and driving around their towns and villages, trying to get on with life and business as best they could as the bombs, missiles and mortars rained down in their midst.

Roughly a dozen troops quickly poured out of the armoured vehicle and set up an impromptu roadblock, which was something they continued to do from time to time in order to give the impression that they were still in charge of the situation. Many of the locals, having had enough of the fighting, were trying to flee to safer areas, and it looked to me as if this roadblock was trying to prevent a column of civilian cars from leaving the town. Unfortunately, we didn't have enough fuel to probe the target and had to continue back to Bonzai.

As we landed on back at the camp, I couldn't help noticing the huge change in the reactions of the ground crew. A week earlier, when I had returned from my very first tank engagement, they had all stood around wide-eyed, pointing at the Lynx's empty missile launchers, and then swarmed all over us to get the low-down on the engagement. But now, ten days into the fighting, they barely even gave us a glance as they impassively went about their business, wiping down the windscreen, loading up three more TOWs and filling us up with avgas. Firing missiles had become an everyday event of little or no interest.

The engineers and ground crew, like the pilots, were putting in a huge effort throughout what was quickly panning out to be an incredibly frenetic day, even more intense than the twenty-fourth. From dawn to dusk the aircraft came and went to and from Bonzai, and each of them had to be fuelled, armed and, when needed, fixed, to get it back out to the battle as quickly as possible.

We took off again and, after checking in once more with the fast jets and the artillery boys of 7 and 8 Commando battery, headed straight for a former water treatment works a few kilometres to the south of Abu Al Khasib, where the battle to take the suburb was now in full swing. One of the highly secret intelligence units operating out in Iraq had asked us to try and seek out a radio transmission station which, according to their direction-finding systems, was somewhere in that region. The Iraqis were using the station to broadcast propaganda to the locals about the great progress they were making against the invaders. More significantly, however, this radio post was the hub of the Iraqi communications network, allowing their commanders to direct operations against us in the field. The intelligence boys were convinced that the radio transmitter, broadcasting to the public, was also sending covert messages to its men in the field. If we could locate the radio station and destroy it, we would deal a major blow to the enemy, who would no longer be able to communicate with each other. Without communication, the Iraqi defences would be thrown into chaos.

We were bombed up, armed to our gritted teeth, covered in sweat from the heat of the midday sun, muscles rippling beneath our combat gear, and I was generally feeling pretty damned nails for the battles ahead when I happened to look over my shoulder and immediately did a double-take. There was Guns, sitting on an office chair which he had lashed on to the floor with some rope, spinning himself round and round on its wheels in different directions, giggling to himself like a kid in detention class at borstal. He was meant to be strapped into a little fold-down seat on the back bulkhead, but somehow he had managed to smuggle this swivel chair on board without Gizmo or me seeing.

I wasn't sure whether to laugh or shout. I felt pumped up like a bare-knuckle fighter heading into the ring, half-electrified and half-terrified, and there was our young door-gunner mucking about like he was on a ride at Blackpool pleasure beach. I went for the shouting option, bellowing over the comms: 'What the fuck are you doing, Guns?'

He looked at me, all innocent, like he was humouring a lunatic. 'What's up, boss? What do you mean?' He quickly secured the chair at the back and manned his GPMG, and I couldn't help but smile.

During our relief in place with the outgoing air patrol, Cindy had told us to approach the area with great caution, on the advice of the intelligence unit who feared that the Iraqis might have given away their position on purpose in order to lure our helicopters into an ambush. Either that, or they had simply become more careless with their broadcasts over the previous few days. The water treatment site was a fair distance south of the day's main battle, only about ten kilometres from our new camp, and we had flown past it dozens of times on our way to and from the front.

After we had scrutinised the buildings and the surrounding area for about ten minutes and hadn't found anything suspicious, we moved in closer and I noticed that one of the street lamps running along the road to the front of the complex looked a bit odd. It was missing its light, for a start, and there was also a small box attached to the foot of the post. It just looked odd. I radioed HQ to report what I had found and they told me to engage the target if I was convinced it was a radio transmitter of some description. None of the four of us were 100 per cent convinced and I was mindful of the £30,000 worth of TOW missile I'd be wasting if it did turn out to be no more than a defective street lamp. As mission commander and the man with the TOWs in that air patrol, it was me who'd have the piss taken out of me for months on end if I ended up in a battle with a harmless item of street furniture. Also, the TOWs were our only defence against armour and artillery, and one of them might just save our lives a little later in the mission if we found ourselves boxed in with an Iraqi tank troop.

So I felt a little ridiculous as I launched a sodding great big TOW missile through the otherwise quiet and still morning air at the base of an old lamp post in the middle of nowhere. The missile struck it flush on the foot, destroying the box and making the lamp post keel over a few yards to one side. Bunker immediately came over the radio to take the mickey about my incredible skill and bravery in taking on the might of an unarmed street lamp. I took pleasure in giving them the fingers through my side window a few moments later when HQ came over the radio to pass on information from the intelligence unit that we had knocked out the radio station that had been pumping out the propaganda and the buried military messages.

The main military communications network, though, was still up and running. But, emboldened by the knowledge that we had been sniffing up the right lamp posts after all, it wasn't long before Bunker spotted what we were looking for, roughly 300 metres away, adjacent to one of the buildings inside the treatment works. Still alive to the threat of an ambush, we edged a little nearer to get a better look at the mass of wires emanating from what looked like a civilian VOR transmitter (VHF omni-directional radio beacon) that had probably been used by aircraft approaching Basra airport before the war began. It also had a non-directional beacon, or NDB (another type of radio aviation guide), in it as well as its own generator and solar panels for power. Some ham-fisted attempts had been made to disguise it, but it might just as well have been wearing a balaclava and holding a sawn-off shotgun. There was no doubt about our target this time: immediately I fired another TOW and watched the transmitter, wires and generator rise about ten feet in the air and then flop into a satisfying heap on the ground.

The dust and smoke had barely settled when the ops room came over the radio to say that the intelligence unit had called up in delight to tell them that the Iraqi military's communications system had fallen completely silent. We had struck a major blow to the Iraqi war effort in the south because their troops were now effectively operating in the dark, unable to give or receive orders and unable to pass on information about our movements in the air and on the ground. It was a massive coup for us, and the pace of Iraqi defeats and capitulations along the battle front was now likely to increase significantly, thus saving more lives on both sides. If the Iraqis had struck a similar blow against us, our assault on the peninsula would have been thrown into total chaos. It was hardly our most dramatic engagement of the war, but it was quite possibly the most important.

The rotation of missions continued throughout the day as one air patrol after another flew back to Bonzai as its replacement flew out. We had seen enough armed action already that day to keep most combatants happy for a few years. All four of us were shaken to the core, as well as completely knackered, by the emotional and physical exertions of the earlier engagements when we took off from camp and flew back to the front, fuelled up and rearmed, for the last time that day. There was plenty of warning of what lay in store for us a few kilometres ahead because we could see the artillery shells chasing the outgoing 847 air patrol as the helicopters raced back to camp with their minimum fuel lights flashing at the pilots, urging them to get a move on. Mako and Suicide were crewing that patrol, and in spite of their critical fuel situation they still coolly conducted the RIP procedure with us, informing us that they thought they had spotted some kind of bunker complex west of the suburbs, deep into the featureless, flat expanse of the desert. They couldn't be sure, they said, but they had a strong suspicion that it was from that bunker that the Iraqis had been shelling the British forces all day.

Flying past the southern edge of the battle still raging in Abu Al Khasib, along a skyline now choked with smoke and fire to our right, we headed out into the relative quiet of the desert. We were now the most westerly of all coalition troops operating in the region, and it was almost eerie to find ourselves suddenly flying through a landscape devoid of any obvious activity or significant landmarks: just sand and craters and the odd bit of wizened shrubbery set against a horizon wobbling in the heat haze. It was now mid-afternoon and the desert had been baking slowly all day, absorbing the heat and releasing it back into the atmosphere. In the aircraft we were all soaked to the skin with sweat, and I was sucking hard on the plastic pipe connected to the 'camelback' water container strapped to the back of my seat, while wiping the never-ending stream of sweat running off my brow and into my eyes.

The sweat was making it difficult for me to operate the roof sight and I had just pulled away from it to run a cloth over my face when, without a hint of warning, we found ourselves on the receiving end of an attack. Tracer bullets flashed past the cockpit, interspersed with regular rounds, but that was the least of our problems because simultaneously this enemy we hadn't seen had opened up with some airburst and PD rounds. They must have seen us coming and begun firing at once when the order was given. It all happened in double-quick time, and as Gizmo took immediate evasive action and swung the Lynx round to the right, I looked out of the windscreen and saw what looked like the whole desert rising up towards us as a blanket of PD shells erupted below, around and in front of us. If it had been 100 metres longer, there was no doubt the barrage would have brought both helicopters down.

If I had a choice in these matters I would prefer our enemies to fire overripe bananas, but at that precise moment I was delighted that most of the shells crashing around us were PD rounds and not airburst. It is highly unlikely that a PD shell will bring you down, unless you happen to be very close to the ground *and* it lands virtually underneath the helicopter. Against helicopters, artillery gunners and tank commanders generally use PD in order to get a fix on you before switching to airburst. Airburst is far more dangerous to a helicopter because the shrapnel can take you down from 200 metres if a piece of it pierces the fuel tank or missiles, damages the rotors or smashes through the windscreen, injuring the pilots.

That said, we were hardly clapping for joy to see the PDs as both aircraft went into hard manoeuvres to avoid the incoming fire. We retreated from the scene as fast as we could in order to regroup, gather our composure and get eyes on whatever the fucking hell had just attacked us. The attack was all the more disturbing for appearing to have come out of nowhere, and you couldn't help wondering what other enemy positions were lying dug into the sand across this huge expanse of arid, scorched wilderness. It didn't take long for us to identify our foes, as it happened, because they carried on blazing away as we legged it out of range and found a rare hill, more a large dune in fact, behind which we were able to take cover.

I could see with my own eyes the muzzle flashes of their artillery guns, twinkling like tiny sparklers in the distance, and I immediately homed in on the location through the high-magnification sight. I was dumbfounded by what I saw. There, heavily camouflaged and invisible to the naked eye, was a massive bunker complex, the size of two football fields shaped in an almost perfect square. Two sides of it were formed by what looked like the remains of an ancient fort – the kind you see in films occupied by the French Foreign Legion, with crenellated turrets and walls. The rest of the fortifications were made up of giant metal iso-containers, the kind used to carry freight on trains and ships, which had been half buried into sand revetments. Inside the complex there were at least four artillery guns, a number of mortar baseplates and God knows how many troops. I could see at least two dozen men walking or running around, but given the size of the place there must have been dozens of others dug in around the complex, most of which lay hidden beneath a mass of camouflage meshing.

Apart from any other immediate consideration – and there were many right then, not least trying to staying alive – it was a shock to find that, almost two weeks after the war had begun, not one of the hundreds of air patrols that had been flown by the various air squadrons out there had spotted this huge encampment, almost certainly a divisional HQ of some description, sitting right on our doorstep. Suicide and Mako were right. We had stumbled upon the equivalent of Chelsea Barracks. There are four reasons why this HQ had managed to escape our detection for so long: (a) it was very far west, a long way from the main battlefront; (b) it was in the middle of nowhere; (c) there were no roads leading to the fort; and (d) the rest of the desert was a crow's nest of tyre tracks, meandering in all directions. At least now we had discovered the likely source of much of the artillery barrage that had been pounding the advancing British forces throughout the day. The occupants of the fort had blown their cover and, if they had so much as a month's military experience between them, they must have known what was coming their way.

As a lightly armed reconnaissance air patrol, we were hopelessly ill-equipped to carry out an offensive operation against such an enormous enemy position. Firing a TOW missile, even all four of them, at the target would have had roughly the same effect as firing an airgun at an elephant from a mile away. It would barely notice the impact. This was a J-Dam job – but, of course, there were no jets available, busy as they were prosecuting targets in support of the Americans to the north. Our only option was the 105mm guns of 7 and 8 Batteries, 29 Commando, who had moved position from Bubiyan Island into Iraq itself as the battlefront squeezed up the Al-Faw towards Basra.

Aware of the sheer weight of fire that we would be calling in, Bunker and I both understood the importance of getting the fort's grid reference spot on. The last outcome we needed was to direct one of the largest British artillery assaults since the Second World War on to a housing complex in southern Basra. Normally, just one of the pilots in a patrol would work out the grid reference but, to make absolutely sure we got this one right, Bunker and I each set about fixing the location on the map and, reassuringly, we both produced the same figure: 725715.

This is what should have happened next: Bunker would first contact Nomad Bravo, the ground controller, who acted as the middle man between us – as well as the other units out in the field – and the fast jets and the artillery batteries for permission to fire; then Bunker would contact the jets or guns, passing on the grid reference; then the fire would be brought to bear on the target. And then we could all go home for tea.

We needed to strike quickly before the enemy saw our dallying as a window of opportunity to flee the scene and disperse to different locations until they were able to regroup under cover of night. Furthermore, the longer we stayed in the air, the greater the chance of our being shot down. Being so far west, running out of fuel was another consideration.

I soon realised, however, that we had a major communications problem that threatened to scupper the attack on the fort. Nomad Bravo that day was a captain in the US Marines, and I listened in over the radio as Bunker tried to raise him. When Nomad Bravo responded, almost immediately, Bunker remained silent for a few seconds and then came back on to try and raise him again. Again Nomad Bravo replied instantly – but again the Gazelle didn't hear him, and I could hear the growing impatience in Bunker's voice.

It was obvious to me in the Lynx, being able to hear both parties, that we had a comms breakdown somewhere along the line, so I quickly contacted Bunker and told him to relay his transmissions to me. Adding to the confusion and frustration, neither Bunker or I was able to get through to the artillery battery direct, probably because we were so far west and out of signal range. So what should have been a straightforward two-way conversation between Bunker and the artillery unit became a ludicrous game of Chinese Whispers as messages were passed back and forth along the front.

This, then, is what actually happened next: Bunker would pass a message to me; I would then relay it to Nomad Bravo; he in turn would relay it to the guns; they would reply to Nomad Bravo, who would come back to me, who would pass on the final message to Bunker. It was a *Carry On* scene without the laughs. (It didn't help the clarity, either, that 'Bunker' was calling in a strike on a 'bunker'.)

The firing procedure itself is convoluted enough. This, in brief, is roughly what happens when an artillery strike is coordinated from the air by an AOP. Once the artillery battery, which was about fifteen kilometres away in this instance, has the grid reference, the gunners load the information into their computers, adjust their sights and load the guns. They then come over the radio and say: 'Ready, Two Zero, Over' (Two Zero being the twenty seconds it will take the shells to reach the target). Bunker then says: 'Fire, Over,' meaning 'pull the trigger'; after firing, the gunners reply: 'Shot, Over,' indicating the shells are on their way; and Bunker acknowledges that by saying: 'Shot, Out.' Five seconds before impact, the artillery battery comes back on and says: 'Splash, Over,' at which point we appear from behind our dune, or building, to see where the round lands and make any necessary adjustments to the fall of shot. We then repeat the sequence until the gun has found its target and the assault can proceed with the whole battery. If at any point there was yet another breakdown on the radio network, we would be forced to abort the assault, go home and allow a whole Iraqi division to slide away and take their threat elsewhere.

It was a huge relief, then, to see that, after five minutes of Chinese Whispers back and forth on our radios, the first round we dropped as a sighter to test our grid reference landed only marginally short of the fort. The sight of that single 105mm shell landing 100 yards short of the walls triggered an outbreak of wild activity, bordering on panic, inside. As artillery troops themselves, those Iraqis would have known exactly what was happening: we were bracketing them. Bunker made a rapid readjustment – 'Add two hundred' – and within a minute, after the relaying of the message down our primitive telegraph system, we heard the word 'splash' and popped up above our dune to see the second round land smack in the middle of the bunker.

There was pandemonium inside the fort now and, almost as a knee-jerk reaction to the impending assault, all their guns opened up at once in our general direction; but as the gunners were unable to fix us in their sights, most of their rounds fell harmlessly short or wide of our position, and only a handful landed close enough to make us twitch a little. As soon as the second shell landed, Bunker passed me the message: 'Cancel at my command, five rounds fire for effect,' which, translated into layman's language, meant the battery no longer needed our permission to fire and that they were to fire five rounds from each of their six guns.

The first two rounds had each created a modest eruption where they landed, but now thirty rounds were winging through the air, a mixture of PD and airburst, to land in one giant, near-simultaneous explosion. These 105mm rounds are designed to give a 200–metre scatter over large targets, to cause as much damage over as wide an area as possible. It was difficult to count the seconds accurately, given the delays over the radios, but as soon as Nomad Bravo crackled over the comms and said 'Splash,' I repeated the message to Bunker and both the Lynx and the Gazelle rose up above the desert. I can safely say that it is highly unlikely I will ever again in my life see a vision like those thirty rounds bursting on the fort. The whole complex appeared to lift away from the ground as a huge ball of fire and dark smoke, as wide as it was high, covering the whole area, mushroomed skywards. By some distance, it was the most awesome display of destruction I have ever witnessed. For several seconds, all four of us just sat in the cabs of the helicopters, staring out of the windscreens with our mouths open in sheer horrified astonishment at the spectacle.

There followed a number of secondary explosions as the fuel tankers and stocks of artillery shells caught light, but incredibly, once the smoke began to clear a little, we could see that some guns and positions remained intact. Many of the men were dead, even more were injured, and all of them would have been rendered deaf by the compression waves blowing out their eardrums; but in spite of the hell in their midst, the more courageous among them stood their ground to fight. Others, I could see, were running away from the fort as fast as they could, and I certainly didn't blame them.

Seeing that the fort was still at least half operational, Bunker called in 'Repeat' to the commando battery, with an 'Add one hundred' to take out the remaining containers, and a minute later the scene from Armageddon was repeated as another thirty shells landed on top of the fort, sending another mighty fireball and plume of smoke shooting into the air. This time its guns finally fell silent. For almost two weeks, the fort had been happily shelling the coalition forces on the peninsula – no doubt as delighted as they had been surprised by our failure to detect their presence – and they had just come within a few yards of killing all four of us as we headed blindly into their wall of fire. But in the space of three minutes, that fort ceased to exist.

Although I doubt any of us were aware that we had just unleashed the largest artillery strike called in by a British helicopter air patrol since Suez, it was clear that we were all painfully conscious of the magnitude of the destruction we had just brought to the battlefield. And it had all happened in less time than it takes to smoke a cigarette. We flew the fifteen minutes back to Bonzai in total silence, alone in our thoughts about the death and mayhem we had left smouldering behind us on the horizon.

Our patrol was the final mission in what had been the

most momentous day in the history of our squadron. In thirteen hours of continuous fighting since daybreak, 847 Naval Air Squadron's contribution to the battle for Abu Al Khasib amounted to the largest armed helicopter action ever undertaken by British forces. Together, we had flown thirty-four missions, under constant contact throughout the day, firing twenty-two TOW missiles while engaging twenty targets and destroying seventeen of them – a tally that included two T55 tanks, four MTLB armoured personnel carriers, four bunker complexes, three fortified houses, two radio transmitters, one ship and a scattering of snipers. Incredibly, in spite of the heat and the exertions of continuous flying, not one aircraft went unserviceable, which was resounding testament to the skill and professionalism of the boys on the ground.

Pride, however, was not the dominant emotion among the pilots when we all returned to Bonzai that evening – at least, not among the four of us involved in that final assault on the fort. We all felt the same 'shock and awe', to borrow a phrase, at what we had witnessed. 'By the time we landed half an hour later I was wishing the war would end right there and then and that I'd never have to do something like that ever again . . .' was how Bunker described his feelings.

I have no idea how many Iraqi soldiers died in that artillery strike. It was little consolation to know, or to be told, that it just happened to be our air patrol that was ordered to go and look for that bunker and call in the strike. Once we had spotted it – not to mention come under fire from it – there was no option but to follow the established procedure of calling in the big guns to eliminate it. Refusing to prosecute a legitimate and highly significant target, or passing the buck to our colleagues, were not options that we could ever countenance. We just did what we're paid for and had been trained to do. If it had been just plain good luck that we had somehow survived the incredible barrage they had flung at us, equally it was just plain bad luck that the horrible responsibility of destroying the place had fallen to us as the air patrol in the vicinity at the time. I didn't take any joy, satisfaction or pride from the episode, and I can find only scant consolation in the fact that the lives lost in those few minutes are no more than a miserably small fraction of all the millions of combatants who have died on the world's battlefields over the centuries. We had come perilously close to our own deaths on at least half a dozen occasions that day, but that doesn't make killing other people, enemy or not, sit any easier on my conscience.

All five of us – myself, Gizmo, Bunker, John Boy and Guns – were as white as sheets as we staggered out of the aircraft and wearily picked up our field rucksacks and personal weapons before staggering, exhausted, towards the ops room to report to Clubs and Sweetcorn on what had just taken place. I was dead on my feet, mainly as a result of the day's exertions, but partly, too, because I had spent most of the previous night lying in a bunker as the camp came under attack from one of the numerous mobile mortar units that had been emerging under the cover of darkness to target us every night since we had moved up to Umm-Qasr. They may not have scored a direct hit, but disrupting the sleep of men who were already suffering from serious fatigue was effective in its own way. I had slept for no more than half an hour in total that night, and although the adrenaline of the battles had carried me through the day, minutes after landing on I could feel the last remaining reserves of energy drain out of my boots. I could barely talk as I tried to recount the details of the assault on the fort to the men in the ops room.

Afterwards, I was standing in the middle of the complex with Lush and a couple of the other guys, smoking a cigarette as we exchanged stories about the missions we had flown that day. Lush was telling me about an alarming moment in which one of his TOWs had misfired and exploded right in front of the Lynx, when the awful, repetitive sound of the Land Rover siren cut him off halfway through. Twenty-four hours earlier the same sound had us all scrambling for our gas masks, helmets and rifles, then jumping into the bunkers and getting our heads down. On this occasion, though, most people walked towards their sleeping quarters and then shuffled off towards the sandbagged revetments, looking incredibly bored and pissed off. For once, like many of the others, I didn't even twitch a muscle. Our group just stood there, shrugging our shoulders and smoking our fags. 'Oh, fuck that,' someone muttered.

'Hey, look at that TLAM [Tomahawk missile] going in.

Hoofing!' someone else blurted out, pointing at a long flying object in the sky just above us. We had seen dozens of Tomahawks heading north to strike various targets, and we had got used to the sight of them after a while.

'Well, if that is a fucking TLAM, it's going the wrong fucking direction,' said Lush, sounding mildly rattled for once. This missile was heading south and within a split second we all realised that it wasn't a Tomahawk at all but a bloody great Iraqi Seersucker, and it was heading right for us. As it arched towards the camp it looked like a great big telegraph pole, belching out clouds of black smoke from its rear. We all froze to the spot as it dropped almost vertically out of the fading light. As if transfixed by this hellish sight, none of us had the presence of mind to budge before the missile struck, just outside the southern perimeter of the camp, with the biggest explosion I had ever experienced. Everything immediately went into slow motion as the compression waves crashed through the camp. The men at the south of the camp were thrown to the floor and blown out of their seats. It made absolutely no sense to run now, but run we certainly did. Even Lush. It's amazing how quickly an apparently exhausted body can find those extra reserves of energy when it has to, and we all sprinted to the bunkers and leapt into them like Olympic athletes setting new personal bests.

My heart was pumping harder than it had done all day from the shock of the explosion, and as I lay there trying to get my breath back I had an instant understanding of how the Iraqi soldiers in that fort must have felt when the first artillery barrage had landed on top of them less than an hour earlier. The 2,000lb of explosive loaded into the Seersucker packed a similar punch to thirty 105mm artillery shells, and it would have caused even greater carnage had it landed a couple of hundred metres shorter, inside the camp itself. There were upwards of 250 men, half of them elite marines and pilots, inside the camp at that moment, and all of them would almost certainly have been killed or injured in the blast; on top of that, all the aircraft and equipment would have been destroyed. The costs, human, financial and military, would have been catastrophic, and I don't think it's an exaggeration to say that a direct hit would have plunged the coalition into a major political crisis. These are the fine margins within which modern wars are waged, and by which governments stand or fall. If that Seersucker, launched dozens of miles away in the vague direction of the British forward line, had dropped that little bit shorter – say, the length of Downing Street – and we had died in our scores, or hundreds even, then those lucky enough to survive might well have returned home to an entirely different political landscape.

CHAPTER TEN

Once the wheels of war had been set in motion, the conflict quickly gathered a powerful, almost unstoppable momentum, dragging everyone along for the ride whether they liked it or not. There was no obvious destination, no notion – among us passengers in the front carriages at least – where the line was to come to an end. There was a headlong rush towards Baghdad, but was that ever, truly, going to be the end of the journey? After three weeks the Americans disembarked in the Iraqi capital and shortly thereafter President Bush flew into the region to declare: 'We've arrived! It's all over now! Hurrah!' – stopping just short of throwing his hat in the air and dancing a jig.

From the moment the coalition forces landed, the prize of Baghdad shimmered in the heat haze in the distance, its capture promising peace, stability and a new golden era for the region. So the troops fought their way through southern Iraq, like men crawling desperately through the desert towards an oasis on the horizon. Baghdad, however, was nothing more than a cruel mirage. Little did we know at the time, but our assault on the Al-Faw had merely set in train a succession of events that steadily gathered a mighty head of steam and finally careered off the rails, destination unknown. Yes, we could take Basra, and yes, we could take Baghdad, but then what? Sailing out to the Gulf, it was plain as a pikestaff to us on board *Ocean* that we had all the tools and the men to overthrow the Iraqi regime. But it was just as obvious, as we looked around at the assembled task force, that it possessed nothing like the necessary resources to rebuild and properly stabilise a country of thirty million people, one riven so deeply by sectarian hatred and division that it makes Northern Ireland look like EuroDisney. While the task force was in a position to offer humanitarian relief and help re-establish essential services, rebuilding Iraq was not one of our responsibilities at the time.

All the death and destruction in which we were involved has not turned out to be the sacrifice some thought was worth paying in order to create a better Iraq in the months and years that followed. I'm just bloody glad I didn't know that that was where the war was heading the night of the Seersucker attack when I collapsed in the bunker, shivering with exhaustion, cold and stress from fourteen hours of intensive combat. At that time, the level of insurgency was just not known.

However, I wish I had known that night that the war for me, and the rest of 847 Squadron, was as good as over. The siege of Abu Al Khasib had ended in victory, with the marines flushing out the final pockets of resistance and taking control of the sprawling suburb as they pushed our front line right up against the Basra city limits and the strategically important Shatt Al-Arab waterway. Within a week, just as the Americans entered Baghdad, our own troops were patrolling in the centre of the southern city. They didn't just walk in, and men on both sides lost their lives in the fighting, but by the end of that week the focus of the operations had switched from all-out offensive to a less combative approach aimed at containment, keeping the peace, expanding the sphere of influence, and bringing in humanitarian assistance and aid for the civilian population.

The men of 3 Commando Brigade, 847 Squadron and the rest of the CHF and the QDG – that is, the original cast in this particular theatre of war – had reached the end of their performance; it was time to hand over their roles to a new group of players. (CHF are now very much back in Iraq.) We had 'kicked the door down' for the infantry and tank regiments. Although we stayed in Bonzai for another two and a half weeks, the fighting was far lighter and more sporadic, and within a day or so of the battle of Abu Al Khasib we were flying only a handful of missions between us each day. Even so, they weren't pleasure trips; the very day after that assault on the fort, Gizmo and I, with Bunker again, flew another mission during which we were invited by an American ground unit to call in a fire strike on a mortar position in a busy residential area just inside Basra.

Every day for a week or so, at almost exactly the same time, a flatbed truck had appeared on a small bridge and fired a series of mortars at British and American positions before driving away and parking up in a street nearby. The American unit we were talking to claimed to have had 'eyes on' the target and asked us to fix a grid reference so that they could fire their own mortars or call in a fast jet, a gunship or an artillery strike to take it out. Bunker pressed our contact repeatedly to confirm that he could see the target, which was obscured for us by a thick row of date palms, various buildings and the drifting smoke that continued to hang over the area. Eventually, he admitted that right at that precise moment he couldn't actually see whether or not the flatbed was there. He could only be sure that that was the location from which the mortars had been fired over the previous days. In effect, he was encouraging us to fire 'blind' at an unconfirmed target, passing the responsibility of calling in the strike to us and thereby, officially at least, washing his hands of any blame if there were any civilian casualties.

Bunker and I ended up having a full-blown row over the radio with my American counterpart, in which we told him that blowing the shit out of a small target, which we didn't even know was there at the time, came nowhere near satisfying our rules of engagement. We were furious, not just because he was trying to get us to do his dirty work for him, but also because it was clear that he had little interest in, or conscience about, the potentially horrible 'collateral damage' that would be caused.

In the end we fired three virtually harmless smoke rounds to fix and record a grid reference as a target, told him to punch it into his computer and suggested sarcastically that he waited until the enemy was actually *in situ* and that no locals were present before prosecuting it. When we returned to camp after that argument, we flew close to the location and, looking down the high-magnification sight, I was able to see, to my combined horror and relief, that there were several Iraqis, teeming around the grid reference we had given. A row of young boys sat on the bridge itself, waving and smiling at us as we raced by. Twenty-four hours later, the flatbed turned up on the bridge, the grid reference was taken from the computer, a surgical strike appropriate to the size and nature of the target was called in, the truck was destroyed, the bridge remained intact and no civilians were injured.

To be fair to the American on the ground, the engagement of targets became considerably more difficult once the fighting out in the open had come to an end, and what remained of the Iraqi resistance had disappeared into the relative sanctuary of the built-up areas. The challenge of fighting an enemy hiding among civilians was highlighted by a nail-biting engagement led by Lush and Naphtha in the

Lynx. For several days, air patrols had noticed an Iraqi MTLB parked up right next to a bus stop along one of Basra's main roads, safe from an air attack – or so the crew must have thought. Using local communities as human shields for their armour and troops was common practice among the Iraqis. There was no thought of our attempting to engage the tank if there was any chance of civilian casualties, and so word was put out to an informer to provide us with the rough times that the buses stopped at that location along that route.

The following day, Lush's air patrol hovered in the distance out of sight, ready to strike. The bus duly arrived, picked up about twenty passengers and then disappeared down the road, leaving the location completely empty of people. Lush had no more than a minute to get his missile away, and he had to be absolutely sure of hitting the target because (a) he didn't want to hit an innocent target by mistake and (b) the MTLB would move off at speed as soon as it came under attack. Lush had had a run of bad luck with his TOWs, but on this occasion the system came good for him as he hit the MTLB flush on the turret with a precision strike. A minute or two later, the air patrol witnessed the surreal sight of Iraqi civilians forming another queue at the bus stop, casting only mildly interested glances at the smouldering wreck a couple of dozen yards away. Burning tanks had become an everyday feature of the landscape in southern Iraq.

The flight programme demanded I returned to *Ocean* on

2 April, and this time I was grateful for the opportunity to recuperate. I was feeling positively diseased by the time I came aboard with a heavy cold and some kind of stomach bug. It didn't help that I hadn't managed to sleep for more than a few hours at a stretch since being called forward. The morning after my return, I was just standing up after finishing breakfast when I staggered a little; it felt as if I was about to pass out. I was incredibly confused, as if someone had drugged my tea, but managed to get out of the canteen and beat a retreat to my cabin.

The symptoms are difficult to describe, but chief among them was an overwhelming sense of dread, as if I was just about to drop dead. I crashed into my cabin and sat down on the edge of my bunk, breathing hard. My whole body was shaking, my head was swooning and my heart was racing at about 200 beats per minute. I gripped the sides of the bed and hung on as if I were at the front of a roller-coaster ride. The worst of it passed after a few minutes, but I was still freaked out by the episode and resolved to go and see the doctor. He told me that I had probably had a panic attack. Like many combatants, he said, my mind and body had temporarily buckled under the exhaustion and stress. My nervous system had become jangled, triggering a violent 'fight or flight' reaction that pumped adrenaline into my system. A period of rest and removing the sources of the stress should do the trick, he said.

Rest and relaxation, however, are not exactly easy to come by in a war zone, in this case not least because *Ocean* was still in a state of high alert. I was finding it difficult to sleep at night anyway, as the grotesque images from my engagements, made weirder by my dreams, rose up to torment me. One nightmare in particular haunted me – a burning man crawling towards me with his hand reaching out towards my face.

The performance of 847 Squadron was later singled out for high praise by both the QDG and 3 Commando Brigade for having gone well beyond our basic brief in order to prove our worth to the operation. I'm sure we could have, and would have, fought just as hard for another two weeks if we had been asked to, but I dread to think what kind of a state we would have been in by the end of it. Already, some were starting to make basic mistakes, and, for a small few, their behaviour became increasingly erratic and eccentric. One morning, for instance, I watched one of the ship's officers eat two breakfasts. He had his first, went back to his cabin, fell asleep, and then got up an hour later having forgotten that he had already showered and eaten.

'Tommo, haven't you already had breakfast?' I asked him as he stood vacantly in the queue holding his tray.

'Don't be stupid, Scoobs, I've just got up,' he replied dreamily. I left him to carry on, oblivious to the fact that he was about to load up with his second full English of the day.

On 19 April we began to ferry the marines of 40 Commando back on board; then we picked up all the vehicles and other heavy equipment, ready at last to set sail for home. We didn't exactly break out dancing on the flight deck when the news came through that we were heading back, but you could feel relief throughout the ship. It would be six weeks before *Ocean* docked in Plymouth, and the wait was too much for a handful of the men who, to the great envy of the rest of us, were flown home from either Kuwait or the UAE. Most had legitimate excuses, such as family illness or bereavement, and one pilot, Pingu, managed to arrive at his wife's hospital bed half an hour before she gave birth to their second child. But there was one character whom I almost punched out at the telephone kiosks when I overheard him saying to his wife: 'Well, love, you know what to do. Just call the airbase, tell them you can't handle it any longer and they'll arrange for my flight home in the next few days.'

The journey home was a catalogue of frustration, illness, exhaustion and boredom, punctuated by many happy highlights. Handing in our personal weapons as we left the Arabian Gulf and then heading up on to the flight deck for some morning sunbathing was one of the better moments. A few days later, however, the weapons were brought back out and the machine gunners took up their positions again on the flight deck as we headed back into the Red Sea and up the Suez Canal.

Perhaps the most enjoyable day, though, came when *Ocean* was close to reaching Gibraltar and we took out members of the ship's company, including the cooks and the stewards as well as the medics and dentists and other support staff, for a series of flights in the Lynx and Gazelles.

They were genuinely thrilled by the experience and it was good to be able to thank them in some way for looking after us so well over the previous four months.

Ocean docked at Gibraltar for two nights, giving everyone on board the chance for a run ashore. Most stayed on the Rock, happy to pack the bars and pubs there, but a handful of us decided to head further afield and took a couple of taxis across the border to the resort town of Puerto Banus near Marbella. We did exactly what you'd expect a group of British servicemen to do when let loose ashore after returning from war: we drank barrels and barrels of rum, caught the pox, set the town on fire and then ran down the beach pursued by the Spanish constabulary and an angry mob . . . I may have slightly embellished a few details there, but I do remember eating in a very fine restaurant, relishing the delicious food, and toasting our lost friends from 849 Squadron. I also have a dim recollection of trying to gatecrash a party on a yacht thrown by 'Croydon-born pop sensation' Dane Bowers.

I shared an apartment with Hovis while we were there, and one moment I won't forget was going to the bathroom on the second morning to find my old chum spread-eagled naked on the floor, apparently dead, surrounded by hundreds of Twiglets, with the empty box still gripped tightly in his hand. It must have been the additives. Above all else, however, I remember the relief and release of laughing as we messed about on the beach and in the bars, like lads on a weekend away. It was the first time any of us had raised more than a tired chuckle for over two months.

Laughter was what we were hoping for, at least, when on the last night of our stopover the comic Jim Davidson, a great supporter of the armed forces, came aboard *Ocean* to put on a show. Jim is unlikely to agree, but in my view perhaps the funniest moment of his appearance came before he had even taken the mike. Jim was suffering from a huge hangover after a particularly heavy night on the sauce, and we heard that the doctor had had to give him an injection of some sort in his arse so that he could perform without being sick.

A week later *Ocean* entered the Channel, and the weather was so atrocious we could barely see the end of the ship, let alone the coastline. It was only when I turned on my mobile phone and five signal bars appeared on the small screen that I knew we were truly home. Foolishly, perhaps, I had volunteered to organise and lead the helicopter fly-off from *Ocean*. The whole TAG (tailored air group) included the six Lynx and six Gazelles of 847 Squadron plus the twelve Sea Kings of 845 Squadron. The fly-off's organisation involved sorting out the crewing, the fuel levels and the pre-designated flight route, co-ordinating with the air traffic controllers and the air stations, and alerting the media so that they could put out the timing of our arrival for people to come and welcome us home.

The preparation was fairly onerous, but I was happy to be given something substantial to get on with just to break the crushing boredom of the final few days of our voyage. In the event, the fly-off itself ranked among the most stressful tasks of my entire deployment! The horrific weather was the main problem, and we had a number of alarming scares simply taking off from the ship. So bad were the wind and visibility that at Culdrose Spidey had to do a 'radar let-down' after he became detached from the rest of the air group and got lost in thick cloud. It seemed for ever before he landed on safely, and it was extremely fortunate that it had been Spidey at the controls, and not someone of lesser composure or competence. At Culdrose we refuelled before returning to the skies, which had started to clear a little as we headed over Dartmoor towards Plymouth.

Thousands of people had lined the route, all waving madly at us as we flew over. There were many Union Jacks fluttering among the crowds and at one point my attention was caught by a very large banner reading: 'Well done boys. We've unlocked our daughters!'

When working out the route, I had arranged for us to fly over the houses of the commanding officers of several Naval Air Squadrons and ships. All their families and friends were there as we shot by and I'm glad that we had gone slightly out of our way to pay special tribute to our bosses, especially Clubs. It was thanks in large part to him that all his men and all his aircraft had come home intact. We headed onwards, first to 42 Commando's base near Plymouth and then on to 40 Commando's headquarters just north of Taunton. Yeovilton was the last stop, and I was delighted we had decided to abandon plans of putting on a mini-display for the waiting crowd. (Explaining to us the difficulties presented by helicopter display routines years earlier, one of our instructors at Culdrose had said: 'Helicopter display flying, boys, is a little like masturbation. Great to do, horrible to watch.')

My stomach began to tighten as I came to the hover and saw a crowd of about 500 – family, friends and press – gathered close to the airfield to greet us on landing. As soon as we had shut down the rotors and turned off our engines, the ground staff lifted the cord and everybody swarmed forward to greet their returning loved ones.

On 3 January 2004 I headed to the airfield at South Cerney in Gloucestershire from where 847 Squadron were to fly out to Norway for our annual Arctic training exercise with the marines. It was while we were out in Norway that I first got wind of the rumour that I was in line to receive some kind of recognition for my efforts back in the Gulf. A couple of the boys hinted that I was up for a DFC, but I hadn't received an official letter or message of any kind since arriving at our encampment in Bardufoss, so I just laughed it off – and when the supply officer approached me and asked if I had organised my travel arrangements for the investiture at Buckingham Palace, I almost fell over with shock. An invitation from the Palace had indeed arrived at my home in Bath, but it hadn't been forwarded. When it did eventually arrive, I was as thrilled as I was stunned when I tore open the envelope. It was particularly gratifying that my citation had been endorsed by the QDG.

Amid the pride and excitement, however, I felt a little uncomfortable too that I was the only 847 pilot to be awarded a valour medal. (Clubs and Geek were both awarded MBEs, Sweetcorn a QCVS, Coco a MID and the CO of the Commando Helicopter Force received an OBE.) All our pilots had flown with great skill and courage under intense pressure in extreme conditions. Not one man had been found wanting. I suppose the difference was that I happened to have found myself in the thick of some of the heaviest fighting. I was in the right place at the right time – or the wrong place at the wrong time, depending on how you want to look at it – but the fact was that I still prosecuted my targets. Still, it made me feel a little sheepish around the other boys to know that I was the only man serving in the Royal Navy able to pin a DFC medal on my chest.

The Distinguished Flying Cross is awarded for 'an act or acts of valour, courage or devotion to duty while flying in active operations against the enemy'. Today, I still can't work out whether my actions were brave or not. I was certainly professional in the execution of what I did, and as mission commander and aircraft commander I was the one who bore the responsibility for our actions. But 'brave'? I'm not so sure. If someone shoves into you in a pub, you can walk away and say you're not prepared to fight. If they come running at you or one of your close mates with a knife or a broken pint glass, then you have little option but to stand your ground and take him out. That's a little how I feel about those three tank engagements.

Strictly speaking, I was awarded the medal for my contribution to the battle on 24 March – my first full day at war – when I spotted and reported on the taxis, destroyed three T55 tanks and eliminated a command post. But I suspect that the events of 30 March, when we took out the radio transmitters, destroyed an MTLB and helped call in the strike on the huge fort out in the desert, would also have had a bearing on the decision to put my name forward. Those two days saw the most intense fighting of the conflict for our squadron and I happened to end up in the sharpest of the engagements on both.

You won't normally find me mouthing a bad word about the Fleet Air Arm or Royal Navy, but you'll have to excuse me while I take a little pop at our bean-counters for the way my DFC was handled. For me, going to Buckingham Palace to receive a medal from Her Majesty The Queen is about as good and proud a moment as a man can expect to experience in his career, and I would have bitten my own legs off to be there on the day – but our budget had become so tight that I was told I would either have to make my own travel arrangements home or have the medal sent out to Norway, where the most senior officer present would stand in for the Queen and pin it on me.

It was difficult, to say the very least, to get excited about the prospect of receiving my award from an officer of my own rank in a frozen Portakabin deep in the Norwegian wilderness, under the tittering gaze of my piss-taking colleagues. It would have rankled with me for the rest of my days if, for the sake of a couple of hundred quid, I had missed out on a once-in-a-lifetime trip to the Palace, to meet the Queen, with my Mum and Dad looking on proudly. When I called Clubs, who was back at Yeovilton, to tell him what was afoot, he went absolutely potty. For him it was a slight on the squadron as much as anything else. The matter was resolved within a few minutes of my putting the phone down – a simple misunderstanding, as I knew it would be, and a seat was promptly found for me on a flight on the eve of the ceremony.

My parents had driven up from Devon for the occasion, and I felt very proud and emotional as we headed up the grand, wide staircase inside the Palace, at which point I was led away into a room full of other servicemen to be honoured that afternoon. It was an incredibly opulent setting: huge paintings by famous artists including Rembrandt adorned the walls; the bright red carpets were spotlessly clean; and the tables and chairs had been so well polished you could see your reflection in the wood.

Amid the hum of nervous chatter – we were all clearly feeling a little on edge – one of the distinguished old men on the Palace staff entered the room, resplendent in his lavish military uniform. 'Right, I want to split you into two groups,' he said. 'Those of you who deserve your decoration over to the right please, and those of you who are here because of other buggers' efforts, on the left please.' Everyone laughed, and the atmosphere relaxed a little. There were a lot of RAF and army present and a few marines, including Clubs, but as far as I could see I was the only navy representative that day. Two of the marines were young lads who had been awarded the George Cross for 'conspicuous gallantry' during the Al-Faw assault and I felt immensely proud for them. Clubs gave me a big handshake and huge slap on the back. He was obviously proud that one of his boys was there that day, and he beamed at me like a proud dad. Bless him. (We are going to miss him when he retires at the end of the year.)

Before we were called through into the investiture room, there was an amusing episode. I was standing with one of the marines when an elderly chap ambled over to our group. He must have been getting on for ninety, and his big, bushy white beard made him look a little like Uncle Albert from *Only Fools and Horses*. He looked slightly dishevelled and you could tell from his dress that he had not been a high-ranking officer during his time in the services. You didn't, however, have to be a great military historian to work out that at his age he must have been there to receive an award of considerable significance. We all shook his hand and he turned out to be a lovely character with a wicked sense of humour and a sharp tongue. One of the RAF boys wandered over to join us, and began to take the mickey out of the old boy, calling him 'Pops' and making jokes about his slightly threadbare suit. ('You could at least have dressed up for the occasion, Pops . . .') The rest of us stared with stony faces at this pilot, and after about five minutes the young marine whispered in my ear: 'Permission to bang out crab [RAF] wanker, sir?'

'Certainly, but wait till we're outside,' I replied.

Pops, though, could clearly fight his own battles. He let the man humiliate himself for a while and then cut him off, as if he had heard enough, and said: 'So, young man, what brings you here today?'

'Oh, nothing really, I'm getting a DFC. I had a missile lock on to me but I managed to take evasive action.'

'Oh, congratulations, you must feel very proud. I've already got two DFCs . . . to go with the rest.'

A fabulous silence descended over our group and we let Flight Lieutenant Crabfat stew in his own embarrassment for a few seconds. Then he began to backslide out of the conversation. 'It must have been a while since you saw service, so why are you here today then?' he asked.

'Oh, I'm just picking up my knighthood.'

The investiture itself was a tremendous experience. It was funny to look along the line of dozens of servicemen, all there to be recognised for gallantry and devotion to duty, but now reduced to twitching, shuffling wrecks as they waited for their names to be called out. The army warrant officer behind me was so nervous he was fidgeting with his uniform like a madman. I tried to calm him down with a quick conversation, but he was stuttering so much he couldn't get a word out.

We had all been briefed about the procedure, so when it was my turn I walked forward as instructed, stopped, then took two paces, bowed, and took the Queen's outstretched hand. 'Don't shake it, whatever you do! Just hold it,' we had been told. 'And it's Ma'am as in Mam, not arm.' Once she had pinned the medal on, each recipient was to walk away backwards. 'Never, ever show your back to the Queen!'

Three things struck me about the Queen: she was much smaller than I had imagined, she was very well-informed and she was very funny. I felt instantly at ease in her presence as she asked me a series of quite detailed questions about 847 Squadron and what I had done in Iraq.

'Are your family here today? They must be very proud of you,' she said.

When I told her that I was currently on exercise in Norway, she replied: 'Well, I sincerely hope you've got one of our sleeping bags.' A few days earlier, there had been a story in one of the papers about some of our marines returning from Arctic training with frost nip as a result of the poor quality of bags which they had bought. I burst out laughing, and she let out a little giggle too.

The Distinguished Flying Cross is a very heavy medal, and the Queen had a little trouble pinning it on. When she had finished, she gave me an ever so discreet push through the handshake to indicate that it was time to move on.

WHERE ARE THEY NOW?

Clubs: Recently spotted slapping on the factor zero on a beach on a Pacific Island. The MBE he received from the Queen marked the end of a long and distinguished career with the Royal Marines. Moved abroad.

Hovis: Left the Royal Navy at the end of his commission and is now a Captain with a major airline. Recently became a proud father to my goddaughter, Elizabeth. Has reluctantly given up processed cheese and blue-coloured sweets; life for the rest of us is a little duller.

Slaps: Recently returned from another tour in Iraq. Currently flying the Sea King Mk4. He is perhaps the most deployed man in the Armed Forces.

Spidey: He has just returned to work following a skiing accident. Suggestions from his colleagues that he might have been better off learning to ski before taking to the 'black slopes' met with frown and growl. Currently coordinating aviation policy at a military HQ.

Coco: One of the squadron's longeset serving members, he has recently converted to a different helicopter type and is about to return to operations in Iraq. Awarded a MID for his part on the Al Faw.

Lush: After handing in his weapons and 'tash', he now works as a Sea King Rescue pilot, plucking ramblers and dogs from cliffs in the West Country. He feels he still has a few years left to top up his massive list of military operations.

Cindy: Recently completed a tour in the Commando Helicopter Force Headquarters and is currently back on the squadron. Started to lose weight and take on an even healthier lifestyle. We prefer the old Cindy.

Bunker: Reluctantly left his beloved Royal Marines at the end of his commission and has moved abroad to raise his family. If you meet him, don't eat his lunch.

Bozo: Has cheered up and mellowed a little since we last saw him! Left the Royal Marines a happy and contented man after an impressive career.

Deps: Still wishes he was up to his elbows in grease and oil fixing aircraft, he is however, serving in the engineering implementation team. And still dreaming of becoming a pilot!

Gilbert: Back in the Commando helicopter force flying Lynx AH7, about to begin an exchange posting. Worried now Jonny Wilkinson is fully fit.

Naphtha: Currently on exchange with the United States Marines Corps, deployed in Iraq flying Cobra attack helicopters.

John Boy: Still serving with the Commando Helicopter Force; recently qualified as an Instrument Rating Instructor on the Lynx AH7. Looking for a new tune to replace 'Painted Cow'.

Leatherman: Still serving with the Commando Helicopter force. He recently completed his course as a Night Vision Goggles instructor. The tac call sign is still about right (ultimate *tool* that everyone carries).

Sonic: Currently engaged on operations with Special Forces. Let's hope he remembered his parachute.

Sweetcorn: After receiving a Queen's Commendation for Valuable Service (QCVS) for his work with 847 NAS he went on an exchange with the RAF and distinguished himself on operations in Afghanistan. Awarded DFC.

Gizmo: Coming to the end of a very long career in the Royal Marines (he turns 92 this year) and making plans for a new adventure: travelling the world. I wish him every success and a long and happy retirement. Yours aye, mate.

ACKNOWLEDGEMENTS

The production of *Armed Action* would not have been possible without the help of a great many people, and I'd like to thank as many of them as possible for their contributions.

There is one person who *must* come first, for once. There is one person who deserves so much more than the lines in this book, someone who changed my life completely. Without whom this book might not have been written. More importantly my life would not be as happy as it is today. To you Donna, my love and depth of feeling cannot be expressed in so few words or sentences.

I must continue by expressing my gratitude to Simon Butler who was of great help in the early stages; his sound advice set me on the right track from the start. Les Wilson deserves lavish praise for, amongst other things, introducing me to the appropriate people in the publishing world. As a serviceman I wouldn't have had a 'Scooby Doo' where to have begun without Les steering me in the right direction. He has been extremely kind and generous with his time and he's also responsible for some of the excellent photographs in the book, which cast me in far more flattering light than I could have imagined!

I am also very grateful to Marilyn Warnick of the *Mail on Sunday* who was quick to see that, behind my stumbling and stammering, I had a half-decent story on my hands. It was thanks to her that I was introduced to the superb publishing team at Headline. I would have been hard pushed to find a more professional and friendly group of people than I met there. I am especially grateful to Val Hudson for her enthusiasm for the book and for her tremendous support throughout its production. Jo Roberts-Miller has been brilliant, as well, in editing the book thoughtfully, meticulously and imaginatively. She, too, has become a good friend. Big thanks also to Kerr, James, Caitlin, Amy and Philippa – and anyone else at Headline involved in the project who I never met.

Niall Edworthy deserves a whole chapter of his own but he will have to make do with a few lines. His wit, good humour and sheer hard work made the whole process a wonderful but challenging experience. Without him the book would not be as good as the one you are about to read. I know I have made a lifelong friend.

To write a book – albeit in my own time – while still serving in the Royal Navy requires a flexible, open-minded and supportive employer. I have exactly that in the Fleet Air Arm. Commodore S Charlier ADC RN, Captain C Alcock OBE RN and Colonel J McCardle RM all deserve a substantial heap of gratitude for their support and counsel. Gilbert, Spidey and Doormouse also deserve special thanks for allowing me to use some of their pictures in *Armed Action*. I am very grateful to you both.

Finally, to the heroes who feature in the book – my friends and colleagues in the Fleet Air Arm, particularly those I fought and lived alongside in 847 Naval Air Squadron during those highly challenging few months in the Gulf. It is worth pointing out here that editorial constraints have prevented me from mentioning every last member of 847 Squadron, let alone every member of the Commando Helicopter Force or every significant mission we flew during the conflict. But those who go unmentioned – you know who you are – deserve as much praise and admiration as those who feature more visibly because they were directly involved with my personal experiences of the war. Any man who has been to war has a story to tell and I hope, by writing mine, I have succeeded in capturing feelings and experiences that were common to us all out there.

We risked our lives for our country and came home to tell

the story. Many, however, did not. This book is dedicated to my friends and colleagues who were tragically killed in Iraq in May 2006.

Alto Ex Concutimus
For Zulu 37

Lt Cdr James Newton DFC RN

Index

AAD (abandon aircraft drills) 130
Abu Al Khasib 2, 214, 273–4,
  281–305, 311
AEW (airborne early warning)
  helicopters 191–5
air patrols 44–5
airburst ammunition 6, 7, 8, 295
aircraft carriers, US Navy 155
aircraft carries, US Navy 117
Al-Faw 115, 153–4, 171, 189, 202, 310
American and British forces, contrasts
  199–200, 269–73
American-controlled zone 12
AOP (air observation platform) 110
Ark Royal, HMS 125–8, 155, 156,
  170–1, 191, 193
assault rifle loading 145–6
AWACS aircraft and controllers 200,
  281

B52 bombers 177
Ba'ath Party 261, 267
Bab El Mandeb 118
'baggers' (radar and surveillance
  aircraft) 192
Baghdad 310
Balkans 21

Bardufoss 148–53
Basra 199, 267
battle bags 159
Belize 252–3
bingo [low on fuel] 17
biochemical attack 72–3
biochemical flying suits, AR5: 112
Bish (Reverend Peter Scott) 59
Black Watch 187, 267, 273
'blue-on-blue' 12–13, 72, 155, 227
Bowers, Dane 318
Boyce, Sir Michael 158
Bozo 60–1, 263, 276–8, 330
Brims, Brigadier 199
British Military and Naval Units
  1 (UK) Armoured Division 172
  3 BAS (Commando Brigade Air
    Squadron) 67
  3 Commando Brigade 170, 219
  7th Armoured Brigade 172, 187, 199
  16th Air Assault Brigade 171
  29 Commando (Royal Artillery) 171,
    283, 298–303
  40 Commando 37, 42, 68, 156, 158,
    170, 273, 283, 316, 320
  42 Commando 68, 156, 171, 320
  539 Assault Squadron 183

845 Naval Air Squadron 42, 157
846 Naval Air Squadron 131
847 Naval Air Squadron
  Abu Al Khasib 304
  air patrol make up 162–5
  aircraft serviceability 165
  armed escort role for landings 156
  awards 322
  CO's skill 278–9
  crewing pairings 160–4
  emotions on going to war 57–9
  experienced helicopter unit 30–1
  'find and strike' capability 114
  flexibility 68
  flight commander replacements 158
  flying practice changes 108–12
  friction within squadron 160
  friends and colleagues 335
  heavily loaded helicopters 227–8
  invasion start 186–7
  largest British helicopter action
    281–306
  most eventful day 214
  negative personalities 60–1
  Operation James 273, 281–306
  praise by army units 316
  role in Iraq 4
  screen role before main landings
    156
  smoking 262
  stretched to the limit 274–5
  taking off in sand 226–8
  tiredness 196–7
  tiredness and stress 259–63, 274–8
  'Where Are They Now?' 329–32
849 Naval Air Squadron 185, 191–5
Bruce 87–8
Bubiyan 171
Buckingham Palace investiture 324–7
Bunker 141, 282, 292, 299, 305, 312,
  330

Camp Bonzai
  description 268–72
  engineers and ground crew efforts
    288–9
  nighttime attacks on 305–6
  Seersucker missile 306–7, 310
Camp Viking

air raid warnings 209–11
  anxiety to reach 190
  arrival for combat duty 195–6
  base in Kuwait 159
  leaving 268
  sandstorm 252–3
  view from the air 208–9
campaign awards 182, 322
Central America 21
CH46 (US) helicopter crash 188
Chainsaw 226, 229
Chapels 131
chemical attack warnings 177
CHF (Commando Helicopter Force)
  28, 67
Chinook helicopter 125–8, 157
Cindy 33, 68–9, 109–10, 144, 202,
  229, 273, 291, 330
CIWS (close in weapons systems)
  109
Clubs 27, 34, 58, 112, 156, 158, 163,
  191, 218, 223, 251–2, 265, 278–9,
  305, 322, 324–5, 329
COCHF (C O Commando Helicopter
  Force) 143, 322
Coco 160, 234–51, 322, 330
Cole, USS 136–7, 256
Colin 92
constraints 14, 144, 238
Cortez 144
CR (combat ready) status 27, 30, 66
Culdrose 193–4, 321
CWP (central warning panel) 134
Cyprus, assault rehearsal 50, 103–15

D-Day landings 115
Davidson, Jim 319
'day sacks' (field rucksacks) 224
'dead ground' 108
'Dear John' letters 59
'Deps' (deputy air engineering officer)
  43–4, 225, 331
'dislocation of expectation' 110
'Ditching Club' 130
DJ 62–4
Djibouti 118
DMZ (demilitarized zone) 172, 187
Doormouse 201
Dutton, Brigadier 170, 219, 229

E&E (escape and evasion) 74–5,
77–101
'Emcon silent' policy 137
emotions on going to war 57–9
engagements
Iraqi Fort complex 294–303
Iraqi mortar in residential area
312–13
Iraqi MTLB armoured troop carriers
284–7
Iraqi radio transmission station
289–93
Iraqi T55 tank outside abandoned
school 1–17, 232–3
Iraqi T55 tanks and command post
234–52
rules 10–11
'Engines' (air engineering officer)
43–5
escape and evasion guidelines 50
EWI (electronic warfare instructor) 23

F16 bomber 216
Falkland Islands War 21, 42, 145, 281
'famil flight' (familiarisation with
conditions and landmarks) 207
family and friends 24–6, 38–9, 141–2
First Gulf War 21
FLET (forward line enemy troops)
75–6
FLOT (forward line own troops) 75
'Flyco' (flight controller) 126, 128
Fort Austin 23, 131
friendly-fire incidents 12, 72, 155, 227

G-spot 127
Gazelle helicopters [AH1] 4–11, 29
Geek 4–16, 201, 226, 229, 229, 322
Gibraltar 318
Gibraltar, Straits of 58
Gilbert 234–52, 331
Ginger 61–2
Gizmo 4–17, 163–4, 195, 200, 221,
225–6, 228, 233, 234–52, 271, 275,
281–305, 305, 312, 332
'goffers' (fizzy drinks) 54
GPMGs (general purpose machine
guns) 47
GPS devices 47–8

grid reference importance 301
'ground cushion' 132
Guns 9, 17, 204, 221, 225, 243,
289–90, 305
gunship 'Spectre' AC-130: 177, 180,
183
gunship 'Warthog' A10: 237, 247–9,
254

'Hail Mary' mark 127
Halabja 73
'Hammersmith' (pre-set route) 222
'Hamster-Rat' technique 110–11,
126
Harriers 177
HEALT (helicopter employment and
assault landing table) 113
helicopter flying
collisions 71
constant practice necessary 67–9
hovering low 110
pilots as high value assets 76–7
risks 71–2
HELO (helicopter control) desk 187
high explosive missiles 45
Hormuz, Strait of 153
Horn of Africa 118
'hot-gas' leak 134
Hovis 19–24, 26, 34, 144, 186, 196,
263–5, 268, 318, 329
Hurricane Mitch 252–3
HVAs (high value assets) 76–7
Hyena 126–8, 129–30, 136–8

information, 'one-up' and 'two-up' 77
Iraq
ambulances 232
bombing of defence system 153
civilian behaviour 205–6, 288
invasion objectives 172–4
legitimate targets 217–18, 313–14
quality of Iraqi army resistance 184,
189, 206–7
sacrifice worth paying 310
T55 tanks 204, 223
tank battle 260–1
taxis used by Fedayeen 217–20,
229–30
Islamic culture 50

J-Dam strikes 'smart bombs' 10, 216, 298
Jack 182
John Boy 282, 305, 331
Johns, Captain 170, 268
'Junglies' 67

Kuwait City 267–8

'lads' (engineers and mechanics) 45, 49
'landing on' 49–50
largest UK military deployment since World War II 171
LCJ (load-carrying jerkin) 224–5
Leatherman 282, 331
Liverpool, HMS 192–3
London milkman in WWII 206
LTDRF (laser target designator and range finder) 47, 248
Lush 31–2, 47, 56, 119, 144, 144–5, 159, 166, 200–9, 210, 221, 230, 282, 307, 313–14, 330
Lynx helicopters [AH7]
    ditching procedure 130–1
    preparation 29

Mako 144, 187, 272, 274–5, 294, 297
Messenger, Gordon 170
mines 72
'misrep' (mission report) 251
MLA (minimum landing allowance) 127, 135
MOAT (mobile air operations team) 182, 209
mobile telephones 52

Najaf 189
Naphtha 123–5, 144, 168, 263, 313–14, 331
Naps and Bats injections 158
Nasirayah 189
NBCD (nuclear, biological and chemical defence) 29
New Forest girl 89–91
Newton, James
    biggest decision in Fleet Air Arm career 219–20
    Dartmouth cadet class 20

Distinguished Flying Cross 321–7
    emotional impact of combat 252
    emotions on going to war 57–9
    family 40, 257–8
    first full-on war 21–2
    first operational flight over Iraq 200–9
    fitness programme 120
    Fleet Air Arm as ambition 121–2
    fly-off on return to UK 319–21
    frustration of being held in reserve 190
    heat acclimatisation 120–1
    kinship with enemy 238–9
    most momentous day (24 March 2003) 213
    only fight during service 62–4
    pairing with Gizmo 163–4
    panic attack 315
    promotion to acting Lieutenant Commander 143
    recuperation 315–16
    responsibility conflicts 30
    sanitising 224
    'Scooby' call sign 23–4
    television interview 257–8
    TO1 (Training Officer One) 31
Newton, James – flying incidents
    collision near-miss 123–5
    ditching near-miss 125–8
    engine failure 132–5
    ship not found 136–8
    snowstorm in Norway 148–53
Newton, Mr and Mrs (author's parents) 39–40, 41, 57, 257–8, 324
Newton, Suzi [author's wife] 26, 57, 30, 141–3, 159
Nick 92–5
Night Navex (night navigation exercise) 88–91
'nine-line brief' 248
Nomad Bravo 299, 300
Northern Ireland 21, 146, 269
Northumberland, HMS 42
Norway, annual training exercise 147–53, 321–2
nuclear attack 73
NVGs (night vision goggles) 65, 67

***Ocean*, HMS**
action stations 105–6
AOR (amphibious operations room)
113, 170–89
briefing room 51–2
cabins 55–7
Cyprus to the Gulf 115–39
fly-off on return to UK 319–21
'Forum of Fact' entertainment
167–8
intense activity 255–6
invasion start 169–89
Iraqi wounded 266
leaving Plymouth 19, 27–8, 37–41
'Mum' 41–2
outward journey to Cyprus 37–101
passageways 46
poor weather 50–1
return journey to English Channel
317–21
size and equipment 42–3, 45–7,
117, 155
sleeping difficulties 118–19
wardroom 53–5
XO (Executive Officer) 264–5
oil installations 115, 172–4, 180,
184–5
Oman, training 7
Operation Houghton 171–89
Operation James 273, 281–306
Operation TELIC 156
opposed landings 115, 171–2
'Outhouse' 136

Page, 'Jacko' 171
PD (point detonation ammunition) 6,
240–1, 295
Phalanx system 46–7
Pingu 317
Plymouth 19, 40
'pop-up unfriendly' 226
'Procedure Alpha' 37, 41
protestors against the War 38–9
PTT (press to transmit) device 48–9
public support 37–41, 174

Queen's Dragoon Guards 2, 12, 156,
203–5, 214–18, 223, 234–5, 254,
273, 283

Officer commanding 2, 204
Queen, HM 323–7

R2I (resistance to interrogation) 75,
95–101
radalt (radar altimeter) 179
RAF Akrotori 107
Raidex (raid exercise) 105–14
rations 197–8
RDF (radio direction finder) 137–8
Red Arrows episode 107
respirators, S10: 112
RIP (relief in place) procedure 108,
164–5, 294
Royal Engineers 273
Royal Fusiliers 187
Royal Marines
combat helicopter pilots 27
preparation 28–9
reconnaissance force 156
sense of humour 32–3
'shock troops' 28
size of men 31–2
'theatre entry troops' 28
Royal Scots Dragoon Guards 260, 283
rules of engagement 10–11
Rumaila 171
RWR (radar warning receiver) 226

Saddam Hussein 73, 172–3
Sagger missile system 286
sand 45, 108–9, 226–8
sand and snow 147–8
sandstorm 252–3, 259
SAS 75–6
sausages incident 197–8
SBS 75–6, 256
Scimitar light tanks 3, 203–5, 223
'Scooby' see author
Scott, Reverend Peter 59
Scud missiles 72, 177, 185, 196
Sea King helicopter
collision accident 191–5
ditching procedure 131
engine failure 132–5
'Secret Six' 23
Seersucker cruise missiles 45, 72, 177,
185, 196, 257, 267–8
Seersucker missile 307–8, 310

'shareholders' (daily briefing) 51, 69
Shatt Al-Arab waterway 311
shot down, fear of and options 74
Six Day War 118
'skylined' 109
Slaps 25–6, 32, 144, 230–1, 329
'smart pack' 222, 273
snow and sand 147–8
Sonic 32–3, 144, 160, 186, 331
Spidey 34, 49, 122–3, 135, 213, 219,
    221, 280, 320, 330
'split' manouevre 7
'spoofing' purposes 77
STASS (short-term air supply system)
    130
Suez Canal 115–17
Suicide 294, 297
Sweetcorn 144, 162, 166, 233, 251,
    279–80, 305, 322, 331–2
    disagreements 34–5, 64–9, 138–9

task force 42
TCUP (thinking clearly under
    pressure) 91
television reporting 189
terrorist strike contingency plans 28
'theatre entry troops' 115
Timex 144, 145–6
TLAM (Tomahawk missile) 178,
    306–7
TO1 (Training Officer One) 31
TO2 (Training Officer Two) 31–2
TO3 (Training Officer Three) 32
Tommo 316
Tookie 41, 53
TOW missiles (Tube-launched,
    optically tracked wire-guided)
    appropriateness 4
    cost 144, 291
    firing 14
    first use in anger by author 7
    four hits with four missiles 243–4,
        250
    guidance wires 14
    reliability 144–5
    rogue firing 285–6

roof sight 47–9
training 7
training
    assault rehearsal 50
    critical pressure policy 161
    desert flying 143, 146–7
    detention centre 96–101
    disagreements 64–9
    E&E (escape and evasion) 75–6,
        77–101
    flying in chemical suits 49
    flying practice, intensive 107–11,
        121
    landing on 64–5
    live-firing in desert 50
    live-firing practice 143
    Night Navex (night navigation
        exercise) 88–91
    night-flying 49–50
    Norway 147–53
    R2I (resistance to interrogation)
        75–6, 95–101
    simulated assault 103–15
    taking off 64–5
    variety 29–32
    water, need for 83–4
training exercise
    energy levels 79–81, 85, 86
    squirrel 86
Two-Two 144

Umm-Qasr 154, 173, 187, 189,
    199–200, 261

wartime risks 71–4
Welsh Cavalry see Queen's Dragoon
    Guards
'whistling chicken leg' (unarmed
    Gazelle helicopter) 11
'Winchester' (out of ammunition) 246
Wings (senior air officer) 191
Winters 132–5
World Trade Centre 28

Yemen 118